DELIBERATIVE ACTS

RED

RHETORIC AND DEMOCRATIC DELIBERATION
VOLUME 7

EDITED BY CHERYL GLENN AND J. MICHAEL HOGAN
THE PENNSYLVANIA STATE UNIVERSITY

Rhetoric and Democratic Deliberation is a series of
groundbreaking monographs and edited volumes focusing
on the character and quality of public discourse in politics and
culture. It is sponsored by the Center for Democratic Deliberation,
an interdisciplinary center for research, teaching, and outreach
on issues of rhetoric, civic engagement, and public deliberation.

Other books in the series:

Karen Tracy, *Challenges of Ordinary Democracy:*
A Case Study in Deliberation and Dissent / VOLUME I

Samuel McCormick, *Letters to Power:*
Public Advocacy Without Public Intellectuals / VOLUME 2

Christian Kock and Lisa S. Villadsen, eds., *Rhetorical Citizenship*
and Public Deliberation / VOLUME 3

Jay P. Childers, *The Evolving Citizen: American Youth and the Changing*
Norms of Democratic Engagement / VOLUME 4

Dave Tell, *Confessional Crises: Confession and Cultural Politics in*
Twentieth-Century America / VOLUME 5

David Boromisza-Habashi, *Speaking Hatefully: Culture, Public Communication,*
Political Action in Hungary / VOLUME 6

DELIBERATIVE ACTS

DEMOCRACY, RHETORIC, AND RIGHTS

ARABELLA LYON

The Pennsylvania State University Press | University Park, Pennsylvania

A version of chapter 3 previously appeared as
"Misrepresenting Missing Women in the U.S. Press: The
Rhetorical Uses of Disgust, Pity, and Compassion," in *Just
Advocacy? Women's Human Rights, Transnational Feminism,
and the Politics of Representation,* edited by Wendy S. Hesford
and Wendy Kozol (New Brunswick: Rutgers University
Press, 2005).

Library of Congress Cataloging-in-Publication Data

Lyon, Arabella, 1951–
  Deliberative acts : democracy, rhetoric, and rights /
Arabella Lyon.
     p.   cm. — (Rhetoric and democratic deliberation)
  Summary: "Offers a theory of performative deliberation,
arguing that speech acts, performances, and performatives
constitute citizens, agency, and events. Through analysis of
human rights conflicts, it reveals difference's productivity
and necessity as it demonstrates the power of performative
theory"—Provided by publisher.
  Includes bibliographical references and index.
  ISBN 978-0-271-05974-7 (cloth : alk. paper)
  ISBN 978-0-271-05975-4 (pbk. : alk. paper)
  1. Deliberative democracy.
  2. Performative (Philosophy).
  3. Human rights.
  I. Title.

JC423.L88   2013
321.8—dc23
2012047606

CONTENTS

ACKNOWLEDGMENTS

At a Christmas party in 2008, in discussing the recent election of Barack Obama, a stranger expressed both his pleasure at the election's outcome and his concern for who the man might prove to be. I was surprised; I thought the election said less about Obama and more about the character of the American citizen. A majority of voters had examined their nation, its problems, and their interests and voted for a man of color, a man seemingly outside the machines of media and party, and a man with ties to Africa and Islam. That is, many Americans voted for someone who was not like them; they embraced the natural and endless occurrence of strangers, and they accepted the unpredictable and impure plurality that is real politics. In repudiating torture, war, and economic frivolity, voters performed acts of citizenship.

At that point, I had stopped writing on deliberation, democracy, and rights. The election of Obama revitalized my writing on performative deliberation, and so the book owes its greatest debt to the majority of the U.S. electorate. Even so, this project required the individual help of many people. Perhaps the biggest backers were the scholars who asked me to contribute to their projects in a variety of ways, enriching my thinking and keeping my fingers on the keyboard. I am grateful for the opportunity to write with Roberta Binkley, Elizabeth Flynn, Carol Lipson, LuMing Mao, Eileen Schell, Edward Schiappa, Jan Swearingen, Hui Wu, and always Andrea Lunsford. These scholars are all committed to broadening the Western rhetorical tradition. I particularly remember Carol Lipson's encouraging me to write on comparative rhetoric, and when I protested that I couldn't, as I was leaving soon for a Fulbright year in China, she replied that I must contribute for just that reason. Working with Wendy Hesford, Wendy Kozol, and Lester Olson taught me so much about the connections between rhetoric and human rights; I often felt like a student at their feet. Keeping me grounded in rhetoric, Janet Atwill, Brenda Brueggemann, Suresh Canagarajah, James Fredal, Lynee Lewis Gaillet, Cheryl Glenn, Deborah Hawhee, Krista Ratcliffe, and Jack Selzer have given me important opportunities to think and speak. On more than one occasion, Carol Colatrella, Robin Grey, and Alan Nadel have given me directions. Always, the crowd at the SUNY Council on Writing gave me plenty on which to ruminate: I have grown from my work with Pat Belanoff, Cynthia Davidson, Tom Friedrich, jil hanifan, John McGinnis, Kelly McKinney, Michael Murphy, and Melissa Tombro.

The project benefited from my seminars on human rights and the thoughtful engagement of my graduate students, especially Banu Ozel, Hyeon Jeong Lee, Swati Bandi, Anita Song, Yvonne Fulmore, Jonathan Fernandez, and Laura Felschow. A conversation with Nilufar Muhammedova initiated a discussion on the different origins of women's rights. My brilliant colleagues Carrie Bramen, Tom Burkman, Ken Dauber, Roger Desforges, Carine Mardorossian, Alex Reid, Jeff Stadelman, and Jiyuan Yu are the Steinways of intellectual sounding boards. Each gave me strength at the right moment. Steven Mailloux and an anonymous reviewer helped me summate and refine *Deliberative Acts*. At Penn State Press, Kendra Boileau helped me envision the manuscript as a book, and the eloquent copyediting of Laura Reed-Morrisson aided that vision. Laura Taddeo offered me the chance to speak on Amy Tan, one of my very few forays into literature. Cindy Anderson lent me her issue of *Marie Claire*, and the Petrocellis introduced me to popular books on political lies. Maeve O'Neil offered her precocious knowledge of language games. These friends have made my work and my mind better.

I am grateful to the National Endowment for the Humanities for the opportunity to participate in three summer seminars on politics and political theory, two particularly on China. The seminar with Roger Ames at the East-West Center in 2001 has influenced my thinking ever since. My time in Asia broadened my understanding of deliberation and rights; for that time I thank the Fulbright program, especially David Adams, for an opportunity to live and work at Sichuan University, and University at Buffalo's Vice Provost of International Education, Stephen Dunnett, for my year teaching at our Singapore campus.

Portions of the chapter 3, "Narrating Rights, Creating Agents: Missing Women in the U.S. Media" first appeared in Wendy Hesford and Wendy Kozol's *Just Advocacy? Women's Human Rights, Transnational Feminism, and the Politics of Representation*. I thank them for the opportunity to write on rights and Rutgers for their generous permission policy.

To my children, Rena and Koko, I owe the pleasure of a chaotic life filled with music, dance, and art, the basic resources of thought; I know you are thrilled that the book is finished. I dedicate this book to my mother, Mary H. Holden, who raised all her children in a world valuing difference and dissension. She taught me what I know about the ongoingness of deliberation.

INTRODUCTION:
DELIBERATION IN THE GLOBAL ERA

Deliberative democracy, of course, attempts to formulate an ideal rational/political structure, one which is both normative and prescriptive: it says that rational debate among equal actors ought to constitute the process of democratic decision making.

—Benedetto Fontana, Cary J. Nederman, and Gary Remer, *Talking Democracy*

America, this republic, the democracy in which we are, is a living thing which cannot be contemplated or categorized, like the image of a thing which I can make; it cannot be fabricated. It is not and never will be perfect because the standard of perfection does not apply here. Dissent belongs to this living matter as much as consent does. The limitations on dissent are the Constitution and the Bill of Rights and no one else. If you try to "make America more American" or a model of democracy according to any preconceived idea, you can only destroy it.

—Hannah Arendt, "The Ex-Communists"

Shall we speak of Abu Ghraib and torture; shall we educate the children of illegal immigrants; shall we guarantee health care for all or for most; shall we intervene in the governance of other nations; shall we ban the *hijab* (head scarf), medicinal marijuana, and prayer in the schools; shall we find one hundred million missing women, the lost boys of Africa, and *los desapareci-dos* (the disappeared)? Virtually every page of a good newspaper asks citizens to consider matters of human rights: we are asked to deliberate on rights every day. In response to the significance of rights talk within politics and the world order, both international and civil rights have grown as areas of academic inquiry. Search the keyword "human rights" in a research university library, and over twelve thousand books come up, the vast majority published since 1994.[1] Human rights, exemplified by the Universal Declaration of Human Rights (UDHR) of 1948, have become a key discourse in international politics after the Cold War, and they have become a key analytic in academic inquiry in fields from law to social work. The UDHR and the proliferating supporting documents have created what Michael Ignatieff calls an advocacy, juridical, and enforcement revolution (5–12). Hence, in the transnational order emerging after the Cold War, rights have become the grounds for questioning the legitimacy of laws and nation-states, a legitimacy increasingly tied to democratic elections and popular representation of rights.[2] In the struggles for representation and legitimation, human rights rhetoric has become a key strategy in political deliberations both nationally and internationally.

The political forces turned loose by human rights talk, even when rights are imagined as universal, are not committed to universalism but rather to competition for dominance by the ideologies and cultures made manifest through our globalization. The clashes call forth complicated deliberations, deliberations whose complexity troubles earlier theories of persuasion, dialogue, reasoned argument, and identification. One might consider briefly the 2001 struggle to claim the rights of Afghan women. Seeking to expand U.S. dominance in the region, then President Bush linked the Taliban to the abuse of Afghan women, joining the U.S. rights organization The Feminist Majority in the position that the Afghan state did not represent women. In response to the process of (mis)representing Afghan women and co-opting their agency, the Afghan feminist group Revolutionary Association of the Women of Afghanistan (RAWA), founded in 1977, criticized not only U.S. governmental imperialism but also that of U.S. feminism. Here three players claimed a legitimate role for themselves in representing Afghan women (a representative of the U.S. government, a U.S. feminist organization, and an Afghan feminist organization), but these three claimants are not the only possible claimants here. The Afghan government, individual Afghan women, and international women's groups, such as Women Living Under Muslim Laws, come to mind immediately. All claimed to represent Afghan women, even though each of these claimants represents very different cultural positions, definitions of (Afghan) women, and relationships to rights.[3] The multiple disputing interlocutors create tensions around religious rights and civil rights, individual and cultural rights, and international and local interpretations of rights as well as colonialism and liberation. In the twenty-first century, human rights deliberations particularly demonstrate the cultural conflicts and competing claims in global deliberations *because* rights are quintessentially cross-cultural engagements in a human world increasingly recognized as multicultural.

Rhoda E. Howard-Hassmann characterizes globalization as the "second great transformation," an evolving phenomenon potentially as transformative as what Karl Polanyi called the great transformation from an agricultural to industrial Europe. Contemporary globalization is moving the whole world to industrialism, entailing a myriad of changes. The transnational circulation of people, ideas, and capital places new pressures on deliberative theory, but these pressures are not new to deliberation. Rather, they have been acknowledged inadequately within deliberative theory, which clings to models formed under earlier power elites. Only now, in new frames of global capital, transnational networks, and weakened nation-states, do the limitations of earlier theories become clearer. Consider that existing nation-states number a scant two hundred, but they are home to five thousand identifiable ethnic groups; hence, even within most established nations, multicultural citizenship is unavoidable (Kymlicka 196). Given historically close proximity, ethnic groups necessarily deliberated over resources, capital, ideas, and relationships, but the ruling patterns of earlier elites overshadowed these local engagements across differences, and thus the elites' understanding of deliberation dominated historically. The significance of multicultural deliberations has recently increased owing to changes in relationships among cultures, capital, and nation-states, and as a consequence of these changing structural relationships—most particularly the destabilization of the Westphalian state system—competing ideas of justice and the good vie more publicly. As Nancy Fraser observes, "[G]lobalization is changing the way we argue about justice" (*Scales* 12).

Although this book's primary purpose is to develop a theory of performative deliberation—a theory of how performatives (speech acts), performances, and performativity produce citizens, events, and politics—its examples and case studies involve human rights advocacy, representations, and deliberations for two reasons. First, human rights deliberations are difficult because they are deliberations across extreme difference, troubled by recognitions, competing values, and political hegemonies. As Julietta Hua writes, the "problematic of difference lies at the crux of human rights debates around how to define universal principles and how to represent the varied victims of abuses" (2). Depicting universalism as a limited concept of modernity, she argues that the issue of difference is deeper than accurate representation; rather, the significance of difference lies at "the moment of the conferring of subjectivity and humanity" (2), for in that act of conferring a subject, a human, becomes legible. Although representation helps in conferring rights subjectivity, the recognition of the rights subject and the recognition of difference precede representation, she argues, making issues of rights less questions of representation and more ones of onto-epistemology.[4] Thus they are issues that inquire into the nature of being and the knowledge of other minds. Even if we see recognition and representation as simultaneous, the difficulty of recognizing and representing the subject of rights defeats facile assumptions of shared values, identities, and rules of reason, procedure, and judgment in analyses of human rights deliberations. Hua might say that for Afghan women, the issue is deeper than who represents them and how. The issue is one both requiring a situated knowledge of their lives and a legible, active engagement with the women as subjects of rights, sharing rights claims and yet distinct from other subjects of rights. Since human rights deliberations require examinations of both being and situated knowledge for the many coming to action, an action potentially transformative of being and knowledge, they are difficult deliberations.

As globalization brings culturally different peoples together in institutions within and beyond the nation-state, deliberations become more visibly concerned with difference, differences not settled quickly through persuasion, identification, or reasoned argument. Confronted with competing claims of justice, calls for recognition, and the struggle over the appropriate means to respond to grave injustice, global citizens and their representatives are regularly asked to understand alien cultural traditions, assess the representations and structural causes of rights violations, and articulate responses to conflicting rights claims, responses that may transform the being and knowledge of all participants. In responding to rights conflicts, citizens are asked to *deliberate,* to recognize interlocutors, to comprehend their competing claims, and to weigh definitions of the issue and the consequences of their decisions on people whom they have never seen. Furthermore, they have little sense of how to intervene effectively, because the terms of judgment and application may be alien, perhaps incommensurable with their cultural assumptions, and yet in the service of peace and the planet, global citizens cannot reject difference as disruptive and are required to engage it as diversity. Even if there is a general agreement on action—say, the rejection of the 2011 Mississippi referendum on personhood at conception—there may be little agreement on what that action means and how that action crosses cultures. Voters may have rejected it for reasons of women's right to autonomy, desire for self-determination through in vitro fertilization, or confusion over its implications. Even in shared action, difference remains, making rights actions multivocal and heterogeneous at their core.

Sally Engle Merry characterizes rights decision-making as translations for rights are in need of local interpretation. She argues that human rights declarations need to be remade into the vernacular in such a way that local agents and advocates concerned with histories and cultural contexts can respond to visions of a unified modernity. In her analysis of how violence against women might be controlled, she observes, "Human rights documents create the legal categories and legal norms . . . but the dissemination of these norms and categories depends on NGOs seizing this language and using it to generate public support or governmental discomfort" (71). The difficult remaking of discourses to reflect the local is a quintessentially a performative act of deliberative rhetoric. Merry's vision of NGOs seizing and translating legal norms into local language extends the process of rights deliberation beyond accurate translations to founding acts of ownership, and this suggests the second reason for my focus on human rights deliberations: the deliberative nature of rights themselves. Although there are definitions of rights based solely in their claims to universalism, human rights law, or the normative force of laws, these are not the only approaches to understanding human rights.[5] Singular interpretations of documents and limited recognitions of difference particularly trouble rights talk. Consequently, universal claims to human rights have been soundly critiqued.[6] From its inception, the UDHR has been haunted by the tension between universalism and cultural relativism, its rights analyzed as either innately human or culturally relative (i.e., Western). Even in its initial drafting, participants such as René Cassin and P. C. Chang attempted to avoid metaphysical and natural foundations and to allow for cultural differences.

To avoid a dogmatic understanding of human rights as law, a textual truth, or a universal standard of what it means to be human, throughout the book, I consider rights as performative deliberative practices leading to the constitution of a new form of life. Rights are community decisions developed through a wide range of deliberative practices. Yes, there are human rights laws, but as Joseph Slaughter notes, they are "a notoriously feeble legal regime" (24). In fact, Amartya Sen stresses their lack of legal standing, arguing that their (legal) existence is less important than their "really strong ethical pronouncements as to what should be done" (*Idea* 357). Inherent in appreciating the force of rights discourse as ethical pronouncements, or as cultural norms, is the understanding of rights as defining relationships among people. Even at the beginning of the twentieth century, the jurist Wesley Newcomb Hohfeld argued that rights were not absolutes; rather, they were relationships between people based in claims. In the tradition of relationship, rebutting rights as universal ethics, true or false constatives, or ethical pronouncements, Beth Singer characterizes rights as decisions based in cultural norms internally formed in reciprocal relationships, where community members both claim and respect similar rights. In placing rights in a "normative community" and conceiving rights as justified through the requirements of social interaction, Singer presents rights as "modes of behavior, institutionalized ways in which the members of a community behave toward one another and which must be learned" (35). Rights, then, are not universals, declarations, religious demands, or natural to being human, but instead are acts of participation formed in conversations among community members and carried out in repeated behaviors or actions which re-enforce them as norms. When rights are considered as relationships defined in behaviors, their deliberative and performative aspects become all the more significant to understanding the meaning of right and the nature of deliberation. As political performances, more so than ethical decisions, human rights become a paradigm of performative deliberation. Indeed, given the basis of rights in learned behaviors and actions that may change cultural norms and hegemonies, rights discussions and enactments quintessentially demonstrate the performative nature of deliberation.

If rights are seen as relationships defined through speech acts and practices, concerned with the contingencies of being and situated (epistemic) discourses, one might imagine rights as ongoing politicohistorical projects, designed through local deliberations. As norms—that is, social coordination or "general rules of action and institutional arrangements" (Benhabib, "Toward" 70)—human rights are subject to subscription, and that subscription, even choice, is locally made.[7] As norms, they do not describe facts, the world where humans act, but make claims about human dignity which, in turn, call upon us to subscribe to those norms and then oblige us and guide our actions. Abdullahi Ahmed An-Na'im observes, "[S]ince people are more likely to observe normative propositions if they believe them to be sanctioned by their own cultural traditions, observance of human rights standards can be improved through the enhancement of the cultural legitimacy of those standards. The claim that all the existing human rights standards already enjoy universal cultural legitimacy may be weak from a historical point of view in the sense that many cultural traditions in the world have had little say in the formulation of those standards" ("Toward" 20).

Following An-Na'im, *Deliberative Acts* conceives rights as culturally sanctioned through historically based translation, negotiation, and deliberation, formed and performed in dialogue. In doing so, I acknowledge the limitation of dialogue, hearing Hua's warning that "the values validated through cross-cultural dialogues are exactly those values that enable cross-cultural dialogue" (16). Hua would require us to acknowledge an onto-epistemological privilege to certain perspectives, perspectives that may place Western values at the core of rights deliberation. Acknowledging her cautions on dialogue, in later chapters, I demonstrate more robust dialogues and imaginative translations of terms and thus suggest that there is the possibility of dialogic and diverse engagement within politicohistory. Adequately critiqued, deliberation remains our best possibility for communication in the state of diversity. Furthermore, rights as conceived in this book are understood as quintessentially political, subject fully to political pressures from self-interest, historical privilege, and economic license. Since even what is claimed as universal is dependent on subscription, built upon what An-Na'im calls *"internal cultural discourse and cross-cultural dialogue"* ("Introduction" 3; emphasis in original), it is urgent that citizens understand the nature of rights deliberations in ways that move away from dichotomies of universalism and cultural relativism, politicohistory and onto-epistemology, enlightened savior and brutal (tribal) savage.[8]

In claiming deliberation's force in global politics, one should neither discard the shawl of skepticism nor deny a crisis of confidence about the human capacity for political judgment. Deliberation is an act fraught with hierarchal power, contingency, and manipulation. Human rights deliberations have been demonstrably subjected to shameless strategy and instrumentalism, and they often are used to promote the self-interests of nations, communities, and dark powers lacking respect for human dignity and difference. As Wendy Hesford observes, "human rights are never pure, or culturally and politically unencumbered" (203). Even so, despite the dark side of rights advocacy, the century is marked by falling poverty rates, decreasing world violence, and increasing voting rights.[9] Human rights talk has turned loose a myriad of complex, contradictory, and constituting forces, both because of and despite being "situated as a universal and uncontestable ethics of cross-cultural relations" (Whitlock 118). To deliberate in responsible and effective (if not ethical) ways, interlocutors cannot discard skepticism, nor can they work within a single interpretive frame. To that end, scholars struggle to describe the workings of rights deliberation.[10]

Using the powerful purposes of human rights deliberations, *Deliberative Acts* develops a new approach to deliberation, focusing on performatives, performances, and performativity as transformative in the contingency and diversity of deliberations. Rather than conceiving deliberation within the frameworks of persuasion, identification, or procedural democracy, deliberation (dramatistically) is reoriented to its initiating moment of recognition, a moment in which interlocutors are constituted in relationship or position to each other and so may begin constructing a new lifeworld. Recognition, as demonstrated in performance and performative, engages interlocutors in shared acts and agencies—felicitous and infelicitous, cooperative and agonistic—but whether the utterances are cooperative or agonistic, they still act upon the event and the interlocutors. In offering a theory of performative deliberation, *Deliberative Acts* provides the means to approach questions such as these: How do diverse peoples recognize and respond to each other while respecting differences of being and knowing? Can citizens recognize and engage each other to create global justice, or are they trapped in home discourses, demanding institutions, and material, historical, and cultural circumstances that primarily benefit elites? What are their responsibilities to each other? How do mainstream and marginal rights communities, even within the same nation-state, articulate and balance their rights norms? How does a thinking and located citizen weigh the normative imperatives of rights, her home culture, and her nation-state to make decisions about her prospects and those of others? How can she do this in multicultural situations in harmony or conflict? Are there resources within traditional deliberative theory that might help explain contemporary decision making? Or are Western traditions of deliberation, as exemplified in the Athenian *polis* and nineteenth-century civil rights advocacy, inadequate to describing and assessing the political rhetoric of the twenty-first century? What is the nature of a deliberative act, its production, and its reception?

Deliberation and Deliberative Democracy

Due to their prominent concern with deliberation, theories of deliberative democracy seem a likely point of entry to political analyses of deliberation.[11] Certainly many rhetorical scholars have considered deliberative democracy, particularly as proposed by Jürgen Habermas, to be an appropriate entry into theorizing argumentation.[12] For instance, Patricia Roberts-Miller finds it "most persuasive" (17), and Douglas Walton contends that it offers "the most plausible and strongly supported type of *ad populum* argument" (319).[13] Aside from its deliberative name and influence within rhetoric, there are other reasons to consider deliberative democracy. Deliberative democracy, like human rights discourses, shares commitments to create and support universal norms of justice and legitimate political institutions that guarantee fair and just procedures.[14] Furthermore, it is a discourse gaining prominence at the same time as the current rights revolution. Search the keyword "deliberative democracy" in a research university library, and over one hundred books come up, virtually all published after 1994. Although the concept of deliberative democracy is primarily an academic concern, not a popular or political concern, deliberative democracy responds to similar global apprehensions about the appropriate means to maintain human dignity in an age of clashing and merging civilizations, new technologies of mass media and manipulation, the erosion of state power and the ideal of communitarian democracy, the invidious spread of consumer capitalism, and the vilification of democracy in its (neo)liberal guise. Finally, even though deliberative democracy indicates a set of theories of deliberative *politics* for modern societies and is not a set of theories of deliberative *rhetoric,* deliberative democracy is deeply concerned with discourse and how nations legitimize decisions. Following in the tradition of democracy as "government by discussion," deliberative democracy imagines political procedures dependent on practical communication to produce understanding and regulate public action. These factors all suggest that deliberative democracy would be helpful in understanding deliberation, but upon reflection, its limitations demand alternative ways to discuss contemporary deliberation. If the concept of deliberative democracy helps develop a contemporary deliberative theory, it does so through demanding a response.

The tensions around deliberative democracy reenact the ancient tensions between philosophers and orators in ways that demonstrate its limitations and the need for alternative discussions of deliberation.[15] Troublingly, the focus of deliberative democracy is not the promotion of talk *per se,* but the political legitimacy of institutions through idealized procedures and discourses. Early theorists of deliberative democracy—John Rawls, Joshua Cohen, and Jürgen Habermas—wish to salvage the project of modernity by finding ways to imagine democracy not as a society made of individuals (liberal democracy) or as a singular society embodied by the state (communitarian democracy or civic republicanism).[16] Instead of focusing on individuals or society, theorists of deliberative democracy focus on procedures of decision making and argue that *legitimate law* results from public and/or legislative deliberation by reasoned arguments among equal participants. Deliberative democracy acknowledges the democratic requirement of dialogue, but in defined and regulated ways. Finding justice in *procedural participation,* rather than the populist will (rule by the majority) or equitable distribution of power, opportunity, and rights, deliberative democracy depends on normative commitments to institutionalized, rational deliberation.[17] Committed to one type of democratic deliberation, one leading to consensus, deliberative democracy does not value the contingency and conflict inherent in deliberative rhetoric, and it does not address deliberation or justice outside of the frame of democracy, modernity, and reason. Rather it offers an ideal model of legitimation, and thus the utopian aspects of political philosophy diminish its ability to illuminate the specificity of deliberative rhetoric, particularly in cross-cultural relationships. Even though Rawls requires political philosophy to be "realistically utopian" (*Law* 11–16), political practices inadequately constrain normative political philosophy, and political philosophy remains a tool better applied to writing utopias or critical assessments. The internal logic of philosophical utopias provides insights into the legitimacy or morality of an action, but it makes utopias limited in their ability to describe, explain, or adjudicate cross-cultural claims, contingent relationships, and strategic communication.[18]

Counterfactual ideals obscure deliberation's contingent and organic nature. In presupposing that any citizen can participate and make claims and that citizens see each other as equals and refrain from compulsion, direct or indirect, theorists of deliberative democracy create a counterfactual, although that may not be their intention. Seyla Benhabib, in describing her purposes, writes, "The deliberative model of democracy that I am advocating seeks to bridge the gap between high and low politics by raising the quality of ordinary people's everyday deliberations. . . . My assumption is that the more such ordinary political deliberation approximates the model . . . the more the likelihood increases that it will be informed by constitutional principles in the 'right way'" ("Toward" 89). She sees her philosophical model as directly and significantly related to the practices of common political deliberations within *low,* or ordinary, politics. However, the relationship between constitutional principles and everyday, popular, contingent practice is unclearly drawn. How ordinary political discourses, the tool of ordinary people, might come to approximate her model is undesignated, perhaps because the ordinary people do not see a purpose to critical or regulatory norms or models as they negotiate and deliberate on their needs, aspirations, and justices. Ordinary people, who are the substance of democracy, do not imagine their democracy as a model (or as low politics) but as a situated practice to be worked for their welfare and the welfare of their nation. They may value relationships, stability, self-fulfillment, and emotions more than reason. Due to their "interests and appetites"—the bane of Plato, Kant, and deliberative democrats—in ordinary deliberations, reason will be contaminated, and deliberation will become "mere rhetoric" (Fontana, Nederman, and Remer 10). Alas, neither politics nor democracy exists without taint. In the second epigraph to this chapter, Hannah Arendt writes that American democracy "is a living thing which cannot be contemplated or categorized . . . it cannot be fabricated. It is not and never will be perfect because the standard of perfection does not apply here" ("The Ex-Communists" 599).

Deliberative democracy provides a standard of popular sovereignty based in communication, and as such, it has use in analyzing and assessing political practices. The utopian aspects of deliberative democracy, however, limit its ability to engage with concepts that do not conform to its norms and prescriptions of a procedure of rational, democratic debate among equals. In prescribing procedure, presuming equality, privileging rationality, constricting the discourse of deliberation, and overvaluing consensus, it moves away from recognizing and maintaining difference. In effect it finds difference disruptive rather than productively diverse. Its utopian concern with legitimation renders deliberative democracy inadequate to recognize the irrational, unequal nature of deliberative practice. Radical democratic pluralists such as Chantal Mouffe, pragmatists such as Richard Rorty, and postmodernists such as Jean-François Lyotard argue against efforts to find one politically neutral foundation for democratic practices because such a foundation would only be a self-referential language game, a tautology. As Mouffe writes in critique of Habermas, there is no view "above politics from which one could guarantee the superiority of democracy" ("Deconstruction" 4); the terms that define superiority script the answer. In a similar critique, Rorty questions the natural starting point of philosophical reflections and the idea of a philosophical "subarea" as prior to others, be it justification, reason, or literary (*Contingency* 83). Lyotard, too, dismisses metanarrative, understanding society as an aggregate of diverse language games where the rules may well be incommensurable (*Postmodern*). In contemporary deliberative theory, many are suspicious of reason as a syllogistic technology of connecting propositions and do not see it as a unique tool for reflecting on the material world and oneself or creating human relationships and attachments.

The discomfort with the contingency and conflict of political discourse is visible in at least three patterns within deliberative democracy: the demand for procedure, the bifurcation of communicative and strategic speech acts, and the insistence on consensus.[19] These patterns—because their assumptions are so deeply embedded in political and rhetorical traditions—help expose the blind spots of contemporary deliberative theory. In what follows, predominantly developed through a reading of Habermas, I provide a brief overview of these limitations; later chapters elaborate a performative response to them. Habermas, who longingly reconstructs modernity, has written copiously over a span of fifty years.[20] The complex evolution of his thinking is difficult to capture in the following sketch, but in focusing on his relatively early theory of communicative action (1971–82) and the monumental *Between Facts and Norms* (1998), his major description of political and legal theory, my goal is to engage the work most related to political communication. In doing so, I reluctantly bracket his work on consciousness, materialism, ethics, religion, and postnationalism. Though this material would buttress my argument, it would also redirect the book away from a critique of contemporary deliberative theory and the gift of an alternative.

The primary limitation of deliberative democracy springs from its origin as procedural democracy (legislative procedure) rather than deliberative politics. Despite its appeal to many rhetorical theorists concerned with deliberation, Habermas does not call his political theory deliberative democracy, perhaps because he well understands the rhetorical and strategic genealogy of deliberation and instead wishes to discuss the crisis in contemporary democracy without the ancient echoes of Athenian democracy and civic republicanism and without its place for strategic speech acts that might move men in mechanical or emotional ways. Although deliberation is often described in linear and temporal ways, the focus on democratic legislative procedure and legal requirements differentiates a Habermasian approach to democracy from other forward or future-looking approaches to deliberation. In the work of first Joshua Cohen and then Habermas, deliberation is described as a procedure that moves through an exchange of information and reasons to a change in attitudes and preference of legislators (Habermas, *Between* 305–6).[21] Since speech only becomes political power when "it affects the beliefs and decisions of *authorized* members of the political system" (363), speech in other areas of civil society, the periphery, has less power. In foregrounding procedure and legal administration and minimizing what is said, by whom, where, when, and why (especially by extra-institutional actors, such as citizens), theories of deliberative democracy tend to omit the difficulties of engaging cross-cultural discourses and people who may have fraught relationships with the legislative institutions. It is also limited in its ability to describe extra-institutional deliberations, such as those of NGO translators (who wish to make international human rights propositions locally intelligible) and the citizens who engage them (Merry). The foregrounding of procedure—a procedure limited only to democratic legislative practices, depending on and insuring practical rationality—upholds, *as intended,* the values of the Enlightenment and Western modernity. In finding justice in open and fair democratic procedure, Habermas seeks to secure legal legitimacy, but in doing so, he embraces the culture of modernity inherent in defining procedures and rationality.

Through its concern of the telos of procedure, moving from beginning to end, deliberative democracy neglects focused analysis on the particularly difficult moments in deliberation. As it celebrates democratic process, it elides the preliminary moments of deliberation when particular people or their issues are recognized or engaged, and it assumes an end, a moment when the vote is taken and all is resolved. The initial moments of recognition, the multiple meetings and alliances, the publicity of the problem, emotional urgency, concurrent deliberations, external disruptions, and so much more demand a critical stance to theories of linear procedure. In the abstraction of argumentative theory, it is easy to develop a vocabulary that omits key practices, the rarely occurring or most difficult practices that define the limits and obstacles. As Russell Bentley observes in "Rhetorical Democracy," abstract principles of communication—such as reciprocity, publicity, and accountability (and, I add, procedure)—might define fair deliberation on an issue, but they are limited as they fail to acknowledge adequately where and how issues arise, their discursive definitions, and the experiential nature of issues and deliberation.

A second difficulty within deliberative democracy is its constraints on what constitutes deliberative speech. Responding to the inadequacies of instrumental, scientific-technical rationality, theorists of deliberative democracy privilege reasoned argument and understanding, a move that foregrounds the intersubjective, reflective nature of public reason, but at a cost.[22] As it values certain speech acts, it diminishes and even delegitimizes others—not only strategic persuasion and emotional appeals but also the political discourses of negotiation, eristic, inquiry, and information seeking (Walton). That is, in the service of reason, deliberative democracy regularly omits the significance of bodies, emotions, histories, relationships, intuition, and existing power dynamics, all forces infiltrating and defining reason.[23] In effect, the project discounts interpretative differences, historical moments, and the complexity of human relationships and situations.[24] In response to criticism, Habermas occasionally acknowledges the limits of reason and allows for "facticity of existing contexts" and the need to relate reason "to the value orientations, goals, and interest positions" of a legal community (*Between* 156). That is, he recognizes reason as a limited but *necessary* means of reflection, pacification, and legitimate decision making. Some of his disciples, such as Benhabib, go further and modify his ardor for reason, "[saving] discourse ethics from the excesses of its own rationalistic Enlightenment legacy" (*Situating* 8). Yet reason remains deliberative democracy's controlling ideal, despite its limits as a technique in certain communities and arguments where emotion underlies human attachment.

From his early work on discourse ethics and communicative action to his later work on democracy, Habermas is suspicious of rhetoric, labeling it strategic action, limiting it to persuasion, and basically considering it sophistry. Habermas argues that communicative action, which coordinates action among subjects, is the basis for reaching mutual understanding. In approaching symbolic actions as hermeneutical, founded in understanding and oriented towards agreement, he privileges reasoning, inclusion, and noncoercion and conceives strategic action as concerned with power and influence through threats and promises (*Moral* 71).[25] Although strategic communication might be normalized and institutionalized (tamed), it can never justify legitimate power; for Habermas, it is always tainted because it objectifies the other as a marker to be moved. Consequently, a communicative ideal—an inclusive discussion where interlocutors are equals engaged in reaching consensus on shared concerns—forms the basis of his democratic decision making. In his speech act theory, Habermas adapts Austin's definitions of illocution (intention) and perlocution (effect); rather than seeing them as aspects of an utterance, he separates them into "mutually exclusive attitudes" within an agential speaker (Fultner). Illocutionary acts are located in what is said and so can coordinate action. Perlocutionary acts, oriented to changing another's behavior, conceal a speaker's intention. They depend on meaningful illocution and hence are parasitic. As he writes in *The Theory of Communicative Action*, "I count as communicative action those linguistically mediated interactions in which all participants pursue illocutionary aims, and only illocutionary aims, with their mediating acts of communication" (295).[26] But utterances do not divide this way.

Can one slash strategy, negotiation, inquiry, and eristic from (political) communication? Can one slice reason off from the facticity of existing contexts? Reason has its persuasive effects and consequences, just as do the metaphors in the two questions above—slash, slice, and cut off. In first typing those metaphors, at least part of my intention was to create a reasoned academic argument, but the violence exceeded the reason. I may have some unconscious desire for some effects of the violent metaphors, but I certainly do not know, nor can I fully control, the perlocutionary consequences. If I revise the questions to limit the violence, does my reason grow and my violence wane? Or have I simply strategized reason? The unavoidable and generative surplus of any speech act—metaphors, internal oppositions, contradictions, ideologies, privileges, connotations, paradoxes, narratives, tropes, interpretations, *ethos,* and *pathos*—infiltrate and strategize the purest and plainest of reasons, constatives, and warrants.

Habermas wishes to script truth, knowledge, and understanding through a theory of communicative action, but in doing so, he fails to script a place for the daily difficulties of "subaltern counter-publics" (Fraser), the impossibility of impartiality (Benhabib; Young), and the necessity of situated knowledge (Haraway), difficulties suggesting the requisite of strategy with all its resources. In sum, to arrive at a truth found through illocution and not strategic battle, Habermas argues that only a reasoned procedure, one allowing only communicative action, legitimates democratic decision making. In so arguing, he creates the illusion that reason is an achievement that corrects the violent excesses of language. As Benedetto Fontana, Cary J. Nederman, and Gary Remer observe of Habermas, "The only force recognized as legitimate is the force of reason" (12). In his own words, deliberation depends on the "unforced force of the better argument" (*Inclusion* 37), a transcendent view privileging the cultural and formal structures of reasoned argument. This is a kind of strategy in itself, for as Richard Rorty has pointed out, propositions and arguments are context bound ("Response" 59).

Some theorists of deliberative democracy, such as Seyla Benhabib, Joshua Cohen, John S. Dryzek, and Amy Gutmann, among many, tolerate some rhetorical dimensions beyond a reasoned argument.[27] Others, such as Simone Chambers in *Reasonable Democracy,* specifically add rhetoric or persuasion as a supplement to reason, consensus, procedure, and the denial of difference. These modifications, however, do not render conflict as productive and tend to desire a reasonable and consensual end to disagreement.[28] Remaining committed to the legitimation of law, some deliberative democrats accept a limited role for specific rhetorical strategies within the early stages of opinion formation, which, by definition, precedes the work of writing law. For instance, Gutmann and Thompson see deliberation as entailing a two-part movement, a rhetorical one of "impassioned and immoderate speech" preceding the legislative moment and actual, reasoned deliberation within the legislature. Tellingly, their example of an impassioned speaker—successful, but in ways inappropriate to the real work of the U.S. Senate—is Carol Moseley Braun (Gutmann and Thompson, *Why* 135). In July 1993, faced with the routine renewal of the patent on the Confederate flag insignia, Braun—the only black member of the Senate—first worked through regular channels to block the renewal, but Senators Jesse Helms and Strom Thurmond attached the patent renewal to a major bill where, seemingly, it would pass. Through tears and threats, Senator Braun forced an ending to the patent on the Confederate flag insignia, arguing, "[T]here can be no consensus. It is an outrage. It is an insult. It is absolutely unacceptable to me and to millions of Americans, black and white, that we would put the imprimatur of the United States Senate on a symbol of this kind of idea" (qtd. in *Why* 135).

Rather than examine how and why impassioned, strategic oratory and resistance to unity or consensus might be necessary, realistic, and more than ethical for minorities and women, Gutmann and Thompson marginalize rhetoric and strategic oratory as functioning in opinion formation, which only functions to make issues visible before they are subject to the *real work* of legislation. Effectively they diminish and marginalize the importance of the political discourse of Senator Braun, describing the rhetorical moment as preliminary. In doing so, they minimize issues of power difference, the advocacy necessary to legislative acts, the requisite of refusing some under-standings, and the force of key rhetorical concepts, such as identification, position, timing (*kairos*), character (*ethos*), affect (*pathos*), and performance, all concepts necessary to describe the types of political action available to marginalized peoples. In making these concepts "preliminary," they frame power inequality as separate from legislative moments. They bracket Sena-tor Braun's strategic means of intervening and label her deliberative acts as opinion formation, not legislative acts, even though she speaks as a senator within the Senate.

In addition to demonstrating the limitations of bracketing rhetorical speech and devaluing opinion formation, they demonstrate the difficulty of procedure, as it conceives deliberation as focused on the end of a process. By focusing on the end process, the legislative outcomes, and not the primary, initiating rhetorical utterances, they omit the originating temporal-spatial moment in which interlocutors are defined and define in turn a delibera-tive event. That is, in defining deliberation primarily as a procedure, they belittle the moments when Braun rises to confront the Confederacy patent with every strategy she can muster and when twenty-seven senators change their minds and oppose patent renewal. These are moments when politi-cal being and episteme changed. The moments of radical courage, innova-tion, transformation, and constitution need deliberative theory's attention. Characterizing deliberation as a reasoned procedure leading to agreements, unitary outcomes, or consensus deeply damages the concept itself, for the model is inadequately descriptive of what constitutes deliberation.

Even so, I must admit that there is a certain appeal to procedure and illo-cutionary ethics in defining deliberation. The image of orderly, productive management from dispute and discord to a just judgment enchants, and so it dominates our thinking, extending well beyond the work of deliberative democrats. Consider, for example, Iris Marion Young's procedural definition of deliberation: "A politicized public resolves disagreement and makes decisions by listening to one another's claims and reasons, offering questions and objections, and putting forth new formulations and proposals, until a decision can be reached" (*Justice* 73). Even the postmodern theorist of incommensurability and the differend (difference in dispute, without a common rule of judgment), Jean-François Lyotard, imagines a deliberative process ("Memorandum"). For many years, I myself defined deliberation through an adaptation of Lani Guinier's procedural definition, a definition that approaches deliberation as procedural problem-solving. Keeping her problem-solving approach, I modified it with speech act theory (with my more rhetorical additions in brackets here): "The process of [articulating and] framing issues to be resolved, proposing alternative solutions, examining the reasons for and against the proposed solutions, [advocating for specific solutions, recognizing and responding to the concerns of others], and settling on an alternative [action]" (Lyon, *Intentions* 256). Some of Guinier's language clearly is related to procedural and deliberative democracy: for instance, her emphasis on reasons, procedure, and end. The definition, however, avoids the requirement of consensus and instead proposes "settling" on solutions and alternatives. Although settling is a concept without transcendent vision, it also ignores the transformations inherent in effective deliberative action; that is, it provides no appreciation of how deliberations transform participants, the scene, the future, and the past. In addition, "settling" is limited further in that it ignores commitments to sharing solutions and highlights negotiation. As Anthony Simon Laden observes of the difference between negotiation and deliberation, deliberation creates solutions which "each of the parties can regard as expressing their investment in the issue under discussion" (210). In a problem-solving model of deliberation, claimants work toward a resolution or end from a set of proposed solutions, conceivably through bargaining and compromise, without ever really changing their own standpoints or those of others. Since problem solving ignores a participant's investments in problems and solutions, this procedural model—even with the augmentations of speech, act, and other, even with its gesture toward diversity through alternative actions—basically ignores hegemonic power dynamics internal to deliberation and the transformative work performed by deliberation in favor of an imagined, nondiscriminatory procedure. Furthermore, in focusing on procedure, it minimizes the constitutive aspects and initiating moments inherent in recognizing interlocutors, developing approaches together, and enacting them through the speech acts of deliberation.

In response to the procedural or process emphasis of many conceptions of deliberation, I want to explicate briefly my prior suggestion that deliberations be considered as "examinations of both being and situated knowledge for the many coming to action, an action potentially transformative of being and knowledge." Although "examinations" and "coming to action" might imply a process, that interpretation builds on traditional assumptions about deliberation. If one considers the acts of examination and action as intertwined, then a better interpretation of my prior definition might be written as "the many becoming action." Although the many becoming action has a terse difficulty and an inadequacy of reference, it is shorthand for my larger argument about deliberation happening as interlocutors engage. As the book develops the significance of speech act, performance, and performativity in deliberative acts, it will show that deliberation, performative deliberation, entails discourse's transformative effects both in the material world and among interlocutors as they deliberate. In contrast with constrained procedural approaches, which cut off linguistic resources, performative deliberation acknowledges the linguistic and dramatic power of deliberative acts.

Deliberative democracy has a third conceptual basis that limits its use for describing deliberation, particularly cross-cultural deliberation. It values consensus. Habermas acknowledges the difficulty of using the procedure and seeking truth, and he struggles with the difficulty of achieving consensus, but still he argues that mature thinkers distinguish between conventional, ethical rules of the good life and just and true norms "that could meet with the consent of all affected" (*Moral* 197). As Habermas writes of communicative action, equal interlocutors of good will committed to reasoning and freed from constraint will consent to the same deliberative end (86–94, 306). Habermas returns to consensus as the democratic principle in the more legally based *Between Facts and Norms*, writing, "Only those statutes may claim legitimacy that can meet with the assent (*Zustimmung*) of all citizens in a discursive process of legislation that in turn has been constituted" (141). In the formalized procedure, participants rationalize public opinion and will formation, and they become discursive rather than strategic speakers, developing mutual understanding rather than arguments for effect and behavioral change. Through this ideal, they achieve closure in rational consensus (Chambers). Implicit through various accounts and elaborations of moral communicative action, Habermas consistently seeks fair and equitable discursive procedures that lead to *unanimity or the support of all affected,* finding consent not simply an end goal or ideal, but fully part of a procedure leading to a generalized truth.[29] That is, he argues for cognitive consensus to the universal norms of justice.[30]

Deliberative democracy's discomfort with diversity creates problems for theorizing rhetorical deliberation, because it is hard to imagine even basic norms of justice achieving practical consensus.[31] Beyond the most abstract of terms (education, security, opportunity), there is little consensus in politics. The long-standing promise of free speech in the Bill of Rights has never had the consent of all. Consider the Convention on the Elimination of All Forms of Discrimination Against Women (CEDAW): Despite having the support of 186 states, it is unsigned by the United States, which, through its inaction, joins the company of Iran, Somalia, and Sudan. All do not consent. Recognizing the practical difficulty of consensus formation, Habermas does make exceptions for moral integrity and self-understanding, exceptions acknowledging that "citizens could find themselves in irreconcilable but *reasonable* disagreement" (Rehg and Bohman 45; emphasis in original). The examples of free speech and CEDAW, however, suggest that irreconcilable but reasonable disagreements may be common. More recently, in *Postmetaphysical Thinking,* Habermas also grants the limits of his view; there he acknowledges the recalcitrance of difference, in that the One and the Other are dialectical and impossible to eliminate. Despite his philosophical acceptance of the necessity of difference, however, he does not give up the ideal of consensus (48, 125).

Even if we were to understand consensus as a cognitive process of recognizing just norms, not a political one, Habermas's call for consensus is deeply problematic, as consensus values homogeneity. Consensus explicitly devalues diversity, resistance, and marginality and thereby fails to perceive them as valuable or useful ends in themselves.[32] Furthermore, the value of consensus, by its definitional force, fails to sponsor institutions that respect and preserve difference (Young, *Justice* 47). Given its commitment to the values of modernity, including rationalism, secularism, rule of law, and progress, deliberative democracy implicitly supports a singular convergence of cultures, a mass move to modernity; more explicitly, in its insistence on consensus, it supports a convergence of deliberative outcomes.[33] Many theorists of deliberative democracy struggle to make consensus more tolerant. They acknowledge and qualify their project with John Rawls's idea of "overlapping consensus," agreement on fair laws between citizens with different doctrines or conceptions of the good, or they nod to G. B. Madison's *"dissenting* consensus," which acknowledges the place of difference as a part of a whole.[34] Others point out the limits of consensus itself and the troubles of deliberative democracy's deep discomfort with the messiness of popular or low politics, ordinary language and ordinary citizens, emotional states, cultural differences, and clashing, competing rhetorical acts, all of which enact politics.[35] To demonstrate this point briefly by copia: Simone Chambers observes that Habermas does not deal with the possibility that citizens lack interest in or capability for understanding each other ("Discourse" 247). Of the conflicting rights norms of the right to life and to bodily integrity, Donald Moon writes that "even these examples are problematic, inasmuch as a consensus on such norms is likely to mask deep conflicts over their application and the conditions under which they may be overridden" (152). To extend Moon, a norm may be accepted generally—such as a call for literacy—but reasons, intentions, and desires supporting a claim can be radically different, as can the practical applications.[36] Abdullahi Ahmed An-Na'im writes that "total agreement on interpretations and standards" is unrealistic, as it presupposes "the existence of the interpretation to be agreed upon" (18). Iris Marion Young also critiques the project of consensus as unrealistic. Although she characterizes consensus as assimilating standpoints, a definition that acknowledges the differences from which we begin deliberation, she is deeply concerned with whether we can recognize each other sufficiently to form consensus or assimilate each other's standpoints ("Communication" 127).

In ways helpful to understanding deliberation in a global era, many scholars not only diminish the practical possibility of consensus but also value difference, diversity, dissent, and even dissensus over legitimation and consensus. From Athens forward, many have conceived democracy as generating a dissensual and critical culture, which sustains not just a plurality of values and commitments but their defining and redefining.[37] Consensus becomes a suspect value even for deliberative democrats such as Gerald F. Gaus, who sees dissensus at "the very heart of a healthy democracy" (237), but postmodern critics and radical democrats are more adamant. Responding to what he characterizes as Habermas's false belief that humanity seeks the regulation of language games, Jean-François Lyotard observes, "Consensus has become an outmoded and suspect value. . . . We must . . . arrive at an idea and practice of justice that is not linked to that of consensus" (*Postmodern* 66). In responding to Habermasians, Chantal Mouffe argues that consensus in liberal democracies is "the expression of a hegemony and the crystallization of power relations" (*Democratic* 49), asserting that what is legitimate and what is not should remain politically contestable. Hailing contestation as a legitimate force, Ewa Plonowska Ziarek constructs an ethics of dissensus, which acknowledges "the irreducible dimension of antagonism and power in discourse, embodiment, and democratic politics" (1). In bridging the gap between ethics of freedom and obligation to the Other (Caputo), Ziarek successfully destabilizes dichotomies, such as politics and ethics, to imagine an ethics responsive to situated domination.

Still, even consensus and dissensus can be a false dichotomy, bogeymen to scare off either tolerance of difference or the hegemonic and necessary power of acting together. Consequently not all radical democrats, postmodernists, or pragmatists value all diversity in its more extreme manifestations. Constraints on what constitutes legitimate difference, however, ignore the most difficult types of deliberation, ones in which cultures with deeply differing values must make decisions about human rights, economic survival, or the future of the planet. Even if one would not issue a permit allowing Nazis to march in Skokie, few would argue against engaging Nazis in political dialogue and the project of changing their position. As Young has argued in "Difference as a Resource for Democratic Communication," remedies for "disadvantages and exclusions" depend on recognition and inclusion of differentiated social groups, groups whose unique positions create a plural public, one not easily subsumed under norms of rationality, procedure, and argumentation.[38] The democratic value of differentiated groups arises because a plural public motivates appeals to justice rather than self-interest, teaches the partiality of any perspective, and exposes the situatedness of all knowledge. Differences enrich democracy, pushing it toward discourses of justice and away from narcissism and self-interest, she argues. Desirable difference redirects attention from legitimacy and procedure toward differentiated (even disruptive) social groups as political resources whose expressions and exchanges create reflection on "the experience, knowledge, and interests of others" (402).[39]

In the service of deliberative differences, long before the copia of voices against consensus, Arendt writes that "[t]o hold different opinions and to be aware that other people think differently on the same issue shields us from that god-like certainty which stops all discussion and reduces social relationships to those of an ant heap. A unanimous public opinion tends to eliminate bodily those who differ, for mass unanimity is not the result of agreement, but an expression of fanaticism and hysteria" (*Jew* 182). If she writes in the aftermath of fascism, her point can be extended to the philosophical promise of reasoned unity, consensus, and universalism. Despite the appeal of transcendent justice and the reconciliation of our differences, ubiquitous human difference denies the possibility of a healthy or ethical consensus as it demands a constant and unstable deliberation on (political) relationships. Certainly participants consent to their community's practices and to political decisions—with reservation and without—but it is not the end of a process. Rather, it is a tentative recognition and engagement with an alluring claim upon the self by the lifeworld, a normative claim always subject to revocation and appeal.

A Better Consensus

Before critiquing more rhetorical traditions of deliberation in the next chapter, I would like to consider an alternative way to conceptualize unanimous agreement for the purpose of understanding consensus and dissensus as less a dichotomy and more a continuum of political perspectives. The decision processes of the Religious Society of Friends (Quakers) create a kind of consensus in a particular situation. I do not consider Quaker decision making as a model for cross-cultural political deliberation, given their close community and its transcendent, universalistic assumptions, but I offer it as an established tradition and practice that considers deliberation differently. In self-selecting communities, such as Quakers, consensus may be used to indicate a common commitment to the good, based in community values, formed over time in a safe, open space, committed to light, peace, and harmony (Morley; Sheeran). Barry Morley, however, observes that "consensus" arose as shorthand for "sense of the meeting" and that the term "consensus" is inadequate for describing the spiritual work and transformative nature inherent in "sense of the meeting." Consensus, according to Morley, is "achieved through a process of reasoning in which reasonable people search for a satisfactory decision," a definition surprisingly in step with those of deliberative democracy (5). Quakers, on the other hand, should be using "sense of the meeting" to indicate their openness "to being guided to perfect resolution in Light, to a place where we sit in unity in the collective inward Presence." Inherent in approaching "the sense of the meeting" are two presumptions: (1) each member of the meeting seeks the best solution and (2) the group, in searching together, guided by their collective presence, can create and be constituted in concord and unity, even truth. These assumptions underlie the community joined in common presence and together minimize a value of difference.

Despite the limitations of its community of belief and its transcendent language, the Quaker process of decision making is a kind of deliberation with implications for secular discussions of consensus and its alternatives. That is, it can redefine what consensus entails and what resolutions demand of interlocutors. Morley quotes another Friend as observing the difference between willfulness and willingness, considering where consensus reveals a willed decision found through a (reasoned) competition of ideas and where sense of the meeting reveals a willingness to be led, to listen, to weigh. When one considers the transient and sensory implications in the concept of sense of the meeting, one can see how the recognition of others and their potential for difference are connoted within sense of the meeting. On a first reading of Morley, it might seem that sense of the meeting emphasizes textual reception, or listening, but the process is deeply discursive, involving sensory actions of many in producing ideas within a more open forum, where the outcome is secondary to the sharing. As Morley writes later, "Consensus involves a process in which we promulgate, argue, and select or compromise ideas until we can arrive at an acceptable decision. When we seek the sense of the meeting, the decision is a by-product. It happens along the way. The purpose of seeking the sense of the meeting is to gather ourselves in unity" (15). Within societies, including that of the Friends, rituals cause transformation—from man and woman to husband and wife, from dissent to unity. In attaining the sense of the meeting, Morley maintains that "[w]e form invisible bonds among ourselves which transcend the petty and make the next sense of the meeting more desirable and more readily attainable" (24). Thus the act of attaining a sense of the meeting creates bonds in ways that consensus as a rational process does not consider. Sense of the meeting emphasizes a significant power in simply recognizing and engaging the other. It understands the practices of recognition and sharing in open-minded presence as more important than the end of willed and reasoned consensus, and it values the creation of ongoing social bonds over a rational outcome.

Sense of the meeting, formed in acts of recognizing and engaging, responds to the limits of consensus, and provocatively, its implied critique arises not in philosophical debate but in the practices of religious community. First, sense of the meeting values the members of the community over political outcomes, while consensus denies the primary place or value of disagreement and difference among political participants and so obscures the greatest obstacle to deliberation, which is the failure to recognize the other's standpoint. Until participants in disagreement can become interlocutors and achieve a kind of presence, there will not be deliberations. The initiation of deliberation may be a more difficult moment than the moment of outcome. Deliberations have no procedure until both parties understand a use, need, or purpose to the other's position. Second, the meeting is achieved over time and with regular interactions; the meeting is ongoing. Consensus limits our temporal understanding of what it means to settle or end deliberation successfully. The ending that consensus imagines is too tidy; its ideality reduces complexity, making it less complex than the messiness of majority voting, less complex than minority struggles for recognition, and less complex than the meeting of tweets and blogs. Too easily consensus conceives its ending without acknowledging hegemony and the ongoing life of an issue, and thus it rarely concedes the impossibility of settling once and for all. A third pathology of consensus: It characterizes the outcome of deliberation as a rational state of being rather than an action or practice embedded in a commitment to sustaining recognition and engagement even in a fractured, fractious, transient situation.

Deliberative Acts

Deliberation within much of contemporary political theory emphasizes consensus, rationality, sincerity, reciprocity, and reflection and allows little space for strategic discourses, the pluralism (even incommensurability) of cross-cultural communication, and incorrigible, inflexible political positions. When political theory does recognize the boisterous possibilities of deliberation, as in radical democracy, theorists offer little definition of the structural possibility and limitations of speaking; although radical democracy's theorists, such as Mouffe, abandon abstract universalism and the danger of consensus, they offer little in terms of discursive theory. They understand the rhetorical nature of politics, but they are not rhetoricians. Responding to the need for a deliberative theory based in rhetorical traditions and embracing difference, *Deliberative Acts* develops a theory of performative deliberation, where deliberation is an action or a practice. In taking a performative approach, it offers a deliberative theory based in the present tense of iteration, the bodily moment of recognition, and the constituting speech act. To emphasize the significance of initial recognition and engagement, performative deliberation is only incidentally concerned with outcomes. Rather, it privileges the speech acts that constitute deliberation itself. To define how interlocutors might come to deliberate across difference, this book offers a new critical vocabulary for discussing rhetorical deliberation. It extends speech act theory and notions of performativity into political contexts to demonstrate the constituting power of deliberating. Within these chapters, participants in performative deliberation enact difference, and in performing cultural differences and diversity, they are agents inhabiting discourse and negotiating particularities together. Building on Arendt's concept of an in-between space necessary for interlocutors (citizen agents) to meet and share inter-ests, *Deliberative Acts* extends the concept of performativity to include agency through the analysis of specific moments in human rights history to describe how agonism and difference are reified or bridged.

The first chapter, "Defining Deliberative Space: Rethinking Persuasion, Position, and Identification," analyzes traditional understandings of rhetorical deliberation. Beginning with Aristotelian rhetoric's dependence on outcomes, persuasion, and audience, it contrasts persuasion with the Confucian concept of remonstration to expose the limits of a means/end approach and the assumption of a docile audience. In developing a frame for engaging equal or superior interlocutors and positing the primacy of initiating deliberation over its outcomes, the chapter examines the concept of position or standpoint, emphasizing the inherent potential within a position. From analyses of the Chinese concept of *shi* (positioned potential), feminist standpoint epistemologies, and James Kastely's "play of position," the chapter describes an alternative spatial and temporal concept of deliberative relationships, focused on the moment of recognition. Through Hannah Arendt's concepts of the in-between and inter-est, the position and relationships of interlocutors are redefined, away from persuasive power and toward presence and unequal reciprocity. Identifying difference as generative and constituting, the chapter ends with a careful critique of why the commonly used concept of identification, no matter how complexly articulated, is inadequate for describing cross-cultural communication within contemporary acts of decision making. Identification, like consensus, refuses difference.

"Performative Deliberation and the Narratable Who" theorizes deliberative utterances as performatives, performances, and performativities on a continuum of form and forming. Performative focuses on the structural or *formal* effects of utterance and reveals the rituals of the discursive system, the security system that bolts language to history and culture (J. L. Austin). Performance connotes the *forming* aspects of discourse as seen in dramatic, embodied situations where acts are less scripted and ritualized and so less stable; performance potentially cracks fastened meanings and creates the space which constitutes the subject's identity and the social forum (Kenneth

Burke). Performative utterances and performance alone are not enough to describe the constituting effects of deliberation, because the concepts insufficiently denote ideology. Performativity engages discourse and the power relationships inherent in discourse that constrain and implicate us in what we would deny (Judith Butler). These three theoretical approaches to deliberation suggest that performative deliberation—the individual and embodied utterances of political rhetoric—can form and transform a culture's citizens, definitions of justice and equality, the laws and declarations of the state, and ultimately a form of life.

Much of the work of the chapter is to enrich these theories, which emphasize utterance and discourse—an emphasis appropriate to philosophy and hermeneutics but not to political action. The agential citizen requires a significant extension of a theory begun in ordinary language philosophy and developed in postmodern erasures of the subject. The performing citizen needs a body, but she also needs agency. Coupling Hannah Arendt's work on natality and Adriana Cavarero's concept of the narratable self to introduce the problematic ethics of recognition within deliberation, the chapter proceeds to develop a concept of agency appropriate to deliberation. In a deliberative situation, neither resistance nor compliance adequately describes the action; although liberal theory values resistance and rebellion, neither concept is adequate to recognition and deliberation. Saba Mahmood's redefinition of agency as a negotiation of lived, learned, and strategically engaged norms allows a richer conception of a citizen subject, who is not just formed and conforming but also performing and forming. Citizen agents involved in deliberating locations and histories have a variety of means to make their presence politically effective.

Recognition is the founding act of deliberation: Unless one sees the difficulty that needs address, unless one sees the human who disagrees, there is no moment of engagement, no dialogue, no performative moments. "Narrating Rights, Creating Agents: Missing Women in the U.S. Media" examines the place of compassion as a performative emotion, and in doing so, it combines Cavarero's requirement of a narratable self with Arendt's analysis of political narrative to examine U.S. media depictions of missing women—specifically, the one hundred million missing women in Asia. Focusing on representations of missing women in China, it argues that media stories distort and destroy the possibility of recognition by representing women as abject, a creation that demonstrates cultural assumptions about acting and suffering. Furthermore, missing women are misrepresented to represent liberal rights valued in the United States, not the communitarian values of their own cultures. After reviewing a number of U.S. newspaper stories, the chapter examines Amy Tan's *The Joy Luck Club* to suggest that cross-cultural deliberation within human rights debates benefits from texts that articulate the consciousness of others and their cultural values. Even aesthetic forms that present narratable and recognizable others compassionately are preferable to abjection. The agent seen in conscious action is more recognizable than the one seen in journalistic reports.

"The Beauty of Arendt's Lies: Menchú's Political Strategy" reconceives the ethics of lies, arguing that they are examples of imaginative, performative acts in the service of (potentially new) political regimes. In arguing for the legitimacy of strategic communication, the chapter builds on Hannah Arendt's discussion of truth, lies, and opinion, suggesting a more rhetorical, deliberative, and layered approach to political discourse. Arendt claims that lies—as substitutes for more violent means—are often considered legitimate within politics and diplomacy and are relatively harmless compared to apolitical, "despotic" truth, which is beyond agreement, dispute, opinion, or consent. Despotic truth has a coercive force outside the wishes and desires of citizens and tyrants because truth, which is normative, forecloses desire and discovery. While Arendt is deeply worried about modern systemic lies that attempt to create systems unrelated to factual truths, she is sympathetic to traditional political lies told to enemies. The chapter then examines the Rigoberta Menchú controversy. Menchú, having won the Nobel Peace Prize, was found to have omissions and inaccuracies in her highly regarded and well-read *testimonio* (memoir), *I, Rigoberta Menchú: An Indian Woman in Guatemala*. Responding to academics' attempts to explain away her lies, the chapter suggests that she told traditional political lies to enemies for legitimate political purposes. To argue otherwise reduces her political agency and marginalizes her. If deliberation depends on recognizing difference, it also depends on seeing the other as an agent capable of negotiating norms.

Deliberations over new rights, such as gay marriage and universal health care, represent key transformations in how citizens conceive and enact themselves. Although contemporary struggles are ongoing and unresolved, older rights disputes can illuminate the transformative potential within current events. "Voting like a Girl: Declarations, Paradoxes of Deliberation, and Embodied Citizens as a Difference in Kind" looks back to the initial deliberations over women's suffrage and argues that the performance of citizenship, even if illegal, was a deliberative step necessary for the development of the subject of human rights as well as the culture that would support her rights. Beyond speech acts, citizen performatives demonstrate their position as rights subjects. Linking the negotiation of norms to the paradoxical nature of rights declarations, the chapter examines how the women of Seneca Falls used a paradoxical utterance in the Declaration of Independence to extend suffrage rights. Extending the uses of infelicitous performatives to Susan B. Anthony's act of voting in 1868, the chapter also considers how the performance of voting rights and citizenship reconstitutes the world, arguing that these acts of performative deliberation brought a convergence if not consensus among citizens.

Rights achieved in performative struggle are *different in kind* than rights mandated by outside political forces. Beyond simply speech acts, these citizen acts constitute the subject of rights. In contrast, women in Uzbekistan received rights as Communist Russia moved to hinder Islamic religious forces; Mao Zedong proclaimed that women "held up half the sky" as he undercut Confucian family values; and Douglas MacArthur gave Japanese women the right to vote in the U.S. effort to sweep out imperial rule. All three state actions had positive effects on rights, but they represented nation-building over citizen performance and failed to value citizen agency. Through performative deliberations, including recognition and engagement with all participants, human rights may become an authentic part of a culture's form of life rather than a colonialist mandate. Although mandated rights—through daily performances and practices—eventually may become part of a culture, the lack of deliberative performance limits decision making and early cultural ownership. Furthermore, clashing cultural values can increase violence and resistance to rights mandated from outside.

Deliberative Acts replaces goal-driven theories of deliberation. Performative deliberative theory begins in the meeting place or contact zone among cultures and describes the performative acts that arise in those locations. Rather than characterizing deliberation as collaboration or competition, performative deliberation conceives deliberation itself as a formative act. In doing so, it emphasizes the speech acts of deliberation using the methods of both formalism and rhetorical analysis to demonstrate the discursive choices interlocutors make while deliberating together. By examining the moments when recognition and engagement take place, the project moves the concept of deliberation from a procedure to the moments of recognizing political difference and the practices of interlocutors during those moments. Such recognitions move difference and sufferance from the shadows of the public sphere and, in doing so, change the interlocutors, interpretive horizons, and discourses of justice. Performing such deliberations makes the participants anew.

I

DEFINING DELIBERATIVE SPACE:
RETHINKING PERSUASION, POSITION, AND IDENTIFICATION

"Wherever you go, you will be a *polis*": these famous words became not merely the watchword of Greek colonization, they expressed the conviction that action and speech create a space between the participants which can find its proper location almost any time and anywhere. It is the space of appearance in the widest sense of the word, namely, the space where I appear to others as others appear to me, where men exist not merely like other living or inanimate things but make their appearance explicitly.

—Hannah Arendt, *The Human Condition*

As a radical standpoint, perspective, position, "the politics of location" necessarily calls those of us who would participate in the formation of counter-hegemonic cultural practice to identify the spaces where we begin the process of re-vision.

—bell hooks, "Choosing the Margin as a Space of Radical Openness"

Political speaking urges us either to do or not to do something.

—Aristotle, *Rhetoric*

To do or not to do, that is the question—Aristotle's founding question for political speech or deliberation.[1] For in doing, or even not doing, in speech or act, one might make one's presence known to others, but more than making presence, one also creates the possibilities of position, space, situation, recognition, event, experience, and sundry unknown contingencies. Hannah Arendt would have the space of human appearance, the public space where we recognize each other, created by speech and act, the very verbs of human existence. Extending space and who appears and participates, bell hooks requires presence in the spatial margin as a prerequisite to re-seeing and re-vising the public space. By defining human events as located within the doings of speech and action, three very different theorists argue that being human is not a matter of what one is or what one knows, but the eventfulness of what one does and where one does it. To approach deliberation as a performative and constitutive engagement in the moment, a doing based in speech and act and not in persuasion and identification, this chapter critiques and reworks some of the key terms of traditional rhetoric, terms that have held rhetorical thinking in bondage too long.

Persuasion, audience, and identification all have limitations for conceiving deliberation as engaged doing or the many becoming action, in part because they emphasize a process of persuasion, but also because they are limited in their ability to critique hegemony and the necessity of difference. If one briefly tosses aside persuasion, identification, audience, and a bagful of familiar rhetorical terms, whatever their use, one might discover or invent new words and worlds that note communicative acts invisible to the common traditions of deliberation. Working from classical understandings of Aristotle and Confucius to feminist standpoint epistemologies and positional rhetorics, this chapter develops an alternative spatial and temporal concept of deliberative recognitions and relationships. It ends with a careful critique of why the commonly used concept of identification, no matter how complexly articulated, is inadequate for describing communication within contemporary acts of decision-making, in a time and space where cultural difference and inopportune futures cannot be glibly swept away.

Persuasive Limitations

In the West, deliberative theory begins with Aristotle. Certainly earlier dramatists and philosophers demonstrate rhetorical deliberation—the common soldiers deliberate in *Antigone*—but Aristotle is the first to develop a systemic theory of rhetoric, based on persuasion and its methods as a productive art (Atwill).[2] He defines deliberation as one of rhetoric's three genres or branches, the others being epideictic and forensic. In moving from the performances of deliberators within plays and Socratic dialogues to theoretical overviews, Aristotle focuses on particular aspects of collective deliberation at the cost of other features, and he sets key assumptions within rhetorical theory. The loss of immediacy in the dialogic and performing deliberations in the earlier plays and dialogues are subsumed under a system that divides rhetorical branches by time or tense, ends or *telos*, and content (*Rhetoric* 1358b). His vision of moral suasion and contrasting branches has dominated thinking about deliberation, and escape from his legacy of persuading speakers is difficult even today, in the full presence of modern democracy's massive scale, representative systems, increased freedom and equality, and tolerance of diversity.³ Consequently the work of contemporary deliberative democrats shows Aristotelian effects through the dominance of his terms and concepts. Their concern with a forward-looking procedure, the means to shared ends, and crafting the right discourse are found in Aristotle, though they resist his legacy in that they constrain the use of strategic speech, limit the place and vigor of public argument, and lack a realistic, if platitudinous, sense of politics (Yack). Furthermore, they assume a place above politics from which to judge, and as Martha Nussbaum observes, Aristotle takes no "stand outside the conditions of human life" (*Fragility* 190).

In defining rhetoric as "the faculty of observing in any given case the available means of persuasion" (*Rhetoric* 1355b26–7), Aristotle characterized suasory rhetoric as a teachable art, one basic to civic practices, and thus necessary and available to citizens broadly. Persuasion dominates his definition and a long tradition that follows, and although Aristotle's definitional terms of "observing," "available," and "in any given case" together situate and modulate ruthless acts of persuasion, as do proofs of ethos, logos, and pathos and the need for an audience's judgment, persuasion by the crafting orator remains a fractious and challenging way of thinking about deliberation. Many—Plato, Kenneth Burke, Jürgen Habermas, to name a few—have characterized persuasion as strategic or manipulative, and others—Thomas Hobbes, Adrienne Rich, Frantz Fanon (*Wretched*), to name a few—argue that far worse persuasion inherently seeks to remove otherness and functions as a violent, imperative, even imperial tool of the cultural or verbal elite.

Although one may be wary of or adverse to persuasion, it describes a historically significant approach to theorizing rhetorical deliberation, one that has survived because of its efficacy. In *Saving Persuasion*, Bryan Garsten responds to attacks on manipulative persuasion. He traces one historical line of persuasion's critique, focusing on the tension between classical views of practical reason and judgment and the early modern view of public reason and state sovereignty, especially as it pertains to deliberative democracy. Cognizant of both persuasion's ability to manipulate an audience and its implicit requirement that a speaker pander to the audience's interests, Garsten still ratifies the political uses of persuasion, and so a rhetoric-as-persuasion model deeply indebted to Aristotle. Garsten takes this tack, in part, because the classical and humanistic tradition of persuasion correctly assumes that, although people disagree, they can and do willingly change their minds and solve problems through language. Garsten rightly would group the persuasion-hostile theorists of deliberative democracy with the early modernists who "aimed to quell controversy by having us alienate our capacity for private judgment" (179). As he interprets it, liberal political theory privileges publicly defined reason and discursive procedures, which lead to consensus, ideally; hence, it assaults rhetorical tools such as interest-identification, negotiation, bargaining, and arguments relevant to specific audiences (identity politics). Garsten decries normative deliberative procedures because they define the better argument in the procedure itself, making deliberation into a discourse of justification and legitimacy rather than one of engagement, persuasion, practical wisdom, emotion, intuition, and the beliefs of fellow citizens. Although deliberative theorists, following Habermas, may characterize deliberation as rational will-formation and an authoritative public standard of reasonableness, Garsten would have us follow the classical and humanistic traditions of "mak[ing] decisions deliberatively" (192) and "think[ing] more deeply" (194).

For purposes of embracing deliberation's more agonistic practices, Garsten successfully defends rhetorical persuasion as a useful art by fending off the attacks of modern political theorists concerned with creating institutional and metaphysical methods of controlling agonism, but he does not address persuasion's other critics—feminist, postcolonial, postmodern—whose arguments are more telling, as they worry not about the people's vulnerability to language but about hegemonic power discursively fortressed and protected by persuasion. Even if persuasion links rhetoric, engagement, and practical judgment as core democratic practices, it remains troubling if it authorizes power-driven establishment politics. On one hand, fearful of the mob and the minority, wary of private judgment and the violence of an agonistic politics, some distrust persuasion and seek to set boundaries to deliberation by positing a unitary public standpoint, be it state sovereignty, shared national identity, or required reason. On the other hand, rather than fear the mob, some fear the state or society, and to prevent oppression, they resist persuasion as a legitimate strategy because the dominant may persuade with more tools and spaces than the marginal and oppressed. Both critiques concur that persuasion may not always be dialogic: in fact, it may never be dialogic.

To understand the limitations of persuasion within deliberation, particularly its hegemonic aspects, I will outline three worries within discussions of persuasion and then develop their implications more fully. The difficulties of audience, process, and commonality do not disqualify persuasion as an undertaking within deliberation. I do not share Habermasian fears of strategy, but they suggest that persuasion is only a partial characterization of deliberation, and scholars should have other ways of describing recognition and engagement as well. First of all, persuasion presumes a powerful speaker (even a demigod) and a docile audience, not a *relationship* between equal interlocutors, let alone a speaker of lesser rhetorical power. Implicit within Aristotle's model is the assumption that an audience is open to persuasion, responds to similar arguments, and will listen and agree with the speaker of good reasons. Aristotle's audience may make judgments, but they do not make counterarguments. Contemporary deliberations, however, often engage members of disparate communities who refuse, counter, or do not attend to the opposing arguments. Furthermore, the power differentials are embedded complexly in cultural differences that minimize any particular speaker's appeal across issues. Second, persuasion is a word driven to hopeful, future outcomes, which may not be the true purpose of deliberation. That is, persuasion itself is a process word, describing an action with an end, but if deliberation is made of constitutive acts, even more so than motivational acts, then an act of deliberation may be *the happening*, organically unfolding and enveloping and not a pathway to transparent goals preordained in the speaker's purposes. Third, Aristotelian persuasion, born of the *polis*, presumes a common core of interests, knowledges, and spaces; perhaps this is best exemplified by the ancient prominence of the enthymeme, with its missing term that glues communal understanding. In the *Rhetoric* and its derivatives, persuasive proofs depend on the socially and culturally embedded knowledge of character, cultural commonplaces, and a community's emotions. In the small community, shared values of character, commonplaces, and appropriate emotions inform decisions on a good life. Intimate optimism and shared values, however, guide few current deliberations, which require different or new proofs. If citizens are to deliberate in transnational or glocal agonisms, they have a critical need for more complex proofs as part of an understanding of who is trustworthy and how one might engage competitive communicative actions.

Addressing persuasion's assumption of the powerful speaker, James L. Kastely aptly observes that Aristotle understands the constitutive force of language and develops a "method of moving from the currently available appearances and opinions to new perspectives and understandings of the world" (9). The new perspectives, however, are based on the discursive powers of the speaker, and due to the centrality of the rhetor and his available means of persuasion, the audience is a targeted spectator to be assessed and swayed to a new worldview. Certainly the rhetor requires judgment from the audience and so is committed to showing his practical wisdom, virtue, and good will. Indeed, the audience has a certain type of power to decide, and the rhetor is dependent upon the larger citizenry. Even if the speaker may have to shape his perspective based on the audience's needs or demands, within the fantasy of Western rhetoric, particularly as supported by mass media culture, a powerful speaker seemingly controls a docile audience, moving them to particular ends. The audience's ability to determine actions is suppressed through a focus on the rhetor's persuasive words and strategy. The power of an interest group is reflected back onto the wise rhetor who strategizes outcomes. Even when Aristotle does consider the possibility of interlocutors, he defines persuasion as a means of succeeding, holding the unsuccessful rhetor responsible for unjust judgments (1354b–1355b). As Plato, Habermas, and so many others warn, persuasion's commitment to power differentials between speaker and audience and its loyalty to a speaker's success make its place in rhetorical deliberation an ethical problem for recognition between interlocutors.

Since audiences in the Aristotelian tradition are fantasized as easily understood by the rhetor (and characterized simply as impulsive youth or cautious elderly), addressing their characteristics and interests is a key part of persuasion. In diminishing the heterogeneous character of an audience, the tradition minimizes the place for dialogic negotiations not solely over outcomes but also over human nature and knowledge. Without acknowledgement of ontological and epistemological difference, the members of the persuadable audience take a spectral role, seated in the auditorium, raising their hands in vote, and then exiting through the fire doors (*theatrum mundi*). Despite its undeniable role in politics, persuasion as theorized ignores the primary requirement of deliberation: willing and engaged participation in the form of speech and act among interlocutors who engage each other and each other's voiced perspective. Since audiences do not speak back, they are always already defined as passive. Luc Boltanski notes that the spectator of distant suffering is at risk of passivity, a passivity I see as similar to that of a rhetorical audience. He observes,

> [t]he criterion of public speech or conversation is precisely what enables us to distinguish between a way of looking which can be characterised as disinterested or altruistic, one which is orientated outwards and which is motivated by the intention to see the suffering ended, from a selfish way of looking which is wholly taken up with the internal states aroused by the spectacle of suffering: fascination, horror, interest, excitement, pleasure, etc. (21)

Just as public speech or conversation is the criterion that may create altruism and activism for Boltanski, dialogic communication oriented *outwards* in public speech creates the deliberative event and its motivations. A spectator appropriate to politics moves beyond the vicarious, internal thrills of a theatrical audience or crowd into the active role of interlocutor. The spectating audience susceptible to persuasion and passivity is taken up with its own internal states and interests—and is subject to demagoguery.

Recognition and reciprocity are the basic conditions of meeting and deliberating across difference. For deliberation to begin, first people recognize other people whose material conditions, beliefs, values, opinions, and purposes differ, and then both sides must have a reciprocal claim upon the other so that they are willing to discuss those differences. Without a doubt, one can say that rhetorical recognition means listening and respecting each other, and then *responding responsibly* to each other. But with more difficulty, once persuasion has been bracketed and the spectator becomes an interlocutor, one still must wonder what is implied and implicated in recognition. Recognition, to which I will return at length, is particularly important to performative deliberation because it considers the discursive acts between interlocutors as constitutive of its participants, their relationships, and the event of their meeting. Yes, the purposes of persuasion are multiple and are of some use. Too much focus there, however, distorts recognition and reciprocity, limiting the outcomes of deliberation in imagining justice, political community, and difference. Interlocutors may not escape perverse persuasion, but in speaking back, their self-defining discourses are offered as evidence of both their being and knowledge, potentially scripting their (fragmented) world into the decision of doing or not doing.

Second, the Aristotelian tradition characterizes deliberation as future oriented, which limits the place and purposes of deliberation. If deliberation is the branch of rhetoric most concerned with the future, Aristotle characterizes all rhetoric as a hopeful, forward-looking art, writing, "Rhetoric is useful because what is true and what is just are naturally stronger than their opposites" (1355a24; see also *Politics* 1281a42–b).[4] Armed with what Robert Wardy calls "epistemological optimism" against the worries of injustice and skepticism about popular judgment, Aristotle audaciously argues that truth and justice will prevail not just through the correct use of language, but because of something intrinsic to the people's judgment of what is true and just.[5] Unlike forensics of the past and epideictic of the present, future-oriented deliberation is particularly concerned with a better future, arising when the consequences of human actions are unclear and the means not defined though the end or *telos* (*Ethics* 1112a18–1112b26; *Rhetoric* 1362a, 1366a).[6]

Aristotle's deliberative rhetoric becomes a calculation of the means to an end, although it is not only vested in means calculation; sometimes the end itself may need further specification (Nussbaum, *Fragility* 297). The calculus of means and ends is not simple, and if their full complexity is acknowledged, the distinctions between them may blur. As Janet Atwill argues, in what might be an extension of Aristotle, the end may be more complexly pragmatic in that the speaker is not simply persuading an audience to act toward that end, but he is also concerned with the uses and effects of persuading in, say, creating a community. In that Aristotle's rhetoric is considered a productive knowledge (rather than theoretical or practical), it is concerned with coming into being (Atwill 172). In particular cases of clashing values, the initial deliberative tasks will include the creation of trust, shared futures, agreement on what is proof, and so on; all of these means serve the end of creating a collective that can agree on an end, a good life. To make this more accessible, let me extend Atwill; it is unlikely that deliberators over abortion or gay marriage find first a common end. Such conflicted interlocutors first might have to decide whether they wish to recognize each other, for what purpose, and on what points. The initial deliberative tasks would not be focused on an end, but on creating the conditions of deliberation. In any calculus of conflict, it may be unclear whether trust, proof, or definitions are ends or means, because they will be both.

Also inherent in optimistic persuasion is a focus on the future event itself. At first glance, this limit seems closely related to the means-ends constraints, but there is a second concern with future orientation. When deliberative theory looks ahead to events, outcomes, and ends, it potentially engages in a type of prediction, a sorcerer's plotting of opportunities in a land where a few citizen soothsayers imagine and speak to a new lifeworld. A future-oriented theory minimizes what is happening in the moment of engagement between interlocutors and bypasses considerations of deliberation as a performance in the present. Thus unlike the deliberations of *Antigone* or the elenchus of the *Gorgias*, both of which demonstrate the significance of engagement, future-oriented theories of deliberation ignore how symbolic acts in the present create a current worldview that is always already constructing the future in an infinite procession. If deliberation is defined not as a procedure with a defined end, not as the futurist branch of rhetoric, not as the vote's legitimate outcome, but as a dramatic event or a series of enactments, then deliberative theory focuses on the discursive acts responsible for altering the subjectivity of the participants, their discourses, and their beliefs. Deliberative acts define ways of responding to the world in which interlocutors exist and make claims. Deliberation considered as performance, performative, and performativity shifts the focus of deliberative theory in significant ways. Future outcomes become less significant than the current engagement, and thus success and judgment become less important than engagement. If democratic citizens and global communities do not share an end or a vision of the good life, deliberation itself may be the good life and an end in itself, for the acts of deliberating require significant understanding of and commitment to recognition and reciprocity. Despite a tradition of outcome-based deliberation focused on a trajectory of means to ends, one might think more productively of deliberation as concerned with constituting the present grounds of engagement, positions of interlocutors, and immediate acts of invention.

Persuasion's third limitation is its focus on shared values, discourses, and rhetorical proofs. When Aristotle holds that a citizenry can come to better decisions on the good life than the individual (*Politics* 3.15.1286a30), he fails to acknowledge the role that a community and its particular form of the good have in creating and perpetuating injustice. That is, although he acknowledges that citizens are enmeshed in struggles—a key moment in embracing diversity—he argues that deliberation ultimately will create or invent the possibilities for justice, in any given case. This optimistic view of deliberation is uncomfortable to modern audiences, who have read and seen fascist propaganda. (Wardy repudiates Aristotle's sincerity about justice over power by examining how victory trumps truth repeatedly within the *Rhetoric*.) Modern rhetoricians, from Kenneth Burke to Stephen Toulmin, consider how deeply persuasion needs a supplement of ideology critique and argument analysis. Throughout much of history, persuasion escapes a critique of communal injustice because historically, the small educated and moneyed elite shared assumptions about a *polis* and a body of reasonable citizens cohesive enough to share ends and conceptions of justice (hear the praise for consensus in the fetal heartbeats of deliberation). Even so, slavery, not even subject to critique in the *polis*, exemplifies how persuasion might work in the service of injustice. In effect, persuasion tends to work in the service of hegemony, for it is easier to argue for what is already present than to imagine futures and find proof for counterfactuals.

In diverse and divided global politics, deliberation cannot be conceived productively as the means to shared or modified ends, because even a glocal audience disputes the nature of justice and the common good at a depth that Aristotle and his followers have not imagined. Not only do barbarians and slaves speak, but women have joined the fray. "The good" seems such a quaint concept amid global diversity. In addressing the active and resisting audience, or rather *interlocutors*, of modernity, a speaker cannot presuppose commonalities, and the site of initiation as well as ends and means may all be the subject of deliberation. Even if the means and ends are easier to imagine after the establishment of a common good, in all likelihood, they are considered continuously and recursively throughout political actions. The complexity of discussing deliberation *apart* from a community that shares common purposes, an already almost consensual community, contributes to why the art of rhetorical deliberation is marginalized within political theory. If rhetorical deliberation is to be understood within global matters, recognition must surmount persuasion as a defining characteristic.

Alternatives to Persuasion

Persuasion, which has so dominated the Western rhetorical tradition, is only one lens for understanding rhetorical deliberation. Other traditions of political communication do not focus formalistically on strategy but rather imagine different types of relationships between interlocutors. Even in Athens, deliberation can be imagined differently, as evidenced in the relational deliberations within Plato and Sophocles. Instead of considering competing strands of Western rhetoric, I want to look globally. Centuries before the Greeks, Chinese scholars considered questions about the state and communication: What is a good state? How does one communicate within a good state? By what discursive means does the ruler lead a people? How do ministers engage an autocratic ruler and fashion appropriate decision making? They did not answer these questions in solitude, but responded to earlier thought and competing theorists, soliciting the support of particular rulers in a variety of ways (Goldin; Lyon, "Writing").[7] Despite the diversity of answers within Chinese classics, without overly generalizing, one can argue that early Chinese political thinking was characterized by authoritarian state rule, communitarian values, and a belief that the dynastic past was even better than the present—and maybe the future. These characteristics worked to orient political communication away from fantasies of powerful speakers, textual trickery, and optimistic ends. With rare exceptions, classical Chinese thinking eschews persuasion and argumentation as dangerous and inappropriate to human relationships.[8] Persuasion and success-driven argumentation were regarded as inept and inapt discursive strategies.[9] Instead, a good advisor spoke to the sage ruler with respect for their mutual positions, the legitimacy of state authority, and the needs of the people.

Although the Chinese traditions of communication are not performative in the sense developed in the next chapter, they offer a number of themes relevant to performative deliberation, allowing us to consider a conspicuous alternative to Aristotle's rhetoric and to begin to define an alternative vocabulary. To sketch out a most ancient theory, I examine Confucius's *Analects (Lunyu)*, a set of dialogues and assertions presented in small excerpts, composed and layered between 479 and 249 B.C.E. Written three centuries after the death of Confucius (Kongzi), *The Analects* advocates remonstrating *(jian)*, as opposed to persuading, within a relationship of trust. Although persuasion and political change may result from remonstration, they are not seen as necessary or even positive effects in cultures valuing stability, as the Chinese did during the Warring States period in particular. In the Confucian tradition, the ruler's power as well as his logical, interpretive, and perceptive skills are more prominent than those of the speaker because the advisor does not—in fact, cannot—assume control of the situation or outcome. Confucian communication begins with recognizing the other and seeks the appropriate level of responsiveness between interlocutors. Rather than actively pursuing a means, ends, or future strategically, or using tropes and figures strategically, or rushing to a persuasive precipice, Confucian advisors acknowledge the value of stability and definite social limits as conditions under which the participants can manifest their particularities. Unlike the promised agency of the individual Athenian orator, *The Analects* imagines communitarian agency contained and restrained by cultural authorities, rites, and traditions. Unlike the showy, forward-pushing Athenians, the speakers of *The Analects* should be both slow to speak and relenting in attempts to engage or convince another (see 4.24, 4.26, 12.23, 12.3). One is to remonstrate, or demonstrate *(jian)* one's ideas, within a relationship of trust (19.10). The communicative act is an opening of the undecided and uncontrolled future to consideration by interlocutors.

Examination of the linguistic roots of persuasion and remonstration reveals their core difference. *Per* and *suadere* together imply a bringing *through by speech. Monstrare*, however, emphasizes the act of showing or demonstrating. Persuasion may be an effect of demonstration, but it need not be, and consequently the audience's interpretive skills and powers of resistance are more prominent. They see the act or demonstration, and based on their assessment, they respond. Remonstration evades defining explicit power differences between the speaker and the listener in the service of developing communitarian values. One can push this difference further with some basic tools of ordinary language philosophy. Building on insights in Aristotle's *Metaphysics*, Gilbert Ryle discusses the difference between terminus verbs and process verbs (102–9). Process verbs, like "seek," describe ongoing action. On the other hand, terminus verbs, like "find," declare an end. "Remonstrate" is a process verb," lacking a *telos*. "Persuade" is a terminus verb. If I say, "I persuaded him that . . . ," there has been an end. The act of persuasion rarely occurs in the present tense, as an ongoing process. It is unusual to say "I am persuading him"; one can imagine a context for this, but it is unusual. Almost always, when one speaks of persuading, there has been a change in him, and the act of persuading is ended. In fact, if we think of this in temporal terms, the future and the past are the realms of persuasion: "I will persuade you" or "I persuaded you." This is all less true of "remonstrate," which even lacks the grammatical object, a person to be moved. If I say, "I remonstrate that . . . ," it is less clear that there has been an end, or what would constitute an end, or who would judge an end. The remonstration simply stops. Hence, the ending of an act of remonstration is very different from the ending of an act of persuasion. In remonstrating, one can run out of time, energy, or materials, but otherwise one can continue the performance, always in the present. In persuading, one has a temporal progression, a narrative from a strategic beginning to an end marked by a change in the audience, reflecting a change in the human realm. The persuader may do most of the action, but the end is in changing an audience. With remonstration, the effect is less clear and unnecessary for judging the speech act: the remonstrator will do all the identified action. The end is when the demonstration finishes, rather than when an audience changes, jointly decides, or enacts an event. Although an audience is implied in remonstration, there is no defined manipulation. The remonstrator simply shows something. Those who observe the performance are free to interpret it, heed it, repeat it, ignore it, or refute it.

Confucian communication thus expands the significance of human recognition within deliberation, considering its hierarchies, difficulties, and ethical implications more robustly than persuasion's focus on rhetor and audience does. In part because the Confucian tradition values engagement over persuasion, the nature of utterance is more tied to relationship.[10] Within an utterance, it is not the saying or locution that creates bonds between people, but the illocution (force or intention) which compels perlocution (effects) and relationships. In remonstration, in the demonstrating or performing of the best course of action, every speech act entails the remonstrator's offer to

make good on its meaning, and every understanding implies an interlocutor's acceptance of that offer of meaning. Yes, the problem of interpretation
is forever and always complex. How do the interlocutors interpret that locution and illocution? Do they understand the perlocution of the utterance?
Even so, in remonstration, it is interpretation and engagement, not persuasive force, that matters.

If, in persuading, there is an audience to be induced or moved toward an
end, then in remonstration, the onus is on the speaker to perform and to represent a position to an interlocutor who is observing, assessing, judging, and
controlling the level of engagement. Despite the intimacy and importance of
harmony implied in the self-in-relationship, *The Analects* provides little sense
that one *must* or *should* reach a consensus with an interlocutor; "people who
have chosen different ways cannot make plans together" (15.40). Accepting
and respecting difference is not fatalistic (or fatal to one's cause), but rather
productive, as an acknowledgement of conceptual pluralism and the power
of the other. Here is a Confucian example of remonstration: When the gover-
nor of She brags that, under his rule, a son will report a sheep-stealing father,
Confucius retorts, "[T]hose who are true in my village conduct themselves
differently. The father covers for his son, and the son covers for his father.
And being true lies in this way" (*Analects* 13.18; see also 1.2, 2.21, 12.13). In
The Analects's brief dialogues, Confucius is almost always the compelling
interlocutor, but he does not force the issue. No elenchus or heavy suasion;
in remonstration, neither the Duke nor Confucius denies the other's judgment. Instead, each offers the other his worldview and consideration of the
way. Of even more deliberative interest in this dialogic exchange, where She
values law and Confucius values relationship, Confucius describes a particular situation, not general laws or rules, and he places intimate relationships
and familial obligations in his village above the law, describing ethical decision making in terms of family and proximity. For this reason, Confucian
ethics are sometimes compared to feminist care ethics, which value caring
for others and relationship over laws, property, and cultural values.[11] In what
Tu Weiming calls "an 'anthropocosmic' vision" (185), Confucian humanism
is located in human relationships, stressing the reciprocity among relationships, not external rules or internal beliefs.

Picturing human relationships through the intimacy of kinship and
entwined lived relationships, privileging attachment over dominance without denying hierarchy, and conceiving deliberative acts through shared perspectives and not subordination or success, Confucian deliberation does not
treasure consensus as an end. It does not even demand an end, and in fact,

Confucian political dialogue is more tolerant, less teleological, and more open to possibility in that the interlocutors may have different ways and need not share plans. Within *The Analects*, there is—instead of a controlling persuasion—the open-ended possibility of change in keeping with the harmony of human relationships. In not requiring consensus, general definitions of a good life, or an ending, and privileging harmony in relationship instead, responsiveness and responsibility become the basis of political communication. If there is not an explicit valuing of difference, there also is not a valuing of sameness, but rather a valuing of amicable relationships and kinship even within state institutions (13.18).

The act of remonstration itself may seem bare of interlocutors and dialogue, and therefore isolating and bare of recognitions, but remonstration does not serve the individual. Instead it works to keep a community engaged in ongoing communication. In the broader frame of Confucian political theory and communitarian agency, individuation is not the purpose of action. Action's purpose is cultivating good character and good relationships in ways that are communitarian, and actions extend from the personal into legal and state matters without boundary (13.18). Also relevant to the critique of remonstration is the fact that Confucian concern with family hierarchies may initially be seen as inappropriate for egalitarian or political engagements. This criticism, however, denies that the scene of speaking is rarely egalitarian or simply reciprocal, and that hierarchy and inequality require acknowledgment in a rhetorical situation, with a hope that the hierarchy is no more extreme than the family. Finally, remonstration may seem inappropriate for hostile or antagonistic engagements, but in refusing process and a clear ending point, remonstration instead may offer a realistic timeline to justice. Although one may desire a more confrontational and level model of argumentation, models of argumentation are limited when they posit equals in a particular instance of sparring in a classroom or a court rather than the ongoing creations of the political realm.[12] In assuming an imperial power not always receptive to recognizing a voice closely placed (the minister is not on the state's margin), remonstration acknowledges the difficulty of being heard, the further difficulty of being recognized, and the possibility of being heard without a change on the part of the more powerful interlocutor. Given these difficulties of initiating deliberation, it privileges the opportunity to go on speaking with a potential for continuous engagement. In many circumstances, Confucian intimate remonstration may be more a productive model of deliberation than counterfactual theories of equal interlocutors or powerful orators who define and control the situation and the audience.[13]

One might ask, in Confucian deliberation, Am I the father or the daughter here? Does the relationship among interlocutors resemble in any way a family with long-term commitments, or is it driven by immediacy and desire? The metaphor of family holds out the promising possibility of ongoing identity formation developed in a specific situation of defined, though hierarchical, engagement. In privileging the continuance of relationship over an outcome-based model of persuasion and the movement of interlocutors to consensus, a remonstrative model of deliberation considers the possibility of proceeding without end, proceeding to exhaustion or engagement, without emphasizing the closure of a singular, future position. In this model, the ethical speaker does not fail if he does not persuade; he fails only if he does not continue to speak rightly or destroys the relationship with his interlocutor. Furthermore, it moves the demand for action from the speaker's words to the decisions of the interlocutors. Although denying power to a speaker's strategy and instead placing power in the relationships of interlocutors—in their mutual recognition, responsibility, and reciprocity—the act of remonstration reveals a deep skepticism about the power of individual speakers and the use of any particular proof or propositions, offering instead the potential of ongoing, evolving political relationship.

Positioned Potential

The concept of remonstration acknowledges both the necessity and the difficulty of recognition and relationship across power differentials and even ideological distances. In offering the possibilities that one might speak and yet not effect change, and that an appeal may be recognized but not judged to need action, remonstration sets forth the problem of position in rhetorical scenes. Where and when does one speak? Where and when does one hear? Act? Judge? The significance of the speaker's position is a common rhetorical trope, where position is understood as temporal and spatial. Often the persuasive tradition scripts a situated relationship between speaker and audience, moving together through a means to an end, but there are many other understandings of position, from the concept of scene in Kenneth Burke's dramatism to the rhetorical situation that creates its own terms of enactment. Classical Chinese scholars recognized the significance of location within the concept of *shi*, a concept with connotations of position, disposition, potential, deployment of power, and strategic advantage. Its rich implications allow *shi* to mark the roles of terrain in military strategy (Sunzi), political status in statecrafts (Han Feizi), and the possibility of moral government (Xunzi).[14] I draw attention to the concept of *shi* to mark the significance of position within deliberative situations across cultures. It is not just an epistemic concern of feminists and postmodernists. Standpoint or position frame human existence, from ontology to epistemology.

In a book-length treatment of *shi*, François Jullien notes that, in translation, its meaning falls between two poles—the static and the dynamic—and hence in its translations, it creates paradoxes that are particularly productive for considering cultural differences.[15] This quandary of whether position is a static mapping and standpoint or a dynamic potential reveals a productive tension implicit in many discussions of rhetorical and political location. Kenneth Burke's dramatism, which acknowledges changing ratios among acts, agents, scenes, purposes, and agency, might be among the more dynamic scriptings of position in part because it does not allow scene or position to exist in static isolation from other dramatic forces. Alternatively, Foucault argues that power is productively disciplining and uses the panopticon as a physical structure that disciplines through its potential. The panopticon overlaps with *shi*, particularly as potential for the concept of *shi* includes the importance of terrain and its productivity of power in war. But the concept of panopticon reveals only one aspect of the terrain. It is static in its view and control, with only one mechanism—whether the prison is in lockdown or riot. Still, both the static and dynamic imply an implicit potential in their possibility and potency. The relationship between position and potential and the possibilities along the unstable continuum from static to dynamic are most important for understanding the effects of location, standpoint, and position within deliberation.

Concerned with success, preferably without military engagement, the early and brilliant *The Art of War* by Sunzi (?5th century B.C.E.) shows that positioned potential within the field of battle takes on connotations of *situational advantage*. A good general's strategy is to calculate all factors in advance of the conflict so that contingencies and the situation are controlled and victory, even diplomatic victory, is a predictable outcome. Although it states that "surprise" and "straightforward" operations present endless possibilities for strategy, there are no fixed strategies, for each situation is different. Still, like boulders rolling downhill (chap. 5, 121), the potential energy of strategic placement and power is beyond the acts of individual humans: "the expert at battle seeks his victory from strategic advantage (*shih*) and does not demand it from his men." Hence strategic advantage, including positioning, defines cowardice and courage (chap. 5, 120). That is, the soldiers' character is defined by the experts' ability to use strategic advantage. *The Art of War's* concern with the advantages of morale, justice, terrain, and opportunity has rhetorical implications.

Positioned potential also has more overt political use within Chinese thought, and it is sometimes imagined as a force of stability rather than as potential energy. Legalism, arising during the Warring States period (480–221 B.C.E.), describes a group of political theories that favor the objectivity and rigidity of the law over the instability of morality and decision making. Han Feizi (?289–233 B.C.E.) is considered the greatest Legalist, because his combination of common law or standard (*fa*), strategic method (*shu*), and the ruler's positioned potential (*shi*) provides a theory of a stable state. Suspicious of humans' ability to administer and worried about the dangers of persuasion, as I have argued at length elsewhere ("Rhetorical Authority"), Han Feizi triangulates the authority to rule within the law, method, and the ruler's positioned potential, and he promotes political stability through their compelling triadic power. Although the law, the ruler, and his methods together are relatively static, their stability authorizes the potential to govern an empire. If the positioned potential of military strategy works to change power structures, positioned potential in Legalism secures stable governance, in that the power is restrained and contained potential in a kind of checks-and-balances system. In placing imperial potential in the ruler's position, balanced with law and method, Han Feizi scripts position as politically central to the state, describing the empire as predicated on position.

Unlike Han Feizi's imperial study of position, contemporary theorists examine the subject's position in relationship to knowledge formation. Feminist epistemologists such as Sandra Harding, Donna Haraway, and Lorraine Code have argued that the concept of location or standpoint is necessary for accurate considerations of knowledge production and political understanding. They argue that situated and embodied ethical speakers cannot have an objective or neutral perspective and should respond to and take responsibility for their position in the world as they create new knowledge. In defining a "feminist objectivity," Haraway describes the situated nature of all knowledge, arguing for the necessity of "a more adequate, richer, better account of a world, in order to live in it well and in critical, reflexive relation to our own as well as others' practices of domination and the unequal parts of privilege and oppression that make up all positions" (187). Inherent in a better account of position is the dynamic potential to change practices. By reflecting on their situated practices and by connecting situated knowledge to practices, feminist epistemologists acknowledge the cultural terrain and historic precedents that create knowledge, discourses, and the potential of their authority. Furthermore, in recognizing and reflecting upon their cultural, discursive, and historical locations and those of others, they can attempt to find choices that are not always already made within a particular historical trajectory. Refusing the possibility of neutral standpoints and original positions, standpoint epistemologists privilege the contextual, contingent, and relational basis of knowledge, and through their reflection on the static tendency of standpoints, producers of knowledge develop the potential to see new directions of research and new ways of speaking.

Beyond analyzing knowledge creation, feminists—responding to simple notions of solidarity among women—also have argued for the significance of positional politics and repudiated essentialism. Position marks political and cultural relationships, the basic starting points which dialogue and deliberation might link. As bell hooks's epigraph exemplifies, engaging new positions potentially generates cultural revision through the formation of counterhegemonic cultural practices. To avoid universal woman, yet retain a ground for strategic action on women's issues, any number of postcolonial and transnational feminists emphasize the potential for women's solidarity in their joint purposes, shared positions, and overlapping practices, arguing for solidarity based in historical struggle and the common positions found through conflicts across the economic landscape. Seeking to break the binary of universal and difference to find a route to solidarity, feminists such as Ann Ferguson, Linda Alcoff ("Cultural Feminism"), Teresa De Lauretis, and bell hooks reconceive identity politics as based in shared position, basing political relationship not in what one is, but in where one stands. In *Feminism Without Borders*, Chandra Talpade Mohanty articulates the changing nature of struggle in a transnational time, writing, "this reterritorialization through struggle . . . allows me a paradoxical continuity of self, mapping and transforming my political location. It suggests a particular notion of political agency, since my location forces and enables specific modes of reading and knowing the dominant" (122). Contemporary political agency and identity, then, depend on recognizing locations or positions and the generic, located modes of reading and knowing the dominant. One might extend this to argue that position forces and enables certain speech acts, a point discussed in the next chapter. Potential for agency as well as the quality and boundaries of that agency are positioned, but following Mohanty, a position (with its agency) can be rewritten through acts of struggle and reflection. Conflict need not be destructive; it can generate agency and new positions of resistance and justice. For Mohanty and others, the conflictual source (of deliberation) is also the constitutive source of agency and change, a return-ing theme.[16]

In keeping with Chinese and feminist insights, James L. Kastely argues for the situated and embodied nature of rhetoric. Defining rhetoric as "the art of position," he argues that this definition constructs the world as "nec-essarily a place of action, a place in which we need to figure out who we are and how we have been positioned" (218). That is, rhetorics of position are concerned with the symbolic map within which interlocutors relate to each other. One might consider the careful mapping of positions as a geo-graphic approach to understanding specific ethical human relationships and the terrain of strategic recognition. Although ethical relationships are not a requirement of deliberation, in considering deliberation as a relational map-ping of interlocutors, one can see how the potential of ongoing actions and positions affects the locations of speakers. In her reading of Carol Gilligan on care ethics, Claudia Card argues that *"the responsibilities of different kinds of relationships* yield different ethical preoccupations, methods, priorities, even concepts" (199–200; emphasis in original). Hence, the situated rela-tionships between mother and child, senator and constituent, or guard and prisoner call for different ethics, but they all entail responsibilities. Think-ing deliberatively, theorists should consider how different kinds of commu-nicative relationships (beyond the familiar templates of equals or of father and daughter, male and female, colonized and colonizer) and communica-tive acts (more nuanced that persuading or remonstrating) allow citizens to respond to differences in beliefs, priorities, and purposes more complexly. In doing so, theorists might conceive more richly how interlocutors come to action.

In discussing the play of two or more positions, Kastely examines contem-porary rhetoric's work in resisting ideologies, epistemological closures, and hierarchies of persuasion. Like remonstration, positional rhetorics imply only the possibility of engaged decision-making and not a commitment to ends, but more than in remonstration, situated speakers reckon their identi-ties and narrate the evolution of their positions. Even so, positional rheto-rics do not simply look backward. As Kastely argues, one cannot understand rhetoric as "the repetition of overturning positions, for since being posi-tioned is unavoidable, one must equally always be trying to do justice to new understandings of past positions and to the consequences of newly assumed positions" (218). Positions, always present tense, must be justified and incor-porated into histories as well as projected as imagined onto possible futures, but not teleological futures. Positional rhetorics do not simply shift from a temporal trope to a spatial trope; rather, they mark a change in both temporal and spatial emphasis, where the present location takes a defining role in deliberations, gesturing toward past, future, and current locations.

Imagining deliberative acts within a dynamic of positions is difficult, in part because most positional models of public discourse depend on continuous ethical reflection on both response and responsibility, an internal GPS that places the speaker in the state of constantly assessing the present position, what Kastely characterizes as "[doing] justice to new understandings of past positions and to the consequences of newly assumed positions." A certain narcissistic and overly intellectual concern with "figuring out who we are and how we have been positioned" replaces righteousness, purposeful persuasion, and the teleological drive to accomplishment. That is, in the case of a deliberation on rights—headscarves or gay marriage, for example— both the defense of and opposition to rights might be lost to epistemic and ontological self-critique in the process of advocacy. If theories of positioned potential aim to identify potential in being and to critique knowledge creation, can they also work effectively as rhetorical tools that mark discourses of subjection and responsibilities in the political?

Recognition

If one imagines deliberation beyond persuading or remonstrating, both focused on the rhetor's performance, and instead sees deliberation as effectively engaging the positions of all interlocutors in their situated relationships, then positioned potential becomes a necessary supplement to the description and analysis of textual production within deliberative studies. With an enriched conception of position and a commitment to engaging difference, however, deliberation needs a fuller account of recognition, one specifically concerned with mutual recognition, and only tangentially concerned with identification (that is, identity formation) and self-recognition (see Ricoeur). The latter two forms of recognition depend on a Hegelian tradition of finding one's self in struggle with the other, a tradition informing many theories of recognition that tend to emphasize traumatic ruptures and the subject's state of being to the diminishment of the daily recognitions in human life. In what follows, while I do not ignore issues of identity, I examine mutual, collusive recognition and develop the possibilities of deliberative recognition, a political recognition fully engaged in struggle, but bare of trauma.

One finds "recognition" prominently in many human rights inquiries, perhaps because it is the second word of the Universal Declaration of Human Rights: "Whereas recognition of the inherent dignity and of the equal and inalienable rights of all members of the human family is the foundation of freedom, justice and peace in the world."[17] In rights talk, recognition, not reason, is the primary assumption underlying freedom, justice, and world peace. Addressing the dominant narrative of rights recognition, in *Spectacular Rhetorics*, Wendy S. Hesford reminds us that the history of human rights can be read as a history of selective recognition, where some people are objects of recognition and others have the power to grant recognition (30). Certainly many scholars have read rights' recognition as movement from object to subject.[18] In such readings, which Hesford finds inadequate, the ability or right to grant recognition then becomes a definition of what it means to be human and to have rights. Kelly Oliver notes that critics of colonialism, such as Frantz Fanon and bell hooks, argue that recognition need not be so pathologized, so tainted with oppression. Although recognition may entitle hierarchies, recognition is more than oppression.

Instead of studying the evolution of rights recognition, a limit case for recognition, this book examines deliberation as a regularly occurring human act. If legal and political recognition are concurrent with deliberation—that is, if we are not examining history, but practices—then present-tense recognition between situated interlocutors becomes key to comprehending deliberation. Performative deliberation must extend the concept of recognition from one of making people politically visible to one of enacting the human; it would have us understand recognition as a matter of being and becoming rather than one of seeing and representing or witnessing. Recognition, a self-willed engagement with another, is more than the condition of seeing and being seen. Indeed, the actual performance of recognition enacts a new relationship and thus creates new positions. Rather than describe recognition as the *condition of possibility* (to have rights), the performance of recognition, its *actual performance* as mutuality in a shared lifeworld (the right of engagement), defines being human.[19] Responding interlocutors enact recognition.

Performing deliberative recognition does not mean imagining another's position, and yet the consideration of alternative positions and difference is part of recognition. This tension haunts theorists of recognition. When Seyla Benhabib, for instance, offers a model of recognition based in reversible perspectives and enlarged thinking, she wishes that interlocutors would place themselves in the position of others, a sophisticated version of "putting yourself in someone else's shoes." She proposes a "universality" which "enjoins us to reverse perspectives among members of a 'moral community' and judge from the point of view of the other(s)" (*Situating* 32). Although she is not discussing deliberation *per se* and she assumes a shared community, Benhabib describes an ideal ethical political community, one that would be capable of deliberation. The moral universality of recognition is based in the human community's ability to imagine the other's position. This is a high standard for recognition, too dependent on the human ability to imagine another's position. Certainly humans imagine the other regularly, but the accuracy of that fantasy is difficult to assess.

Acknowledging the slippage between recognizing a real person and simply imagining another, Benhabib moderates the standard of reversible recognition with a key distinction between the "generalized other" and the "concrete other." To deepen the reversing of perspectives, she critiques the limits of the "generalized other," a most general character described as a moral, reasoning person who can formulate a sense of justice, the good, and act toward their creation (*Situating* 10). This loosest of human description, argues Benhabib, can offer only an other similar to oneself, an other whose standpoint can be imagined and addressed "by the norms of *formal equality* and *reciprocity*" (159; emphasis in original). Benhabib rightly contends that the identity of the other must be imagined as distinct from the self and seen as an individuated other: she writes that the standpoint of the concrete other offers "an individual with a concrete history, identity and affective-emotional constitution." Relationships with the concrete other require attention, the careful consideration of their specific needs, motivations, desires, and bodily otherness as well as a concrete relationship "governed by the norms of *equity* and *complementary reciprocity*." Although not without difficult negotiations, equity recognizes difference better than an equality defined in form, because equity is involved in balancing contingencies. Benhabib reasons that inherent in reciprocal relationship is mutual response to and responsibility for a concrete other as well as self-reflection on ourselves as concrete others, a confirmation of each one's "*humanity* and human *individuality*." The moral respect arising from the shifting and multiple positions seemingly makes vivid the histories of other beings. Here are similarities to Kastely's rhetoric of playful positions, though more morally concerned and less copious in the overturnings and reversals of positions. Still, Benhabib's thought reveals a similarly optimistic belief that the potential of multiple positions releases new civic knowledges, understandings, and actions as well as recognitions.

Alas, Iris Marion Young's response to Benhabib's symmetrical reciprocity provides a telling critique of standpoint reversals and the painless play of positions, one that is relevant to imagining deliberative recognition between interlocutors. Young finds structured reciprocity in communicative action too limited in representing the hierarchies and asymmetries of identity formation. In "Asymmetrical Reciprocity," Young insists that asymmetrical reciprocity offers a more accurate concept of communicative action than an imagined symmetry among positions. She further argues that claiming to know the standpoint of others risks showing disrespect, because it (1) obscures the deep differences of the other's position, (2) ignores the impossibility of reversing standpoints, as standpoints always are defined in relationship to one another, and (3) fails to acknowledge structural privilege, making it politically suspect.

Young observes that one's desire to reverse perspectives may obscure and disrespect difference, a view easily amplified. How can I take the position of a mother in Afghanistan, a widow in Tokyo, or a girl in a wheelchair and then speak to them and for them? Speaking for other people is a fraught activity needing particularly careful reflection, as Linda Alcoff has taught us. I may not wish to speak for them, merely to them, but if we are to be symmetrically reciprocal, if I am to recognize them, then Benhabib would have me reverse positions with them. How could they become me? In deliberative action, desiring relationship and reciprocity, I may wish to emphasize and acknowledge the shared identities or intersections in gender or familial placement with other women, but the fantasies and projections I have for those positions are made from my standpoint, an inherently limited position.[20] As Young writes, "The perspective of the other can too easily be represented as the self's other represented to itself—its fantasies, desires, and fears" (212). The fantasies of and errors in symbolic reciprocity would be corrected, possibly, by the other; one can hope for a stalwart interlocutor who corrects errors in reversed reciprocity and who teaches the depths of differences. Yes, one should listen to the other's voice and repair—as possible, if possible—blunders and failures in understanding and reciprocities. Still, continues Young, if respect is willingness to listen to the other and hear of difference, then what need is there for imagined symmetry? Is there any reason to imagine for oneself the power to stand in her shoes? Sit in her wheelchair? Respectful interlocutors might simply remonstrate and listen, respecting the differences and particularities of our lives while forming relationships.

Young's second concern with reversing positions is even more telling of the limits of standpoint rhetorics in that she argues for the impossibility of symmetrically reversing positions. A standpoint rhetoric based in symmetrical reciprocity might help us *imagine* the agential and scenic constraints, but even if we accept the limits of imagination, as Young and I do, symmetrical reciprocity cannot help us recognize and engage the interlocutors in a consequential way. Although she agrees with Benhabib's definition of how to sustain a relationship—to recognize the other is to know that as I am "I" to myself and she is "I" to herself—Young finds this structural condition of communicative action limited. She contends that reciprocal recognition does not extend to the possibility of reversing standpoints or positions because the relationship between the self and other is asymmetrical and irreversible. She writes, "This structure . . . precludes such reversibility because it describes how each standpoint is constituted by its internal relations to other standpoints" (236). Through interactions with others, argues Young, one is known to oneself as an internal experience defined against the other, and that other's objectification formulates the self-conception. Hence, I am my daughter's mother, and my students' professor: those sustained and ongoing relationships are "asymmetrical and irreversible, even though [they are] reciprocal" (213). The relationships between people define each person's position in contrast and difference, but their identities are also constituted internally by asymmetrical differences. To extend Young slightly: although how others look at us can expand or shrink our positioned potential, it is incoherent to conceptualize reversing our standpoints, as this neglects the mutually defining and asymmetrical nature of the relationship between "I" and "you." The impossibility of reversal is more than saying that a minister is not an emperor, and more than saying that a son cannot shift position with a sheep-stealing father. Physiologically and ontologically, I cannot shift position with you.

Finally, since the symmetrical reversal of perspectives implies an equality or equity of experiences and thus ignores the place of structural privilege in making moral judgments, it is politically suspect. When people attempt multiple perspectives, with multiple identifications, in the service of reciprocity, Young observes, "we have merely aggregated a series of subjective and self-regarding perspectives . . . we still have not represented that upon which these are perspectives" (223).[21] Aggregate subjectivities and self-regarding perspectives may trick well-meaning interlocutors into believing they know the positions of others and can represent them equitably, but in a cooperative setting—let alone in an agonistic one—even those with the best of intentions cannot take the position of another. Pretending to do so, they misrepresent and co-opt voices, ignore the ideological structure, and deny the struggle of deliberation. In effect, the need to recognize, listen, learn, remonstrate, and reciprocate is bypassed in the service of an imaginative perspective which is inadequately dialogic. Rather than aid communication, Young argues, the concept of reciprocal reversals may impede it, because an imagined perspective replaces the interlocutors' expression of their distinct perspectives (215). Listening remains a primary means of apprehending another's history and constructing the history of the relationship, a relationship based in asymmetrical reciprocity. According to Young, our relationships are formed in the particular forces that shape the public world around us: mutual recognition and wonder, the hermeneutical aim of understanding, and recognition of asymmetry together.[22]

If Benhabib's approach to recognition is too impossible and imaginative, Young's critique of recognition is more accurate and descriptive, but not engaged in the contingent interactions required for initiating deliberation. Although Young's work values difference over identity and identification, recognition requires crossing an abyss. How can it be that recognition is so vexed? It occurs regularly. Might we proceed better in describing recognition if we consider it as a regularly occurring practice, not always accurate, but a regular symbolic pattern? Just as Oliver describes a proof of early recognition in studies of human infants' mimicry of the mother, I propose that there is a level of recognition in which we all engage. Some demand more of recognition. Alexander García Düttmann names recognition "the impossible creation of what is given" (4); Krista Ratcliffe would require a rhetorical listening that opens "the exiled excess" (203); Robert Pippin would require a "binding form of human dependence" (162); and Nancy Fraser (*Justice Interruptus*) requires both recognition and redistribution as responses to injustice. Later I will offer more, but for now I offer a simpler definition of recognition, one that acknowledges its central moment of performance, that initiates a relationship without overly interpreting or constraining the nature of the relationship. I conceive recognition in acts where two people understand a connection between them—not a connection of dominance, identification, or projection, all of which deny difference, but simply one of a shared communicative act. This in itself may require a transformative intersubjectivity.

Beth Singer suggests that we conceive recognition simply as sanctioning, in the sense that a chair of a meeting might "recognize" someone wishing to speak; the chair's recognition of the speaker opens space for a hearing (56). If we extend Singer's sense of recognition, it offers a way of conceiving deliberative recognition. Obviously this is a thin standard of recognition, leaving out the difficulties of listening, attention, interpretation, understanding, equality, equity, and justice, but it has significant metaphoric advantages.

Sanction, "a solemn enactment," has both definitions of binding approval and penalty (*OED*). In its ability to authorize and penalize, it is not a benign or stable term, and as the cases within this book show, recognition is not benign or stable, but it is ubiquitous. Furthermore, while sanctioning is dialogic at its core, sanctioning acknowledges asymmetry; in granting authority to someone from the floor, the metaphor of sanction acknowledges power differences in recognition and the need to initiate recognition in a moment of full attention. The speaker rises and speaks in asymmetrical recognition of the chair, but she has the power and place—the positioned potential—of having the floor and the attention and attentiveness that goes with the ritual of speaking. Sanction does not excuse the chair of the meeting from the obligation of recognizing members of the meeting, for it is her duty as well as her power to recognize others who are present, who share a place, and who have a say in the meeting's agenda. Recognition is ritual and repetition; it is a social norm within the meeting. Finally, the chair's act of recognition has both a referential or constative aspect and a performative aspect. In acknowledging a body or voice to speak, the chair ascribes a physical presence, similar to the constatives "the cat is on the mat" or "the speaker is present." Her utterance also performs, in that she utters or declares a relationship, similar to the performatives "I baptize thee," "I declare war," or "I recognize the woman in the back." In defining recognition as sanctioning, recognition's minimal conditions and difficulties are made explicit.

In keeping with recognition conceived as a give-and-take of sanctions and authorizations, Hannah Arendt conceives a public world created in human dialogue and shared among us through objective relationships, relationships based in the cognitive and material objects of the world. For Arendt, the enlarged thought of the public world moves a citizen from a self-regarding position to socially inclusive commitments because "public" signifies the world, the world as human artifact and fabrication. She writes, "To live together in the world means essentially that a world of things is between those who have it in common, as a table is located between those who sit around it; the world, like every in-between, relates and separates men at the same time" (*Human* 52). Arendt's concept of in-between helps define the scene of recognition. In the common lifeworld, people share objects, symbols, events, and actions, all located in-between, seen and known from different perspectives. The multiple positions at the table, that which both relates and separates, makes the deliberation over common objects, symbols, events, and actions both unavoidable and constituting of meaning, identity, action, and the world itself. The in-between, significantly, both relates and separates: implicitly, it defines position, including separation, as central to human life. In-betweens imply responding, if not responsible, relationships and commitments without the interiority of reflection and the demands of continuation or outcome. Closely related to human affairs or the public realm, the in-between makes evident the significance of position to the world constituted, and inherent in the constituted world, relation and separation mark an openness of communicative and interpretive horizons. It does this without an explicit demand or a precluding of full recognition. Rather, it marks the moment and position of meeting in disclosing and sanctioning the world of creation. Deliberation may entail recognition, but initial meeting need not go beyond the acknowledgment of living together in the world.

In *Thinking*, the first volume of *Life of the Mind*, Arendt is explicit about the place of the in-between in the present tense, occupying the ephemeral gap between past and future. This temporal aspect of spatial placement—or more actively, positioning—is important to rethinking deliberation not as a means to an end, but as a performative when and where new identities and political potentials are formed. Arendt characterizes it as "an extended Now on which [man] spends his life" (205). Humans act in the Now, although they may reflect on a past and hope for a future. In her later analysis of the act of thinking, she defines the in-between less as a social meeting and more as a temporal battleground: the "dead weight of the past" drives one hopefully forward as the fear of the future, with its implicit death, drives one back to a nostalgic past. However, reality-forming meetings and separations as well as the significant present tense in creating presence are conceptually important for the in-between, and are even necessary to mark the dynamics of interlocutors in acts of becoming. Neither deliberation nor democracy moves with haste, but their work in the present founds the future and reforms the past. Deliberative time is slow and fragile time in which the enacted moment of recognition becomes a basis of being and continuing.[23] The deliberative present creates a temporal gap and spatial positioned potential where the citizen agent is vulnerable to her own acts as well as the acts of other interlocutors in-between. For these revelations, one must put aside Aristotle's purposeful and outcome-driven deliberation and Habermas's procedures so that one can imagine the in-between, the moment of relationship, and the gap where interlocutors are vulnerable to the present, past, and future.

Arendt's in-between underlines the generativity shared among interlocutors in producing meaning: "Being seen and being heard by others derive their significance from the fact that everybody sees and hears from a different position" (*Human* 57). Just as Aristotle holds that a citizenry can come to better decisions than the individual, Arendt implies the benefits of different positions, but aside from a richness of positions, there is no imperative to recognize others. The in-between does not demand action. For action, Arendt provides a second background concept to performative deliberation, "interest," a concept used to denote what binds people together. Arendt reworks the rhetorical and political tradition of "interest" when she develops her concept of inter-est. Aristotle is concerned with interest in privileging the ethics of deliberative over forensic rhetoric in matters of judgment. He argues that "the man who is forming a judgment is making a decision about his own vital interests" (*Rhetoric* 1354b31), and vital interests may well be expanded to the common good because self-interests require that the speaker, in seeking his interests, do more than pander to the audience's interests. For Aristotle, self-interest creates a more honest speaker, for he builds a relationship with his audience that acknowledges his position and desires in relationship to theirs. Interest may mark a rhetor's moment of considering "What should I do?" in relationship to the audience. Arendt moves beyond this. From the "everything in-between" which is created in diversity, Arendt develops the concept of "inter-est" (*Human* 182) or, later, "interspaces" (*Men* 31) to mark the overlapping concerns that initiate citizens' unique relations and separations. In describing the agent-revealing capacity of action and speech of the in-between, Arendt shows how worldly interests constitute "something which *inter-est*, which lies between people and therefore can relate and bind them together" (*Human* 182). From its start, the question of inter-est considers "what should we do" *together*.

The in-between has two aspects: one as worldly and objective (trees, bus routes, classrooms, voting booths) and a second as intersubjective and intentional, originating in the acts and words that people address to one another in the present. The second is the realm of inter-est as it marks Arendt's web of human relationships which exists—bound to the physical, objective world—wherever people live. In the web of human relationship, the realm of human affairs, inter-est designates the shared actions and words that make collaboration possible, the finding of what is common or cosmopolitan, and the matters that make remonstration effective or that allow deliberation to begin. Unlike the in-between, inter-est is concerned with human relations only, and it both initiates and arises in recognitions. Thus inter-est is not the same as interest that arises from and implies self-serving expediency. In the in-between, inter-est arises and asks, "What binds you to others?" More than something of interest or concern, inter-est implies the multiple ties among people which prompt recognition and the complex openness of shared action. Human relationships and shared actions signify deliberation more than the zero-sum games, compromises, or two separate solutions of interest. Implicit in inter-est is a dedication to finding "shared agency," what Abraham Sesshu Roth calls a participatory commitment to and even obligation in "what "we're doing." Prior to persuasion, negotiation, identification, and other tools that obliterate difference, people discover what matters in-between, asking what binds us together. From that instant, they might decide if what matters and what binds are vital for inter-est and deliberation. Deliberation understood through Arendt would emphasize the spaces in-between and inter-ests shared by interlocutors, shared not in the sense that we are in agreement, but in the sense that we recognize the significance of other people to fashioning who I am and who you are: that is, who we are in apposition, for who we are in apposition forms what we can do together. Successful deliberation would not reflect individual views negotiated, but instead be an enactment of inter-est in an in-between, a shared agency arising in the present moment of engagement.

Inter-est—because it seeks to bind—is the source of human power, "this potentiality in being together" (*Human* 201). In this context, it is important to remember that Arendt sees power as immaterial potential, not force, strength, productivity, or violence.[24] Being together does not obliterate difference, as each person's utterance and interpretation create the public realm, what Arendt calls "sameness in utter diversity," a shared space of difference (57). She is quite clear on the need for multiplicity and the pathology of consensus, writing that if only one opinion arose, "the world, which can form only in the interspaces between men in all their variety, would vanish altogether" (*Men* 31). Appropriate to informing deliberative theory, Arendtian politics is fully engaged in relation and separation, similitude and difference. That is, she theorizes distinction and separation as fully as community. Aristotle, concerned with persuasion, understands speech as naturally binding the gregarious human, enabling politics as the cure for individualism and isolation, and reducing anxieties about difference. Arendt, in contrast, valorizes saying and doing as showing human distinction by demonstrating "qualities, gifts, talents, and shortcomings" (179). Perhaps at times, her sense of distinction is too individualistic and fails to recognize the contemporary politics of identity groups or the cross-cultural difficulties of shared interest. However, Arendt expresses the conviction that human distinction must be recognized for the human to appear, writing, "action and speech create a space between the participants which can find its proper location almost any time and anywhere. It is the space of appearance in the widest sense of the word, namely, the space where I appear to others as others appear to me, where men exist not merely like other living or inanimate things but make their appearance explicitly" (*Human* 198–99). Appearance in the political space of speech and act allows for, though does not promise, difference: both the act and the explicit meeting of difference in the here and now, this space and time.

It is important to note that Arendt's concept of appearance is different from Benhabib's assertion that to recognize the other is to know that I am "I" and she is "I" to herself. Rather than place the relationship within the individual's perspective and reciprocity's potential, Arendt seeks to place the composing of human relationships within the sharing of the in-between and inter-est. In related work analyzing the primacy of voice in politics, Adriana Cavarero helps distinguish Arendt's sense of relationship from that of Benhabib, explaining the interactive politics within Arendt. As Cavarero writes, "The speakers are not political because of what they say, but because they say it to others who share an interactive space of reciprocal exposure. To speak to one another is to communicate to one another the unrepeatable uniqueness of each speaker" (*For More* 190). It is not the locutionary force of utterances but the illocutionary and perlocutionary forces that create the political within Arendt. Implicitly, speech must be received and acknowledged, recognized and reciprocated, for there to be political relationships, but those political relationships are based in the communication of uniqueness, not symmetry. Furthermore, it is not what is said by those in the interactive space that makes deliberative politics. The text itself is inadequate. The in-between space focuses not on agent or act, but on the shared potential of those at the table. Any act within an in-between is not easily owned or attributed. Individuals are not distinct foci, but rather distinguish themselves through the shared symbolic practices of speech and act (*Human* 8).

Since it is not the individual or her act but the recognized and sanctioned speech and act that distinguish agency and act and allows their recognition, it is difficult to characterize a procedure, *telos*, or future action. Deliberation is more difficult than means and procedures. In her descriptions of unanimity as pathology, her prequel critique of consensus, Arendt describes the uncertainty of human action, conceiving the effects of human action as without end.[25] Agents cannot know the end of their actions, a scary predicament for human affairs and a conceptual problem for teleological rhetorics. Arendt observes, "[t]hat deeds possess such an enormous capacity for endurance, superior to every other man-made product, could be a matter of pride if men were able to bear its burden, the burden of irreversibility and unpredictability" (*Human* 233). Since the act's capacity for endurance exceeds an individual's distinction and a community's response, deliberation cannot be imagined in ends, for there are not ends to human acts. Fear of the consequences of action, according to Arendt, turns humans away from their capacity for freedom (though some might think people need to consider consequences more). Still, given the endless openness of acts, Arendt characterizes entanglement in the web of human relationships as making us sufferers of our actions more than authors and perpetrators. The space between us entangles us in consequences of our actions, consequences that we can neither understand fully nor ratify without reservation.

Identification as Magical Thinking

The difficulties of recognition, the sanctioning and authorization of other voices, are too often glossed by positing identification as a rhetorical or psychological goal. The facile move to identification distorts the difficulty of difference, the productive agonisms of deliberations, and the deep struggles over diverse norms of justice, citizenship, and community. Despite its explanatory power in describing certain acts of advocacy and identity formation, identification is limited in explaining reciprocity within deliberation.[26] If persuasion is too hegemonic to adequately describe deliberation, identification is too monologic. Yes, one might identify to varying degrees on different points at busy intersections where identities meet in passing, but still, identification is my feeling about your similarity. Let me explain. As I write this, dear reader, I easily imagine our identification. We share the ideals of political deliberation, the class of intellectuals, and the mediated relationship of reader and author. These three aspects of identification—identity with ideals or values, classifications as "we'," and dialogical relationship—are well described in Allison Weir's defense of identification. To her list, I add a fourth identification based on our sharing a discourse; if you understand my disciplinary assumptions, if you share my language game, then there might be identification. Even so, in whatever of the four aspects that I might imagine our identifications, I do not know you—your ideals, your connection to intellectuals, your relationship to me in reading these words, your ability to find meaning in my discourse. Our identification is all my pretense, cloaking cooptation and narcissism as it ignores differences. In fact, my eager claim of our identification may be better described as a misrecognition, what Lauren Berlant defines as "the psychic process by which fantasy recalibrates what we encounter so that we can imagine that something or someone can fulfill our desire" (*Cruel* 122). Rather then conceive of a hostile, bored, disdainful, or ignorant reader, I fantasize one who identifies with my project, my desire. Both the concepts of identification and misrecognition circumvent the difficulty of explanation, justification, and deliberation, however.

Although identification has its uses, it is a deeply troubled term in deliberative situations. As Frantz Fanon reproaches his readers, "the Negro suffers in his body quite differently from the white man" (*Black* 138). Even identification's defender Weir acknowledges the more political and less co-opting concepts of coalition and solidarity, but she still would redefine and redeem identification, giving it a new complexity not denoted in standard usage. Weir would reimagine it as a dialectical, transformative identification, but I would have us interrogate relentlessly the assumptions within the core of identification. As it is monologic in privileging sameness and bonding, identification is imbued with power's innate normativity, and too often, as a abstraction, it depoliticizes the most political and contingent acts of deliberation—the many becoming action—through its failure to designate inequality, history, parochialism, struggle, and marginalization. Identification is an abstraction without particularities or people, one that forms a structural dialectic between identification and division, same and other, presence and absence. Ignoring the continuum of intimacies within human engagement, identification is a term without an antonym other than in the approximations of division, absence, or rupture, all terms that describe extreme disconnections and failed recognitions among people. Due to these deep definitional problems, despite work on its reappropriation by feminists such as Lisa Cartwright, Julia Kristeva, Maria Lugones, and Allison Weir, identification is inherently committed to each one's reception or consumption of the other and, therein, an obliteration of difference. In its obliteration of difference, the norms of identification are particularly pernicious. Identification characterizes our political unities and solidarities without acknowledging them as "something that has to be worked for, struggled toward—in history" (Mohanty, *Feminism* 116). In recognition based on identification, interlocutors query, "Is that one of us? Is she human? How can we make her one of us?" Thus the questions inherent in identification are not productive for discussions of deliberation across difference, because identification focuses initially and primarily on similitude. In its seemingly abstract impartiality, identification hides the powerful differences of material conditions, suasory practices, semiotic technologies, and discursive structures, all of which lend force to identification as a vehicle for creating outcomes and consensus.

As a normative force, like consensus, the concept of identification corrals diverse citizenries into binaries of same and different, with and without, for and against. Even worse, it pretends to explain when it does not. Unlike a performative recognition which requires sanction and authorization of distinction, identification assumes an impossible similitude. Just as Young criticized Benhabib's concept of symmetrical reciprocity for obscuring difference, ignoring the impossibility of reversing position, and failing to acknowledge structural privilege, with even greater deficits, identification obliterates difference, ignores the impossibility of full and sated identification, and disregards structural privilege in the definitional basis of identification, making it politically suspect in its naïveté.

In view of its limitations, one should not allow identification more explanatory space than necessary.[27] Still, it is difficult to dismiss entirely identification's ability to explain rhetorical acts. In particular moments, identification may be employed as a useful concept in binary rhetorics of praise and blame (epideictic), and at least on occasion, the concept of co-opting identification may help illuminate how some citizens empathize with each other, even if the identification is co-opting and hierarchical.[28] When connected or conflated with acts of identity-constituting, identification sometimes is imagined as necessary to shared meanings and employed as a counterweight to antagonism and division.[29] In some redefinitions and extensions of identification, its limitations are acknowledged and corrected. Although I see the work of redefining identification as unrewarding due to its long tradition of co-opting, Weir's concept of transformational identification provides a useful critique and corrective to identification's limits. Rather than seeing identification as sameness in recognition, feeling, or experience, she describes a transformative identification that involves remaking meaning. She writes, "[t]ransformative identification involves a recognition of the other that transforms our relation to each other, that shifts our relation from indifference to a recognition of interdependence" (125). Arguing for a human interdependence and interconnection, a cosmopolitan core to identification, Weir imagines identification as "an active process of getting to know the other" which creates a new we, located in a web of relations of power and identification. Weir's concept of recognition, through transformative identification, places more demands on interlocutors than Singer's recognition as sanction by the chair of the meeting, one that emphasizes binding in ways reminiscent of inter-est. As an ethical argument, she offers a stronger ideal of recognition, but unfortunately her concept of identification does not describe common practice or usage. Identification may potentially entail transformation, but in my identifications with the Afghan mother or my dear reader, how am I transformed? How might one measure that transformation? Do I feel her pain? Your pain? Weir may be more engaged with semantic transformations than political action. Even if she characterizes a transformative potential within some acts of identification, Weir's redefinition does not transcend identification's established denotations, but maybe another approach to identification can.

Responding to the limits of persuasion, Kenneth Burke developed a rhetorical theory based in identification. Burke is sensitive to the conflicts in identification, and he exploits its connotations and definitional limits, mixing identification and division and demonstrating the instability of both terms (*Rhetoric of Motives* 25). Thus his analysis of identification attempts to balance suspicion and belief. As James Zappen has pointed out (see Burke "On Persuasion"), Burke shapes his conception from the earlier work of Harold Laski and George Herbert Mead. Although Mead characterizes identification as a negotiated relationship between the individual and society, which resonates with Arendt's concepts and Weir's vision, Burke is engaged in rhetorical theory more than sociology or political theory, and so he conceives of identification and its counterpart, division, as corrections to the old rhetoric of persuasion and conquest. Committed to a dialectical transcendence of human divisions, Burke's new rhetoric can be glib about the reversals between identification and division, especially when he follows Spinoza on all definition as negation, suggesting that identification is in effortless symmetry with division (*Grammar* 25).[30] At his best, he conceives identification as multiple, ambiguous, and unstable in relationship to equally multiple, ambiguous, and unstable division.[31] Dialectically they form an unstable cognitive structure for communication and identity, and in turn the structure's seismic movements evolve new meanings and pluralism, which lead to continual deliberation and dialectic evolution.

Burkean identification is an ideal, but it is an impossible, unstable ideal and, as such, a repudiation of consensus and even unity in difference. As Burke describes the necessary movement between identification and division, "Identification is compensatory to division. If men were not apart from one another, there would be no need for the rhetorician to proclaim their unity. If men were wholly and truly of one substance, absolute communication would be of man's very essence" (*Rhetoric of Motives* 22). Any promise of "absolute communication," and even consensus, fails to acknowledge the inescapable division implicated in human identification and identity. In this tautological dialectic (are all dialectics tautological?), identification has little to do with reversible positions, reciprocity, solidarity, or recognition; rather, it is consubstantial "*acting-together*" in "a way of life" that creates "common sensations, concepts, images, ideas, attitudes" (21). Despite his emphasis on acting together within identification, which rightly emphasizes performative aspects of recognition and echoes the physical meetings of the in-between, identification works at a level of abstraction similar to the generalized other, and thus identification remains concerned with denying the presence of difference, for it potentially captures "man's very essence," ignoring the gender, culture, and all manner of contingencies.

Within Burke's dialectics of identification, there is a transcendent premise, incorporating Aristotelian optimistic ends and Platonic truth seeking; all three are concerned with the erasure of difference.[32] As Zappen contends, Burke—responding to persuasion as advantage-seeking—develops a process of dialectical-rhetorical transcendence with Platonic echoes. The process of open dialogue, where good idea is replaced by better idea, finds an end in the mystical or spiritual possibility of ultimate identification and unitary ground, transcending faction by permeating rhetoric with dialectic (Burke, *Rhetoric of Motives* 331). Despite its unworldly aspects, Zappen maintains that transcendence here has pragmatic extensions: through a new rhetoric founded in identification and lifelong education, Burke wishes to cultivate new habits of mind in the pursuit of better, ultimate ideas. This interpretation supports the contention that identification, like persuasion, is committed to an ultimate end that decreases difference. Even when defined dialectically—or, more accurately, *because* it is defined and structured dialectically—identification tends toward transcendent unity, lifted away from difference and division and away from understanding coalition and solidarity as achieved through action over time.

Burke's desire to escape the wrangle has received significant critique. Noting disparities between Burke's Anglo-American world of the 1930s and our global community, scholars like Celeste Condit and Zappen would limit the use of dialectical-rhetorical transcendence for contemporary rhetoric in a pluralistic world. More critically, Robert Wess writes that Burke offers a "utopian vision" which ignores power differentials; ultimately, "[b]eing free to speak means little without being powerful enough to be heard" (216). Even Burke himself repeatedly criticizes the dialectical transcending of reality. He writes of transcendence that "[i]t culminates in pure persuasion, absolute communication, beseechment for itself alone, praise and blame so universalized as to have no assignable physical object (hence it is led to postulate the Principles of Goodness and Evil in general, as the only 'audience' possible for an address so generalized)" (*Rhetoric of Motives* 275). By his own accounting, transcendence lacks objects in the world and a human audience.

Given his own discomfort with transcendent identification, it should be no surprise that Burke critiques false and manipulated identification, particularly scapegoating (*Rhetoric of Motives* 20–21; *Philosophy* 191–220). Through scapegoating, he recognizes the innate violence of identification and the requisite of division, and he implicitly acknowledges that identification exists in a context that is violent, a context that may exceed the agent's horizon.[33] Burke's tellingly Biblical example is the shepherd who may act "for the good of the sheep, to protect them from discomfiture and harm" (*Rhetoric* 27). This, however, is not the shepherd's only identification; he also is "identified" with a project, raising sheep for market. Hidden from the pastoral scene of identification is the slaughter, and inherent in the shepherd's identification with the sheep is also the othering of the sheep, division unto death. Identification, for Burke, is not always a snuggly unity or transcendent Good; it is not intimate recognition of or reciprocity with the other, but a relationship of potential violence. Even as Burke imagines transcendence, he narrates identification's violence. It is worth noting that the good shepherd's identification is both with the sentient sheep and the project of meat; consequently, Burkean identification does not distinguish between persons, belief, or material needs and desires. The confusion of sentient sheep and rack of lamb gestures toward identification's tendency to blur subject and object. In so conceiving identification, Burke reconceives rhetoric not as a relationship of address, persuasion, or recognition among interlocutors, but rather "as a general *body of identifications* that owe their own convincingness much more to trivial repetition and dull daily reënforcement than to exceptional rhetorical skill" (*Rhetoric* 26). Hence, the shepherd need not mask his division from the sheep or himself; the dull repetitions of his daily life convince him of the identification and the division without critical distance. He simply shifts his identification from sheep to human hunger in the daily, trivial taking of meat meals. The dull repetition, what Butler and others call citation or reiteration, normalizes even the slaughter of lambs, perilously hiding the normative force of identification and its hidden violences.

When identification presents itself as a nonpolitical, conceptual tool for understanding the formation of rhetorical and political communities, it tames the other and subsumes and consumes her difference, much as the concept of symmetrical reciprocity does. If symmetrical reciprocity frames the nature of reciprocity in equity, it at least attends to reciprocity. Identification's structure does not require mutual response, and so it lacks a deliberating "I" and "you," moving quickly to a transcendent "we." Unlike the more negotiated, transient, political unities of coalition and solidarity, the dialectical oppositions of identification and division divide or unify under the dominating ideology of the shepherd.

Previous definitions of deliberation—be they based in deliberative democracy, persuasion, or identification—emphasize an end of unified action. If one shifts the focus from the end of unified action to the moments when the many meet, recognize each other, and share their acts and agency, deliberative theory shifts from procedure, outcomes, and suasion and instead addresses the constructions of deliberative events and subjects, the topic of the next chapter. The concepts offered here—remonstration, positioned potential, asymmetrical reciprocity, in-between, inter-est, deliberation in the present tense—suggest new answers to the complex questions of global deliberation. How do people develop multicultural cooperation? How does deliberation construct our identities and positions as it enacts our future? If deliberation does not proceed by reason and identification, how might it proceed? How does deliberative engagement contribute to what David Ingram calls a citizen's "risk of radical self-transformation" (258)? If the answers to these questions are impossibly complex, their answers become more imaginable when approached through performative acts and practices.

2

PERFORMATIVE DELIBERATION AND THE NARRATABLE WHO

Man is born free; and everywhere he is in chains.

—Jean-Jacques Rousseau, *The Social Contract*

To act, in its most general sense, means to take an initiative, to begin (as the Greek world *archein*, "to begin," "to lead," and eventually "to rule," indicates), to set something into motion (which is the original meaning of the Latin *agere*). Because they are *initium*, newcomers and beginners by virtue of birth, men take initiative, are prompted into action. . . . The fact that man is capable of action means that the unexpected can be expected from him, that he is able to perform what is infinitely improbable.

—Hannah Arendt, *The Human Condition*

On 26 March 2011, bursting the boundaries between Libyan citizens and Western journalists at the Rixos Hotel, Libyan lawyer Eman al-Obeidi reported her repeated gang rapes, two days of captivity, and assault by fifteen Gaddafi soldiers. She told the foreign press corps, "Look at what Gaddafi's militia did to me." Her distress, demonstrably scratched face, and binding marks on her wrists—behavior, mark, and gesture—worked as testimony as much as the narrative within her accusations. Responding to her situation, televised internationally, the world quickly deliberated on her fate, on justice, on the place of rape in war, on the future of Libya, on international responsibility, on the nature of journalism, and on the disappeared. It responded with petitions (a million signatures gathered), blogs, Facebook pages, news analysis, and engagement from many governments and NGOs. Dragged out of the hotel and held for ten more days, now in official government custody, she was released on 3 April in response to world pressure. Al-Obeidi, despite her legal education, did not choose a textual representation of injustice; she did not file a complaint with the police or blog about her captivity. Rather she came to a particular position to a particular audience and sat her bruised body down at the breakfast table. In the many following scuffles—involving herself, government minders, hotel staff, and journalists—the embodied

acts of authoritarian government demonstrated its will to violate and its relationship to Libyan people in moving bodies for the world to see.

Through changing her position, al-Obeidi changed the potential of her
situation. Her position and potential were different in the Rixos Hotel than
in the Libyan streets or Gaddafi's courts. As she redefined the event from
state power to state assault, al-Obeidi's testimony offered a new norm of
political speech in Libya, a norm of embodied, positioned politics toward
which revolutionaries and advocates work and which in turn works upon
them. In testifying to rape as a war crime, al-Obeidi first refuses the norms
of rape warfare and then rearticulates them, remaking the silence of attack
and the devastating feminine shame into the voice of an attacked people and
the shame of the patriarchal state. In positioning herself at the Rixos Hotel,
she initiates the events, for all events are human creations, constructed from
raw experiences into rhetorical arguments and identity narratives. Her argument and narrative, dramatically performed, offer physical evidence and a
demand that the world recognize her and reciprocate. Even though journalists at the Rixos responded to her accusations, their recognition and reciprocity could only be asymmetrical: al-Obeidi speaks only for minutes before she
is abducted again, but even her brief speech has perlocutionary effect. As a
speech act, however, her testimony does more than persuade. It makes the
event, the citizen herself, and a worldly response. Her testimony performs a
ritualized act, such as those performed by baptisms, legal sentences, or warn-
ings, but as well it potentially confers a binding power on itself, in that she
refigures the cultural norms of the shamed woman. If a baptism renames a
child, then al-Obeidi's testimony renames shame, shifting shame from the
silenced woman to the shame of the abusive state, moving the norms of degradation, death, and repentance to the state. As the norms are repositioned,
al-Obeidi's refusal of the position of shamed woman potentially renames the
position of the state as shamed and unjust. In refusing the expected position,
her testimony forms new, unstable relationships among herself, the state,
and international communities, redefining their relationships and raising
questions about the nature of agency in transnational advocacy.

Although the international communities recognized her, one of the considerations is *how* they recognized her. How does a lone speaker garner such
immediate and anguished international attention? What characterized that
recognition? A great deal of the recognition that followed could be subsumed
under what Boltanski calls "the politics of pity" and not under the preferred
righteousness of justice. Justice would require deliberation over the specifics of al-Obeidi's life in Libya, but pity only entails a one-way emotional

connection, not political acts. Significantly, in keeping with chapter 1's critique of identification, identification becomes a common means of responding to al-Obeidi's subjection to the Libyan national forces, but it is a means
of recognition that obscures her experience. Despite a Facebook page that
proclaims our identification with al-Obeidi (www.facebook.com/FreeIman),
"We are all al-Obeidi," obviously we aren't all al-Obeidi.[1] Even those Facebook
claimants who have been gang-raped have not experienced Gaddafi's rule
nor risked speaking at the Rixos. Simple identifications that deny difference
thwart meaningful dialogue over located politics, and they haunt and diminish the brave and constituting acts of al-Obeidi even as they build political
support for her.

Monovocal identification fails to support deliberation, but we might
reclaim an aspect of identification for the project of rights advocacy and
claiming. Despite its limited ability to do more than recenter the privilege
and authority of those claiming to be al-Obeidi, identification may help al-
Obeidi herself. Building on Chantal Mouffe's understanding of the non-
individualistic individual always at the intersection of multiple identifications
and collective identities, identifications and identities that subvert each other,
Upendra Baxi connects subversive identification and the bearer of rights.
Arguing for an emancipatory potential in universal human rights, he argues
that if "a being [is] born with a right to invent practices of identification, con-
test identities pre-formed by tradition, and the power to negotiate subversive
subject-positions," then people may claim, from time to time, the universal in human rights as it benefits their identity projects (149). Subjects of
rights, that is, may claim identification as it serves them. Always remaining
"contingent" persons, they choose rights contingently through the process
of what An-Na'im calls "*internal cultural discourse and cross-cultural dialogue*"
("Introduction" 3; emphasis in original), and subjects of rights may use identification strategically and contingently. Finding agency to claim identities
troubles postmodernist theorists, but a performative approach to deliberation shows al-Obeidi's agency manifest as act. To find her agency within the
act, we can recognize her as we narrate her life and she narrates our lives
and inter-ests, working toward discovering the in-between where we might
share agency, not identification. Although she does not control her identity
or govern Libya, she publicly acts and defines the terms of Libyan rights.

This chapter offers a theory of performative deliberation, a theory that
explains deliberative aspects of al-Obeidi's speech acts while acknowledging her agency and the cultural, discursive constraints upon it. Performative

deliberation cannot depend on speech acts and postmodern theories of performativity alone because these theories do not adequately describe agents,
agency, and material conditions, especially the materiality of situated agents'
bodies.[2] To elaborate a theory of performative deliberation which allows
for agency and an agent who both conforms to and forms cultural norms,
this chapter extends conventional speech act theories in four ways. First, it
analyzes tensions between conforming and forming within speech act theories to reveal the agency inherent in discourse. An example: al-Obeidi was
able to shift the focus on rape from the shame of the woman to the shame
of the patriarchal state through both conforming to gendered norms and
forming new ways of casting blame by reflecting responsibility not to the
woman or the rapist, but to the state. Second, given that speech acts such
as declarations and testimonies are not initially or always conventional or
normative (form), but instead are sometimes inaugural and responsive
(forming) instruments, the chapter argues that their position, interpretations, and enactments can be sites of fervent deliberation, and the nature
of the cultural change is visible in abnormal or infelicitous performances.
Al-Obeidi's testifying to Western journalists in a hotel is such an example of
a performance that extends the conventional rules of testifying. If a felicitous
utterance should be executed correctly by particular people in appropriate
circumstances, what does it mean to testify not against a criminal before a
court, but against a police state, before the press, over breakfast? Is infelicity
a revolutionary resource? Third, this chapter develops a stronger sense of
embodied performance, especially in reference to deliberation, conceiving
the agent's physical, embodied position as part of the deliberative situation.
Following Susan Leigh Foster, the performative project must consider "[t]he
possibility of a body that is written upon but that also writes," for this consideration "asks scholars to approach the body's involvement in any activity
with an assumption of potential agency to participate in or resist whatever
forms of cultural production are underway" (15). Inherent in a speech act is
a tension between the speech or text and the act marking the located physi-
cality of speech. Fourth, as part of its analysis of bodily agency as participation in cultural and political production, it argues that the work that agency
does is not only resisting and sustaining norms, but also navigating norms
and the tensions among them, using both felicitous and infelicitous acts to
widen possibilities. To demonstrate agency as navigating norms, the chapter
returns to the narrative of al-Obeidi's life and examines her continued navigation of the norms of political discourse.

Doing Things: Utterances and the Drama

"Performative" and its extension, "performativity," have a rich, although brief, history. J. L. Austin quips of his coinage, "It is a new word and an ugly word, and perhaps it does not mean anything very much" (*Philosophical* 233). Given such humble beginnings, the word has achieved a surprising success, and perhaps because it does not mean anything very much, it has come to be a site of considerable extension.[3] Austin's concept of the performative mostly signifies an utterance's ability to constitute or act. Since Austin's insight that some utterances do more than reveal the world and in fact enact the world, "performative" and "performativity" have entered a variety of academic discourses, from anthropology to theater. In traversing disciplines, the term "performativity" has come to mean quite a lot, thus making the triad of concepts—performance, performative, and performativity—complementary, sometimes overlapping, and occasionally contradictory, but never unitary. In considering deliberation, citizen agency, and political act, we should not be too vexed by definitional slippage. Performance, performative, and performativity are matters of changing standpoints. Austin himself wrote,

> It must be remembered that there is no necessity whatsoever that the various models used in creating our vocabulary, primitive or recent, should all fit together neatly as parts into one single, total model or scheme of, for instance, the doing of actions. It is possible, and indeed highly likely, that our assortment of models will include some, or many, that are overlapping, conflicting, or more generally simply *disparate*. ("A Plea" 203)

Performance, performative, and performativity, the terms used here to describe performative deliberation, may be disparate, but each attends to specific aspects of speech acts and citizens' bodies.

Let me lay out a rough map to usage, a map to be developed further as the concepts unfold. Austin inaugurates the family of definitions with performative, the institutionally embedded, conventionally modulated speech act that not only has effect, but does the act. Performatives do: saying "I do" makes the marriage. As he writes, "it indicates that the issuing of the utterance is the performing of an action" (*How* 6). Butler extends performative, arguing that "[g]ender is performative insofar as it is the *effect* of a regulatory regime of gender differences" ("Critically" 21; emphasis in original). Since performatives are concerned with effect through repetitions of norms, Butler continues and argues that "[t]here is no subject who precedes or enacts this repetition of norms." That is, the repeated, socialized symbolic system of constraint, taboo, threats, and even reward constitutes the gendered subject as its effect. As used here, performativity derives from Butler's concern with the constituting, subjectivizing forces of reiterative discourses, forces more prevailing and systemic than a single utterance. For Butler, performativity denotes "that reiterative power of discourse to produce the phenomena that it regulates and constrains" (*Bodies* 2). Performativity defines the structure and powers of discourse that constrain and regulate what it creates. Performativity, in the context of performative deliberation, recognizes the constraints, regulations, and opportunities in traditions of iteration. Performance, a dramatic term here in the work of Kenneth Burke, acknowledges the contingencies of bodily space and agential purposes in the pentad of act, scene, agent, agency, and purpose. Inherent in the dramatic setting is a situated sharing of utterances and a sense of—Burke's word—*persuasion* in the performing of attitudes (*Grammar* 164–65). If performance is not freely the agency of an agent, both are fabricated in the dramatic action of performance.

As I read Burke, he struggles with the definitional difficulties of distinguishing between scripted performatives and innovating performance. At the beginning of "Words as Deeds," his 1975 review of Austin's *How to Do Things with Words* (1962), he draws a taxonomy of moral models within the larger philosophical tradition. He draws attention to Hume's distinction between two species of moral philosophers: some philosophers consider "man chiefly as born for action," and others consider "man" as "a reasonable rather than an active being" (Hume qtd. in Burke, "Words" 147). Although Burke suggests that the distinction initially may have signaled the difference between an ontological (act) and epistemic (reason) approach to moral philosophy, he discusses the distinction between act and reason as a terministic, not deterministic, orientation and uses the concept of "born for action" as the connection between his dramatism (performance) and Austin's speech act theory (performatives). His primary concern is with terminological screens and dramatism in theorizing human motivation. Even so, Burke's extensions of a philosophical division between action and reason, between performance and understanding, may be used to demarcate two approaches to deliberative theory, and while the drive to divide the concepts of act and reason may well be indicative of the repression of their shared identities and interdependence in describing human judgment, there is usefulness in recognizing the divisions between communicative theories primarily concerned with reason, procedures, textual structures, hermeneutics, and understanding (theorists such as Plato, Toulmin, and Habermas) and communicative theories concerned with worldly action and consequence (Aristotle, Arendt, Austin, and Burke). In the world of action, the agent and agency become more significant. Even though both poles of communication theory acknowledge agent and agency, a rhetoric founded in action directly engages purposes and a doer. So simply put by Aristotle: "political speaking urges us either to do or not to do something" (*Rhetoric* 1358). That is, even though ritualized utterances such as "I do" or "I christen" focus on action, the "I" is more than a discursive placeholder: the "I" is part of and necessary to worldly action and effect. Unlike reason-focused communicative theories, action-oriented rhetorics premise a speaker or doer whose utterances affect her lifeworld, and although she may not be a robust I, she is an I who writes as well as is written.

As Burke accurately observes, Austin and he are two theorists deeply concerned with act. Both emphasize the performing dimension of language, seeing words as speech acts or deeds, and they describe at least some utterances as self-referential, constituting reality in their enunciation. Both agree that the speech act itself is more significant than the truth or falseness (constative nature) of any statement. Burke draws a distinction between the grammatical nature of Austin's action and his own more rhetorical concern with the fulfillment of the act in the uptake of a hearer. Rather than understanding "I promise" in terms of a grammatical or metaphysical I, Burke reads it as the "'two way' consideration," shorthand for "I promise that if we all do what I am advocating we'll all get fulfillment" ("Words" 164–65). In offering a shared attitude which may or may not be taken up, utterances extend beyond the speaker and the rituals of speaking. I extend this, arguing that performatives can be seen as conforming to a script and as the forming of event; together they describe aspects of utterances both as form and as forming. Using this division, Austin emphasizes the pre-scripted, reiterative nature of performatives, what I call *ritualized* or *conforming performatives*. Burke claims for himself the sense of performance as forming the social order, what I call *constitutive* or *forming performatives*, even as I acknowledge that his orientation is to a more drama-based performance and not a speech act performative. Despite their differences, the conforming, conventional scripting ascribed to Austin is as removed from reference and the constative nature of language as is Burke's concern with forming utterances, but in emphasizing the ritual and ongoingness of communication, conforming performatives suggest that we are led through discourses by their repetitions and citational history. Austin's theory, read strategically, is useful for seeing the form of action as revealed in the patterns of propositions and the force inherent in their institutional base.

In accepting the form-forming dichotomy for strategic purposes, it is important to remember that neither theory of utterance offers a clean distinction between form and forming. One must not fall into a false dichotomy, for it is a dichotomy that limits an understanding of agential resources within language. As Carrie Noland warns of contemporary theories of subjective agency, there is "on one hand a determinist, constructivist theory that depicts subjects as pliant material on which culture inscribes and on the other a neovitalist approach that tends to exaggerate the subject's capacity to express and fashion itself" (8). Using the form and forming dichotomy, one might see Austin as understanding language (culture) as inscribing acts on pliant subjects, while Burke allows the agent an ability to inscribe act and meaning. However, rather than place Austin and Burke in the dichotomy between postmodern limitations and materialist exaggerations of subjectivity, it is important to understand the intricacy of each position. Austin's utterances and rituals, for example, may seem deterministic, formalistic, and inscripted, but they are both culture-sustaining and culture-making, reiterating the "experience and acumen of many generations of men," but still "supplemented and improved upon and superseded" (*Philosophical* 185). In that conventions are revisable, they are political and subject to contestation. Although Burke, and others, frames Austin as limited to conforming performatives, Austin frequently acknowledges "a great many uses of language" (234), and he is tongue in cheek about the possibility of classifying utterances, writing that philosophers should be able to describe the uses of language, as the number could be no larger than the number of beetle species classified by entomologists. Furthermore, within Austin's work, performative is an evolving concept. As Jonathan Culler describes the performative's evolution, "Austin starts from a situation where performatives are seen as a special case of constatives—pseudo-statements—and arrives at a perspective from which constatives are a particular type of performative" (505). Even within *How to Do Things with Words*, Austin's theory is a moving target, reflexively moving from a taxonomy of constatives and performatives to one of locution, illocution, and perlocution. Moving from the broad class of constatives to the special case of performatives to all aspects of an utterance, Austin circles, remaps, and toys with utterances that "do" something in a felicitous way: "I do," "I declare war," "Notice is hereby given that trespassers will be prosecuted" (*How* 6, 7, 57). With later lectures, he discusses society's resistance to inventing particular performatives, arguing that since society does not approve of insults, it has "not evolved a simple formula 'I insult you'" (*Philosophical* 245). "I insult you" could be imagined to work just fine if society allowed insults adequate space to formalize, writes Austin (and perhaps, too, if society did not find creative insults so useful and joyous). Austin is not as doctrinaire as Burke (or Derrida) would have him.

Despite his interest in purpose and forming, Burke is also not committed consistently to a subject's ability to fashion herself. Preceding postmodernists,[4] Burke places the agent's identity in the combinations of already produced, already constructed, and incorporated discourses, although he modifies this by acknowledging the distinct corporeal grounding of the individual in bodily motion and symbolic action. Furthermore, despite the tensions within his writing, especially his response to Austin, Burke describes the citational, ritualized power of language. As early as 1969, he recognizes the force of citation and reiteration in discourse; he writes, "often we must think of rhetoric not in terms of some one particular address, but as a general *body of identifications* that owe their convincingness much more to trivial repetition and dull daily reënforcement than to exceptional rhetorical skill" (*Rhetoric* 26; emphasis in original). Trivial repetitions are the speech acts and rituals that incorporate and make an identity, a different kind of identification than that of publicly claiming to be al-Obeidi. Rather than seeing identification in terms of human relationship, at this particular juncture, Burke locates identification in discourse. Rituals and patterns form the subject and her discourse-based relationships more than the occasional persuasive moment when the orator claims to identify with an audience. Burke acknowledges the conforming nature of speech acts, and so blurs the distinction between Austin's *conforming performatives* and his *forming* or *constitutive performative*, suggesting that it is strategic and dialectic, not schismatic.

To read Austin's performatives strategically, then, one must imagine that they play up utterances in defined, ritualized contexts; they are not deliberative but formalized constitutions of a reality. A good extension of Austin: the judge—supported by precedent, the great institutions of law, his robes, court officials, and so on—says, as so many earlier judges have said, "I sentence you to death." With that situated and scripted performance, the speech act causes death, but not in any simple way. The utterance is embedded in precedent, written law, the will of the society, the apparatus of the state, and the material conditions of its utterance. In a felicitous utterance, the judge cannot intend murder because his individual intention is subsumed under the utterance's conditions and the law's illocutionary force. The death sentence, while not one of his examples, is a quintessential Austin speech act in the revelation of violent authority and worldly consequence. Similar too is the teacher's pronouncement, "You fail." Here the institutional regulations on plagiary, the history of copyright law, the technological apparatus that reveals plagiarism, the authority vested in a teacher's credentials, the requirements of the syllabus, and the position of student together allow the teacher to discredit a student's prior productivity over a single act of copying. As each of these examples shows, it is relatively easy to define the terms of a felicitous utterance within a ritualized utterance happening in a clearly defined site of inter-est, Arendt's concept of what engages distinct and diverse people in actions. Austin's felicitous or happy utterance, reported as a singular act *without* a reciprocal act, only requires an accepted structure and effect to be executed correctly by particular kinds of truthful people with particular procedures in appropriate circumstances. Individual agency is subsumed under the felicitous norms because the script in context makes the ritualized act itself more significant than an intending or agential "I" engaged in dialogue.

In addition to failing to consider dialogue, Austin's theory excludes many types of discourse from the performative dimension, and his exclusions place limits on conforming performatives in deliberative settings. Seeking clean propositional examples and evading the complexity of reciprocity, despite his own jokes, Austin does not describe jokes, fictions, or theatrical performances as performative, seeing them as "*parasitic* upon its normal use" (*How* 22).[5] Their uses—whatever they may be—mimic the conditions of felicity; that is, they mimic his criteria of performatives and thus are neither independent nor healthy on their own. Although he does not expand this point, consider the difficulties of describing the criteria for a felicitous joke, perhaps one that creates a laugh. Jokes are too contingent, innovative, and dependent on reception, too elaborate and multiple a language game to normalize. Hence, they cannot conform to the felicitous criteria of procedures executed correctly by particular people in appropriate circumstances (*How* 25–38). Just as "Knock, knock" jokes require a breaking of expectation, the power of all jokes is in transforming expected actions and relationships.

When al-Obeidi testifies against the state in a hotel, it is no joke that she breaks accepted and expected acts and relationships. Still her utterances do things in the world, exactly because they are infelicitous. Since they exceed procedures and conventions and because she is not the right kind of person making a conventional claim (shamed women do not speak), her utterances demand recognition of and attention to their consequence. Unlike the "I do" at a wedding where attendees ritualistically reach for rice, no one is certain how to respond to al-Obeidi or to her first or second abduction. The rupture of ritualistic repetition requires a redefining of positions, an entering into the in-between so that a shared lifeworld can be reconstituted. In such a way, the utterances of poets, jokers, and revolutionaries highlight the forming aspects of infelicitous performatives and the generativity of ruptured, distorted, or ineptly performed rituals. In requiring renegotiation and recentering of a shared lifeworld, the infelicitous performatives cannot be adequately captured by the study of single utterances and normative situations. Certain speech acts can initiate and create without felicitous or happy rituals addressing procedure, execution, circumstance, particular people, and effects. In fact, speech acts may do the most when they craft parasitic parodies and slant imitations of conventions and rituals.

Despite their limitations by monologue and happy conventions, Austin's performatives can reveal aspects of deliberative acts because performatives are not a species of utterance, but a dimension of language. In situations where interlocutors are defining political and cultural norms and conditions, the felicitous or happy utterance may not be delineated as neatly as within a courtroom or a wedding, but there are normative requirements that call for attention. To examine ever so briefly a single proposition that is less than legal ritual and more than a guide, one might look at Article I of the Universal Declaration of Human Rights (UDHR), which proclaims humanity's primary values. The utterance "All human beings are born free and equal in dignity and rights" shares similarities with Austin's conforming performatives. Here, through the felicitous criteria of an international procedure of ratification by a particular kind of people, the speech act constructs norms of freedom, equality, and dignity and the right to influence future conduct. That is, the declarative utterance approximates a performative—even if in application declarations are always partial and exist only in fragile relationship to felicitous, contextual supports such as the historic circumstance of rights and rights declarations, the nation's procedures and executions of internal law, the will and understanding of a particular people (its leaders and citizens), the international willingness for intervention, economic development, and so on. It might be a clearer, more felicitous performative to hear the veiled bride say "I do" in the church than to hear a distressed Libyan lawyer or a condemned murderer quote the UDHR on rights and freedoms, but the United Nations provides guidelines, institutional and legal procedures, that define the appropriate enactment, suitable circumstance, and engaged people before and during the utterance. That is, the UDHR defines its terms of felicity. In claiming universality, however, it undermines the force of its felicity as it claims effect everywhere. It extends beyond ritual. Exactly because the article is uttered and used everywhere, it escapes its felicitous circumstances of courtrooms and assemblies and opens itself to deliberation. When it is used as a guideline or norm, not as a law or ritual, the question of felicity in a UN declaration regularly opens deliberation over how to do things with words in ways that the bride's utterance cannot. The constantly shifting context of the utterance undermines the possibility of pure felicity.

Like many norms, the article is valuable because it is not issued always in fully ritualized circumstances (despite efforts and intentions) and because the choices made in adhering to the norm generate performative deliberations. For instance, although law generally is felicitous utterance, the ability of law to be uttered outside of a conventional setting is one of its primary strengths as a normative instrument: my teen can remind me that she has freedom of speech. Like laws, the utterance of normative rights declarations outside of conventional settings compounds their ability to claim, advocate, and create. Although inconsequential within Austin's considerations, the performative features of normative utterances, especially uttered in new positions, need not be excluded from our considerations. Lacking clear conventions and historical applications, certain utterances create deliberative moments with the potential to form unscripted effects: How to respond to al-Obeidi? What does she do? How might I recognize her, sanction her, authorize her? Hearing infelicitous performatives, critics and advocates struggle with what to do, wondering at their effects, considering appropriate responses, asking what enactments of rights are possible or desirable, and choosing a way of proceeding. Rights declarations and demands are performatives extending felicitous criteria along a continuum, somewhere between jokes and the most conventional "I do."

Ignoring Austin's playful, purposeful struggle with slipping taxonomies and the question of felicity, responding to the simplicity of conforming performatives, Burke claims for himself the sense of performance as forming and constituting. Burke is concerned with the initiating potential of utterance and ignores Austin's engagement with the forming aspects of performing, in part, because he is reviewing *How to Do Things with Words*, Austin's lectures most concerned with felicity, convention, and structure.[6] Burke's reaction may also be against his own earlier, conventional self and a time when he was concerned with formal structures and universal understanding.[7] For example, in *The Philosophy of Literary Form*, composed of writing dating back to the 1930s, he claims that "situations are real; the strategies for handling them have public content; and in so far as situations overlap from individual to individual, or from one historical period to another, the strategies possess universal relevance" (1). Early Burke sees language as emerging from a tangible, public situation where the effective strategy is broadened, even "universalized," to form future patterns of communication. Note that Burke's universalizing itch is not a universality of historical progression, nor is it a generalization abstracted and plunked upon reality; rather it is an expansion of a communicative strategy across human bodies (2), a kind of universal relevance, not a universal truth about reality. Thus early Burke might consider the Universal Declaration of Human Rights not as an abstract requirement of all peoples, but as a normative expansion of a relevant strategy for defining humaneness across one historical period to another. Early Burke sounds not so different from Austin, who writes that ordinary language is the "experience and acumen of many generations of men" (*Philosophical* 185). He too sees language as a public reservoir of embodied experience and thought distilled through relevance and use.[8]

In considering the agency of the individual, Burke uses Austin as a foil to what he wants to say about "the *collective* realm of 'culture'" and "each user's *individual* physiological 'nature'" ("Words" 168; emphasis in original). He considers the speech act as occurring through culture's collective realm, but grounded in an individual's bodily motion as illocutionary or intentional attitude (153). To develop the physiological position of each interlocutor, he examines a tension in saying "I do," a tension between the speech act as embedded in the ceremony and the positioned making of a personal commitment to another very particular person. If Austin studies the institutionally embedded act, Burke studies the self-reflexive act, the speech that turns back upon the speaker, creating obligation to the other. Is the "I do" a ritual utterance, or a self-reflexive, self-constituting, embodied act, or both? Does a ritual utterance have the potential to incite self-recognition, leading to the recognition of another? Burke is never clear on the answer on this question; as Debra Hawhee observes at the end of her book-length inquiry into Burkean bodies, "Bodies and language, then, are irreducibly distinct and yet parallel and complementary, mediated by sensation and attitude—at times undermining, at others duplicating each other, but often, if not always, in effect moving together" (166). The closest to clarity one might get is when Burke argues that performing within immediate experience forms the lived body and, within that body, both "physiological (nonsymbolic) motion and symbolic action meet" (*Permanence* 309). Embodied experience—that is, *performance, not performatives*—allows the physically located and embodied subject not just to be formed by and conform to language but also to perform and form her particular life drama, to be seen in both biological motion and symbolic action. Body and mind are twined together, constructing and constituting each other. In such a way Burke considers himself in relationship to Austin: Austin *might* ground symbolic action in nonsymbolic motion, but Burke's dramatistic performance is grounded in the engagement of motion and action in ways that disrupt binary thinking, which would cut the body off from language, thought, and agency. Burke imagines Austin's speech act, his performative, as conventional and discursive, and he understands his own project as performance, as mind and body's theater in the domain of politics and life. His dramatic pentad, which seemingly borrows the metaphor of theater of the world, actually reorients the metaphor away from spectacle and toward physical participation in that the agent is placed in ratio with scenes, purposes, acts, and agencies, orientations which all make partial. Consider further that his drama has no audience. If the theatrical aspect of performance summons images of spectacle and an observer, Burke's form-ing utterances and his drama suggests an adequately complex way of under-standing how a citizen agent might engage in making a world and be part of the action, but never at its center: al-Obeidi can engage the world with mind and body, but never be center and all.

Despite the value of placing the embodied agent within the drama, for purposes of deliberative theory, Burke's sense of performance still is limited in his consideration of the agent and relationships among agents.[9] Although performance expands Austin's performative to position an agent within sym-bolic and bodily struggles with form and forming, it still leaves questions. What are the agent's and agency possibilities within dramatic struggle? If the agent is only partially in discourse, how does bodily motion work within deliberation? How do agents recognize and engage each other across dif-ference? Austin and Burke lead us toward a performative understanding of the utterance, but a deliberative agent must go into political situations and engage alterity, if not conflict. How does one describe the performances of agonistic interlocutors? How do their performances and performatives inter-act? What utterances engage interlocutors in productive ways? And how might we assess that productivity? That is, Burke's performance and Austin's performative give us a vocabulary that we might use to describe al-Obeidi's dramatic utterances at the hotel, but they do not address the world's deliber-ating response to her utterances and body.

Who and the Narratable Self

Despite their rhetorical interests and ambiguous relationship to mainstream philosophy, Austin and Burke keep asking philosophical questions that do not lead directly to grasping the contingencies of rhetorical deliberation and political engagements among diverse, agonistic, or antagonistic interlocutors. This is in part because they repeatedly ask "what": What is an utterance, what is a performative, what is a motive, what is an agent, what is a body? Little concerned with standpoint, dispute, or the where of meaning-making, Austin and Burke primarily are concerned with causal questions—What is the motive of the utterance in communicative situations? What are the effects?—and so their inquiries circumvent questions of engaged interlocutors representing cultural conflicts. Even Burke's concept of an embodied agent cannot be focused adequately on interactions of divergence, forced confluence, and argument among individuals' and their cultures' perspectives, beliefs, and potential because, in Burke's larger question "What is involved when we say what people are doing and why they are doing it?" (*Grammar* xv), he does not specify differences among people, and the specific agent, the concrete other, is subsumed under his method. Burke only incidentally considers who our interlocutor is and who we are. Mostly he wonders what makes people act and seeks a method describing the motives for their acts.

A shift in focus from questions of "where one stands" and "what one does" to "who one is" helps reveal the agent as unique self, a concrete other, and from that unique, concrete agent, it is easier to depict the conflicting cultural values represented by distinct agents in acts of deliberation, each struggling with recognition and the desire for inter-est. As Adriana Cavarero argues, Arendt understands why "Who are you?" might be a better query for depicting the uniqueness of a life and its action because a "who" is exposed and relational.[10] The question of "who" asks for relationship, for the choosing of words that recognize, and takes us to a narratable self that necessarily involves recognizing the other as different and valuable, because to recognize her is to recognize her life as different but worthy of telling. In narrating another's life, the narrator, an interlocutor, answers the question "Who matters to me?" In speaking beyond the recognition of simply sanctioning and telling the other's life, one permits, consents to, and even endorses a relationship of shared lives. Before drawing out the recognition of the narratable life, though, let's examine Arendt's critique of the question "what." Dismissing disembodied, universal Man and describing human actions within situated politics, Arendt is frustrated by definitional knowledge: When "we want to say *who* somebody is, our very vocabulary leads us astray into saying *what* he is; we get entangled in a description of qualities he necessarily shares with others . . . with the result that his specific uniqueness escapes us" (*Human* 181; emphasis in original). One might say that he is subjected to identification. Even if the who question is asked, she continues, too visibly the whatness of its answer in descriptions and analyses leads us toward classifications and universals (invisibilities). To understand uniqueness, to reframe the who, Arendt would have us consider natality, the nudity and birthright uniqueness of the newborn who arrives where no one was before (177–78). Despite her anxieties about how compelling bodily needs—separated from meaningfulness and lacking in language—disrupt political processes, Arendt places natality, the physical birthing of a new human, at the center of human uniqueness and the political act of founding.[11] In *The Origins of Totalitarianism* she writes against the claims of totalitarianism, arguing for the political promise of human beginnings, beginnings identical with human freedom: "This beginning is guaranteed by each new birth; it is indeed every man" (479).[12] Against the force of totalitarianism and its claim of natural or divine right, she contends that the disruption of each new life raises a voice.

With birth into physical being necessarily comes exposure to others and identity through the question asked of all newcomers: "Who are you?" Exposure to others—exhibition and embodied relationship—initiates, even institutes, the request for individuation, argues Arendt. Even against "the self-coercive force of logicality" and all the ideological force of totalitarianism, there is the chance of speaking back from a new position (*Origins* 472). Arendt's natality is not a conceptual foundation for a romantic individual; rather, it is a statement of the potential of diversely placed and birthed individuals to rupture laws and norms. Still, even if we accept the potential of disruption, a baby—however unique—is not a deliberating citizen, not yet an agent asking "who," let alone responding to Judith Butler's accusatory question, "Was it you?" (*Giving* 11). Arendt's promise of a unique potential for each birthed human seems too confident; should I note again Noland's warning against neovitalistic exaggeration of expression and self-fashioning? Natality, however, is only the beginning of Arendt's conception of the heroic citizen and her larger response to totalitarianism's many "methods of dealing with this uniqueness of the human person" (*Origins* 453). Inaugurated in natality and its endless, unexpected creations of plurality, individuals distinguish themselves through speech and action, in engagement with others. That is, an individual distinction depends on a web of human relationships formed in symbolic action over time, not mythic or romantic imaginaries. "Speech and action," writes Arendt, "go on between men, as they are directed toward them, and they retain their agent-revealing capacity even if their content" is directed toward the world of things (*Human* 182). The exposure of the agent to others is integral to words and physical deeds in the world, and "the web of relationships," with all of its sticky connotations, is important for balancing her individualistic and heroic tendency. The web of relationships—the in-between, and inter-est together—provides a basis for speaking distinctly and audibly in a lifeworld formed in symbolic action. Arendt's acknowledgment of a web of relationships, with its inherent and adhering recognitions, allows one to extend her and consider group differentiation and identity politics, a set of moves she would resist, but one that reveals feats of oppression and solidarity (Young, *Justice* 45–57).

Deliberative politics depend on agents, speaking and acting, revealing their agency. Hence Arendt is merciless toward the innocent Billy Budd, whose silence prevents him from entering the web of relationship and leaves him only violence and harsh judgment. Even so, the action of articulate speakers may be twisted; distinction and exposure are partial, for, within the existing web of human relationships, a plurality of wills and intentions thwarts action. Resonant with Burke's partial act, but *more entangled with the other*, the web allows stories of a life to disclose the agent, although the stories are not the product of the agent.[13] This is perhaps clearer when Arendt writes of narration, "*Who* somebody is or was we can only know by knowing the story of which he is himself the hero—his biography, in other words; everything else we know of him, including the work he may have produced and left behind tells us only *what* he is or was" (186). As she observes, Plato's stories of Socrates reveal who he was, while a study of Aristotle's works more answers questions of what he was, what he valued, what he thought. One can extend this and consider how Plato's stories reveal both Socrates and Plato himself.

In asking "who are you?" (or "who am I?"), interlocutors ask for recognition beyond sanctioning. It may be recognition from different perspectives, but they asking for a recognition of their identity *not* based in a what. Indeed, Seyla Benhabib observes that a "narrative model of identity is developed precisely to counteract [sameness], by proposing that identity does not mean 'sameness in time' but rather the capacity to generate meaning over time so as to hold past, present and future together" ("Sexual" 353). The question "who?" makes a first meeting or a new contingency that requires assessment, proposal, construction, and recognition. Interlocutors are asking for engagement in the present, but narrative implicitly provides an active history and trajectory into the future. As Allison Weir observes of human life, "it is a capacity to experience oneself as holding together, though connection—to oneself, to one's meaning, to other people, to significant 'we's'" (118). *For temporal reasons of connection and action, deliberation's recognitions are tied to the connections of who and not simply to the texts and reasons.* For the action of performative deliberation seeks a significant we, an inter-est formed in coalition or solidarity. One's actions—actions exposed to and through another, actions with others—redefine agents and agency as intersubjective even as agency depends on an ability to initiate events that reveal individual distinction.

To articulate the subject capable of agency yet based in discursive practices, Adriana Cavarero extends Arendt's discussion of narration and distinction. Conceiving identity as a complex narrative construction, she argues that the "unique existent" depends on two things.[14] First, she embraces Arendt's insight that humans depend on narration by others for discerning the narrative of their own lives. From this insight Cavarero develops the concept of the narratable self—not a narrated self, but a self that desires to hear her life story told by another. One might say that Cavarero describes a self in need of a particular kind of recognition, that of a narrative not drawn from myths and ur-narratives, but specific to a life. She wants more than Beth Singer's sanction, a minimal standard of recognition. More than the granting of space to speak and be heard as an interlocutor, more than defining space in the in-between, Cavarero defines interlocutors' recognitions at a point when they are already mutually inter-ested. The narratable self desires to know her own whoness, her self in relationship to another's viewing. Implicit in the narratable self is an interlocutor who shifts position to become a narrator of otherness. Cavarero writes, "Correcting Arendt, we will therefore say not only that *who* appears to us is shown to be unique in corporal form and sound of voice, but that this *who* also already comes to us perceptibly as a narratable self with a unique story" (34). Recognizing that each other has a story, "quite apart from any consideration of the text," narratable selves desire to know who appears before them, and their verbal response, their narration of whom, the life story, belongs to each and reveals who each is. As the unique existent finds out who she is through another's narration, she is thus twinned with the desire for her own story, desiring another's recognition. Identity and the desire for identity are in tenacious relationship with narration by others; what is desired is unique recognition and self-identity (32). Unlike identification's obliteration of distinction, the desire to be narrated depends on recognition of distinction, and I would extend this to suggest that the desire to be narrated implies a desire for inter-est. As it marks uniqueness, it marks sharing and shared agency in the creation of recognition, relationship, and identity. Cavarero is clear that the desire for narration is not a desire for immortality in an immortal tale, but a desire to hear of one's uniqueness in the here and now. That is, the performance of the tale ruptures the epic flow of a life to provide a centered moment of engagement. Narration in the present tense: for Arendt and Cavarero, recognition, relationship, and identity established in the act of telling are more important than the text of the story and its later interpretations. Rather than a hermeneutical, textual subject, who is inscribed upon, interpreted, and interpreting, narratability speaks a relationship between deliberative agents, rhetorical agents who produce actions and speech. Hence if one considers the depths of human symbolicity in politics, it makes no sense to dismiss the productive symbolic drive and the rhetorical human in favor of more passive capacities to experience and read. Thus, narratability, never the narrative, is the focus. Unlike the constituting power of discourses and utterances, which are a performativity, the recognition of the unique other and performance of her telling is the constituting power of recognition and relationship for Arendt and Cavarero.

In application: although she does not recognize the unique individual, the militiaman, al-Obeidi narrates a central uniqueness of Gaddafi's men, and so of Gaddafi in proxy. Even if she does not speak to their individual distinction, she tells who they are in a narrative of relationship: "Look at what Gaddafi's militia did to me." Her telling of Gaddafi's whoness has such force that she must be stopped, even if the events of stopping her paradoxically reveal the accuracy of al-Obeidi's first narrative. More of Gaddafi's agents scuffle her out of the hotel, again demonstrating his abuse, solidifying her narration of him; through his narratability, he is recognized. In al-Obeidi's words, Gaddafi is revealed, through the narratability of his agents, and revealed even to and most significantly to himself in the telling (hence, she must be silenced). The actions reinforce the narrative, but the narrative names the who as a precursor to their public action.

If there was only the narratable self, then Linda Alcoff's critique of the co-opting force of speaking for other people might be valid here ("Problem"). The problem of telling another's story is not so different from speaking for other people. Narratability, however, sets the stage for Cavarero's second conceptual offering, "the necessary other," a robust, distinct other who is fully necessary for narrating uniqueness. With public exposure, narratability discloses the deep togetherness of human life, the specifics that Arendt calls "the prepolitical and prehistorical condition of history" (*Human* 184), and the need for distinction, what Cavarero calls "the ontological status of the who, which is always relational and contextual, for whom the other is necessary" (90). If a life is to be narrated and performed in the moment, then the speaker coincides in "the very same scene—where the other who interacts, watches and recounts is the inassimilable, the insubstitutable, the unrepeatable" (90). The necessary other—she who tells the you—disrupts a simple grammar of "I" and precedes a grammar of the "we" in "a curious morality of pronouns" (91). Instead of the glib, co-opting we of identification, the necessary other, always present in the moment of telling, creates the more fraught position of you, a you who requires recognition, acknowledgment, and responsibility. Cavarero's necessary other indicates a discursive relationship significantly different from identification. Identification recognizes oneself in the other, somewhere along the first person continuum from I to we, and thus fails to capture the deeper ontological and prepolitical recognition of an other as a *unique extent with a tale and a desire to hear that tale told*. Cavarero's ideal ethic and logic of relationship requires and desires another who is distinct and irremediably other (92).

Empathy, identification, and other confusions of identity dismiss the significance of the narratable self whose event-ness is distinct, but without the gulf of difference. Still with some connections that confuse identities, the distinct human is at risk for being subsumed in a shared tale where one finds one's own self in another's tale of suffering or abusing. Cavarero writes, "Following Arendt, the term identity must indeed be understood not as that which results from a process of identification, or from a social construction of that identity, but rather as that which a singular existent designs in her uncategorizable [*incatalogabile*] uniqueness" (73). In this, Cavarero writes against her critique. The fragility of uniqueness in the face of social construction, group oppression, and identity politics troubles readings of an agent's unique identity uniquely positioned. In focusing on individuals' narratives, told with recognition, Arendt and Cavarero bracket the forces of ideology, the prominent politics of identity, the generic constraints of narration, and considerations of how interlocutors deliberate in ways not narrative. They disregard the reiterative and discursive and cultural pressures upon speakers. Even so, the concept of narratability is useful to rhetorical deliberation. In the quotation above, Cavarero brackets identification and social construction to describe the design of being and identity. The concept of design is necessary to describing the rhetorical agents engaged in deliberation because deliberation depends on recognition—at least in sanction, but more robustly in narratability—and the agential designation of common inter-ests and actions.

Even if the narratable self helps imagine the rhetorically competent agent, can deliberators ignore the consuming logic of "we" and "they," identifications that so dominate the politics of community? If they were not impossible to ignore, we might bracket co-opting identification in the context of global differences; the deliberative relationship—even before it is a relationship—is first one of recognition and mutual inquiry into life's narratives, a discovery of the in-between, and a rebuff of any quick summation of relationship under either identification or symmetrical reciprocity. When al-Obeidi narrates Gaddafi's life, it requires that one recognize that she has a particular lifeworld to be told back to her and narrated without subsuming her under a generalizing, co-opting tale of consensus or identification. To advocate with al-Obeidi, her narratable self must be a presence. As Benhabib has observed in ways directly related to deliberation, one can engage "the concrete other." The concrete other, the other with "history, identity, and affective-emotional constitution," is born in relationships, not untied and individuated, although unique (*Situating* 159). To understand a distinct life requires that interlocutors conceptually re-form the life in relationship to history, identity, and affect. Deliberation cannot occur when one imagines others as generalized and interlocutors define their relationship through reasoning "in norms of *formal equality* and *reciprocity*." The possibility of deliberation across distinction becomes distorted in formal equality and reciprocity. In Arendtian terms, when interlocutors are generalized, the initiating deliberate acts of finding the in-between and inter-ests are marginalized, if not omitted, because the political is contingent and it exists in particulars and engagement with the "concrete other." The political causes to which one speaks may benefit from generalizing the other as saint and sinner, but acts of robust deliberation are particular: constituting particular scenes, lives, and laws through a finding of in-between and inter-est.

Benhabib's tension between the general and concrete other in the context of narrating lives has direct implications for acts of deliberation. In theoretical understandings of deliberation, the distorting force of the generalized other tends to obliterate the concrete other. Consider whether a narrative is read as concrete and particular (biography) or general and generic (ur-narrative and myth); each method of reading defines a structural tension within both literary reading and democratic deliberation. Without careful recognition of and commitment to a narratable self and interpretive respect, biography evolves and devolves to myth. Narratives of concrete, unique others become subject to pragmatic reinterpretations through memories, preexisting discourses, and the needs of larger political groups. Just as variations of Little Red Riding Hood are subsumed under ur-narratives of a young woman's sexuality, so too al-Obeidi's narratable and unique self is too quickly subsumed under ur-narratives as the politically oppressed, the raped of war, the outraged, the crazy, the drunk, the whore, each depending on who narrates what in her story.[15] She becomes mythic, as ur-narratives often arise in politically strategic refusals of uniqueness, but this, in and of itself, does not dismiss the pragmatic, ethical, and political desirability of approaching another as a narratable self whose concrete and unique self engages and performs experience and culture differently than those of other narratable selves. Al-Obeidi sets—in those moments on that date—her distinction, and that distinction entails and requires worldly attention, interpretation, and narration. Deliberating interlocutors may never be able to narrate the true tale of another's life, but in imagining a just tale, interlocutors begin to create deliberative spaces and acts more complex than those based only in reason, speech act, or drama. Through those acts they may form inter-ests and shared purposes or intentions.

Within deliberation, always across difference, the desire to be narrated and to narrate another's experiences has the potential to explain the development of a relationship in-between. If narrative desire is not a political force, it still impels political action forward. More than the drive to change and make the lifeworld, the desire to be individuated paradoxically brings humans together across difference. The desire for individuation, narration, and recognition together serve cross-cultural and cross-conflict communication. Inter-ests, with their implication of shared agency, arise in the struggling narration of experiences, values, and cultures not shared. The careful narrator, always an unreliable narrator, suggests and discovers shared inter-ests and intentions as a means of recognizing and speaking a narratable life. A narrator of distinction, who somehow speaks more than the fiction of another's life, potentially tells a shareable faction, a useful mixture of event and fiction, even as the narrator of identification distorts another's life. Although likely the narrator has not participated in the other's events, to imagine and produce the tale, she becomes immersed in the events and the experience of witnessing, somehow witnessing and constructing both the other's particular experience of the events and her own inadequacy in constituting the events.

The recognition of the narratable self, even before the narration begins, initiates inter-ests within the in-between, mandating deliberative engagements on what can be uttered. First constrained as it constitutes iterations of norms and rituals, but significantly opened in narratable relationships, performative deliberation constructs human events. The nonproprietary relationships formed in reorienting narrative frames of experience are relationships that recognize and constitute dissonance and intractable distinction. Even if the willed relationships do not disorient, they require an acknowledgment of difference within the equality of life's narratability. The inescapable narrativity of human existence frames and reframes the value of individual lives and offers a moment of inter-est. Narratability as a forming performance creates the terms and agents of deliberation.

Performativity and the Limits of Agency

Judith Butler's performativity, especially in her early work, mitigates any too-easy recognition of the other as narratable and the too-facile agency implied in story-telling. Since performativity expands Austin's performative beyond the single utterance to include the structure of discourses and applies performative force to identity formation, redefining subjectivity, it is significant for understanding deliberative acts. Akin to Austin's performatives, which arise from conventions, citations, and rituals whose felicity demands procedure, execution, circumstance, particular people, and effects, Butler's performativity depends on the citational or reiterative nature of discourse to constitute the performative subject (and her gender). Rather than privilege the distinction and effects of an individual's speech, act, and agency, Butler argues that discourse's ability to produce material effects not only makes the human world, but also makes the subject, what Kathleen Dow Magnus calls "the subjected subject." The subjected subject is not individual or heroic, but subsumed under the generalities of a shared discourse. In constraining agency, a theme to which I will return (for she does more than constrain), Butler ends the potential for radical deliberative invention; what is possible is constrained by what has been said already. Even so, she does expand the concept of performative beyond tidy operatives and single utterances to consider the larger world of discourse, which is so much more than single speech acts, and her broadening of utterance to discourse reveals cultural norms and constraints within conversations and arguments. Even if not fully embraced, performativity marks the depth at which cultural norms, constraints, and iterations may inform and delineate deliberative possibilities. In performativity, Butler finds the "reiterative power of discourse to produce the phenomena that it regulates and constrains" (*Bodies* 2). Similar to Austin's utterance "I do" in depending on prior iterations of the sentence and to Burke's understanding of identification as based in "trivial repetition" (*Rhetoric* 26), Butler argues that iteration and reiteration both repeat and reinscribe conventions in ways that are almost inescapable (12). In placing human intersubjectivity within the discursive reiterations we share, Butler frames our engagements and responses, our meetings and our interests, within our repetitions. In doing so, she posits deep response and responsibility within discourses we share, but she limits the deliberative potential of interlocutors across discourses as intersubjectivity depends on shared reiterations in discourse, not actions in the world.

This critique of engagement's difficulties springs from the privileging of discourse and internal cultural relationships over subjective and positioned agency. In conceiving a subjected subject, Butler argues that the subject is a performative construction—there is no "doer behind the deed" (*Gender* 33, 181)—and that "the iterability of performativity is a theory of agency" (19). In imaging agency in discourse, performativity ignores the autonomy of distinction, even embodiment. In sum, Butler writes, "[t]he source of personal and political agency comes not from within the individual, but in and through the complex cultural exchanges among bodies within which identity itself is ever shifting, indeed where identity itself is constructed, disintegrated, and recirculated only within the context of a field of cultural relations" (161–62). At the extreme edges of Butler's work, no one "does," there is no subject before the predicate and the active verb, there is no prediscursive I of mind or body. Only discourse, and only the discourse that gives agency, is constructed, disintegrated, and recirculated within a culture.[16] In ignoring the singularity, or at least individuation, of individuals, Butler's performativity identifies the conservative power of norms and reiteration within deliberation, rights talk, and subject formation as the necessary counterbalances to individual and shared agency as well as the linear imagining of democratic progress.[17] In focusing on discursive constitution and ideological control in subject formation, Butler mutes questions of recognition and responsibility and denies the possibilities of narrating new ways of being. In arguing that the already discursively "constituted character of the subject is the very precondition of its agency" (in Benhabib, *Feminist* 45–46), Butler provides one answer to why citizens in a free speech democracy do not engage each other regularly and strategically in deliberating for inventive and workable outcomes, but rather accept, reiterate, and work within the discursive histories that limit their visions and opportunities.

At this point, I have offered two discourse-based theories of agency, each a corrective of the other. The theories resist a prediscursive subject and seek the ways in which discursive variety creates a who, an agent. On one hand, one might conceive agency within deliberative moments as dependent on mutual recognition of the narratable selves as well as on the strategic force of narration to create new lifeworlds. On the other hand, one might acknowledge that agency is constrained by an inability to narrate against and beyond familiar discourses and norms. Rather than the limitless agency of a powerful orator or persuasive narrator, both theories consider deliberative agency dependent on discursive resources and constraints defined beyond interlocutors. One need not choose between them, as the resources of language are copious; it is more productive to place them on a continuum. At one end deliberation quintessentially requires one to be addressed and to speak in discourses not chosen but required by the other and the purposes of recognition. At the other end, in denying subjective agency and placing agency within cultural relations, Butler minimizes the force of individual utterances and the agent's manipulation of discourses. Seen through the lens of performativity, al-Obeidi's expansion of the shame of the raped woman to the shaming of the raping state apparatus would not be interpreted through her subjective agency, her who-ness, or her narratable self, but through the forces of discourses running through al-Obeidi. The contradictory discourses of fundamentalist religion, totalitarian lies, and the liberal nation-state create "a certain agency." Butler conceives "the force of repetition in language may be the paradoxical condition by which a certain agency—not linked to a fiction of ego as master of circumstance—is derived from the *impossibility* of choice" (*Bodies* 124; emphasis in original). That is, in moving among discourses, al-Obeidi appears to act as agent, but the agency is in the language, not the ego's design or mastery of circumstance. Most twenty-first-century theorists would concur that the discourses constrain what al-Obeidi can say and do, and thus they would be closer to Butler than Arendt, Cavarero, and even Burke. But Butler's sense of agency as limited to language raises other questions: How does the shift between the discourses happen so nimbly? So wisely? What kind of agency would explain the shift? Is there design?

Even as performativity expands the speech act beyond the utterance and provides the necessary counterbalance to optimistic views of truth-will-out, the power of subjective agency, and the cornucopia of deliberative possibilities, it is troubled by both its lack of dialogism, a concept necessary to deliberation, and an agency limited to formal mechanisms for resisting discourse. Since the lack of dialogism is a greater problem for deliberation, I will begin explicating that limit first. In Butler, the subject does not respond to another (narratable or not), but rather is subsumed by and subjected to forces of discourse, as are all subjects and potential interlocutors.[18] Butler understands the subject as relational, but relational in and through discourses that do not allow an outside and deny the dyadic relationship. As she puts it, "the relations by which we are defined are not dyadic, but always refer to a historical legacy and future horizon that is not contained by the Other, but which constitutes something like the Other of the Other" (*Undoing* 151). If our selves are not our own but are defined in the alterity of history and future, then, for Butler, there is no "single, whole, or autonomous self." She defines the subject as "a temporal chain of desire" and diminishes the possibility of engagement with the Other and distinction. Paradoxically this is because Butler desires "escaping the clutch of those norms by which recognition is conferred," escaping or resisting oppressive social norms (3), but alas, she does not find the escaping of norms politically possible, for norms frame discourse and deliberation. The redefinition of norms and laws is political change, but Butler conceives redefinition in escape and resistance.

In response to the difficulty of describing a meaningful agency and engagement with another, Butler revisits the limits of agency and subjective responsiveness many times, though for purposes of discussing deliberation, most notably in *Giving an Account of Oneself*. Since "giving an account" places a self in response to another, one might read *Giving* as her most rhetorical text in its acknowledgment of a scene of recognition as well as a response to Cavarero's implicit critique of her subject's limitations. Butler positions herself against Cavarero, who argues that the experience of memory inherent in narration is not simple reflection, but a kind of ontology. Cavarero writes, "I know that I have a story and that I consist in this story—even when I do not pause to recount it to myself . . . I could nevertheless not know myself to be narratable unless I were not always already interwoven into the autobiographical text of this story" (35). Cavarero sees our heroic actuality, our selves in relationship to others, manifested in our stories. Butler rejects the heroic story as she rejects distinction and individuation; instead, our memories—which observe human singularity, specificity, and all that which separates our stories—may be understood in a Hegelian frame, which aligns specificity with generalities. Diminishing singularity, though in some ways acknowledging the dialogic structure of subjection, Butler argues that the "singularizing exposure" can be and is reiterated to establish "a structure of substitutability at the core of singularity" (34–35). Butler views the generalities of discourses, conventions, and norms as collecting the singularities into a we, and so in the end, she subsumes human recognition under generalities of discourses, conventions, and norms.

Although a full analysis and response would take us far from performative deliberation, let me note two deliberative difficulties with Butler's discussion of recognition. First, if human singularity and distinctions are so subsumed under generalities of discourse, it becomes difficult to imagine

how difference and deliberation would arise. One might nod to the temporality of discourse being different from the temporality of one's life: one is
born into preexisting discursive regimes, great historical regimes, and so
the time of one's life obscures its submission to discursive and historical
regimes. Still, somehow, there appears among us great variety. Second, even
if delightful, abstraction at this level does not help delineate how al-Obeidi
was able to achieve worldwide recognition. By what cause? Through what
means? We can imagine the discourse of her patriotic courage, but by what
means does she use it at risk to her existence? How does she know to subject Gaddafi to the discourses of feminism and nationalism? In giving an
account of oneself and in responding to accusation as well as recognition,
Butler builds a theory of recognition as she delineates a scene of recognition
that assumes some causalities within human engagements. For instance,
she writes that sometimes recognition, or rather unrecognizability, marks "a
site of rupture within the horizon of normativity and implicitly calls for the
institution of new norms, putting into question the givenness of the prevailing normative horizon" (24). Ruptured norms potentially initiate a struggle
with norms, which in turn might generate new norms. This recognizes the
primary role of recognition within deliberation. However, it remains problematic for deliberative theory, as the struggle is between norms and not
between cultures, agents, or subjects (26). How norms struggle is unclear.
Where and how does the agency of norms arise?

Theorizing recognition is difficult in the best of times, but Butler's site
of accusation and accounting seems more fraught with desire, distrust, and
disengagement, more difficult and demanding than recognition theorized
through a pragmatics of sanction and narratable lives. To account for oneself
and one's acts toward another, I argue, one must go beyond performative and
constative acts of basic recognition (sanction). When interlocutors go beyond
personal interests and commit to finding inter-ests, they acknowledge the
narratability, the sequence, of another's life and the possibility of inter-ests;
they enter the in-between. If deliberating interlocutors have partially separated practices and experiences of culture, reason, evidence, values, emotions, and assumptions, how can each give an account across practices and
experiences? To give an appropriate account, one must have in mind and
discourse the other and her grammar, logic, rhetoric, culture, form of life,
claims, and narrative. Butler will not help us here, for as she understands
giving an account, one must enter a different frame of recognition, one that
demands re-cognition and understanding of one's self, not the other. Butler's
sense of accounting escapes these operational difficulties of difference and

the other through its solipsism, its concern with mirroring back what is "contingent and incoherent" and wondering how "my own opacity to myself occasions my capacity to confer a certain kind of recognition on others" (41). That is, in Butler, recognition springs from a failed self-recognition, and it comes not from an agent seeking connections, but from becoming disoriented and failing self-identity (42). If Cavarero's subject responds to the desire for recognition by desiring both to hear her narrative and to tell another's narrative, Butler's subject responds to the question "Who are you?"—or more accurately, in *her* scene of recognition, "Was it you?"—with a desire to give a self-reflective account of herself, suggesting a narcissism if not intolerance of the outside (an agoraphobia). The task of (self)recognition may engage both Butler's and Cavarero's subject, but Cavarero's subject produces a narrative within which the other finds her own narratability, and in narrating herself and others, the subject is committed to engaging and constituting an alternative lifeworld. Butler's subject turns back into herself at the point of recognition and recognizes neither the other nor what narrative the other might audit as an appropriate account. Her agential resources are limited to self-explorations and self-reflections and hence cannot lead to deliberation and shared actions.

Performativity, as a deliberative concept, both benefits from and is limited by its minimal agency. Even so, if it serves as a corrective to individualist models of the subjective agency and reifications of the powerful orator, it overcorrects by limiting agency to the incomplete act of resisting the discourses in which the agent is entrapped. For example, in response to the emancipatory subject of early feminist theories, Butler argues that "[t]he feminist subject turns out to be discursively constituted by the very political system that is supposed to facilitate its emancipation" (*Bodies* 4). Trapped in the Enlightenment discourse that made her, Butler's feminist subject is constituted and discursively limited by the very political system that is to provide her emancipation and political possibility. The possibility of political rights is implicitly constructed and constrained by preexisting discourses, and Butler describes the now-familiar paradox of subjection,[19] writing, "the subject who would resist such norms is itself enabled, if not produced, by such norms. Although this constitutive constraint does not foreclose the possibility of agency, it does locate agency as a reiterative or rearticulatory practice, immanent to power, and not a relation of external opposition to power" (15). Located in an apparently closed system, a discursive regime where power cannot be withdrawn or refused, the subject is constrained by what the discourse allows, although it seemingly allows *internal* oppositions.

Butler imagines agency as possible only through variants on repetitions, discursive instability in the frame of parodic and subversive redeployment. The alternating or subversion of the norms is limited to infelicitous moments of reiteration, points at which the reiteration is altered by infelicitous procedure, execution, circumstance, people, and effects. Through embracing the infelicitous possibilities of speech acts (altered contexts, violated procedures, shifted audience, inappropriate speakers), Butler is able to describe deconstructive resources within the compulsory repetition of norms which, if they cannot be thrown off, can provide a means of resistance, subversion, displacement. In recognizing the potential of both consolidating and destabilizing norms, Butler articulates the tension between norms (conforming) and invention (forming) within performative utterances.[20] Emphasizing norms and reiterations, she disrupts the tautological nature of discursive form without abandoning it; she imagines an inventive agency within discourse as she abandons more humanistic or grammatical agents (Ebert 209–15).

Despite the useful broadening of performative in performativity, Butler's subject subjected to discourse lacks in body, so lacks in position and the material conditions that make visible contestation and make possible deliberation in-between. There may be a kind of agency in the reifications and reiterations of discursive regimes, but the reiterations of discourse have limited use in creating robust recognitions and bridging cultural and discursive divides. That is, although ruptures and infelicities within performativity have the political potential to reform norms, even when considered as agency, the political potential is defined in oppositional dialectics and contrarian wishes, possible only through reworking and resignifying of existing norms, regulations, dominations, and constitutions. Butler defines only agency's constraints, as she works toward answering what Saba Mahmood characterizes as a central question of feminism: "[H]ow do women contribute to reproducing their own domination, and how do they resist or subvert it?" (6). Accepting Butler's premises that the body is always already politicized and agency is constrained in discourse, Mahmood brilliantly replaces the question of domination and resistance with the question, "[D]oes the category of resistance impose a teleology of progressive politics on the analytics of power—a teleology that makes it hard for us to see and understand forms of being and action that are not necessarily encapsulated by the narrative of subversion and reinscription of norms?" (9). Rather than imagining agency as subversion or submission, Mahmood conceives agency beyond subverting and inscribing norms. Instead she conceives agency as embedded in an agent's relationship to norms, demonstrating agency's formation through the interplay of citational acts. To describe complex relationships to norms, she conceives the positioned body in ways similar to the concrete other, examining the relationships that a subject forms "between the various constitutive elements of the self (body, reason, emotion, volition, and so on) and a particular norm" (120). Critiquing liberalism's overvaluing of freedom, Mahmood demonstrates how liberal claims have dominated feminist arguments of "self-realization/self-fulfillment," forcing a binary model of subordination and subversion (13–14). She would have us set aside the terms of subordination and resistance embedded in the discourse of freedom and understand agency as historically and culturally specific, embedded within historical and cultural norms. One might think of agency as performance. In this context, agency is defined not just in resisting norms, but also in how an agent *inhabits* norms. That is, the discursive cultivation of norms may reveal "projects, discourses, and desires" which exceed liberalism's autonomy, freedom, and resistance (14–15). To analyze the emergence of agency in one particular mode of being, Mahmood engages women in the mosque movement in Egypt, arguing that when the women face difficulty with authoritative structures, either Islamic or liberal, familial or state, their responses are not adequately characterized by a binary of resistance and subordination. To understand the women's agency, one should approach their discursive traditions and bracket one's own "prejudices against their form of life" (198). Categories of agency, like categories of identity, are cultural productions created in the frames of political possibility. Other realms of experience, other positions, are not impoverished culturally, politically, or agentially. As Mahmood argues, the feminist practice of "solidarity" cannot arise from "the 'ur-languages' of feminism, progressivism, liberalism, or Islamism" (199). These ur-languages (or ur-narratives of redemption) have inherent visions of futures. One might argue that, like traditional theories of deliberation, ur-narratives of solidarity are premised upon teleological forces that move participants from finding the in-between to developing inter-ests to succumbing to persuasion, consensus, and domination too rapidly and too linearly, especially when it is unclear that persuasion and consensus are desirable or possible in a conflict.

Resisting the heroic individual, Mahmood acknowledges the normative subject and the interiority of norms, but rather than restrict the subject to an agonistic framework of doing and undoing norms, she interrogates how "norms are lived and inhabited, aspired to, reached for, and consummated" (23). Acknowledging the Aristotelian tradition of morality realized through outward behaviors, practices, and forms of life, but stripping it of the teleological and collective notion of a good life, Mahmood employs Foucauldian ethics to argue that learned ability, a requisite of agency, requires "docility," the ability to be taught (*doxa*) (29). In turn, docility and the ability to inhabit norms are implicated in the capacities and skills required for certain kinds of moral actions and characterize an agency capable of more than resistance. Learned, lived, and strategically engaged norms are the tools of subjective agency, for agency is always within specific historical and cultural discipline. When agency is conceived more broadly than freedom and resistance, then the acts of citizen agents are framed within norms, not simply against norms. Obedience to certain norms, such as human rights norms or the ethical norms of the mosque movement, has value and represents agency in that it requires a negotiation with contradictory—even paradoxical—messages about the nature of obedience and the value of docility. Given that the norms of any culture are not singular or static, agents negotiate varied sets of norms even within a single culture, and they negotiate them from a number of identities, intersections, or standpoints, which in turn affect their capacity to negotiate norms.[21] Thus acceptance and resistance are a reductive binary of human agency, action, discourse, and distinction; acceptance and resistance elide the scene of deliberative politics. Within deliberative situations—dependent on the exploration of possibilities, shared purposes, and even sacrifice—freedom and resistance may be forms of agency that minimize the pragmatics of engagement, paradoxically increasing division and the centrality of power dynamics. If resistance and acceptance were the only basis of agency, how might global citizens deliberate and collaborate together? How might agents meet in-between and discover inter-ests if they focus primarily on resistance and freedom from domination? If agency is based in resistance, how can a struggle between two sets of norms create a third doxa that is learned and shared in meaningful ways?

As an alternative to resisting agency, consider the discovery of an interest in itself as a form of agency, with agency understood here as the ability to invent or be taught a means of proceeding through and across norms, or the sharing, inhabiting, and consuming of norms in ways productive for the agent. One might extend the agency of negotiated norms to the agent's recognition of narratable selves, the potential negotiation of cross-cultural norms. *The acts of recognition and narrating respect negotiation and resist teleology and universalism, and even agonism, finding meaning only in a present-tense location and among people.* The practice of negotiating is more significant than the agent's willful resistance. One need not turn to the mosque movement in Egypt to find models of agency outside of liberal frames of resistance and emancipation. Confucius's *Analects* is just one of many classical

Chinese theories of political discourse that demonstrate agency without the explicit values of modernism, freedom, and liberalism.[22] In remonstrating and valuing relationships, a political advisor does not give up agency, but rather understands agency as relational to and respectful of difference. The political value of remonstration, which does not require more than the in-between, locates agency in recognizing the positioned potential of the other and minimizing the moves of individuality and autonomy, be they controlling, resisting, or dominating. In remonstrating, the speaker offers a possibility to the other, who may or may not find it of inter-est. If intercultural deliberation is concerned first with recognition, respect, and finding inter-est in-between, deliberative projects benefit from the docile bracketing, at least momentarily, of entrenched cultural and historical norms, offering a first step toward their negotiation.

Agency reconceived as the navigation, maintenance, and construction of useful norms as well as resistance and subordination sets the stage for performative deliberation based in a recognition in-between and an investigation, navigation, maintenance, and construction of inter-ests, inter-ests guided by but not restricted to preexisting norms. Performative deliberation—given its speech act origins—entails reiteration and discursive norms, but it also must allow for meetings across norms in actions such as performances, infelicities, and recognitions. Reconceiving Butler's discursive agency dichotomized as subordination (conforming) and resistance (forming) to norms, Mahmood's theory of subjective agency suggests a richer vocabulary for understanding agency as form and forming, and their necessary intersection within deliberative moments. Performativity, as I employ it here, acknowledges crevices between and surpluses in discourse and a present, but limited, human agency in constituting relationships with norms. In conceiving agency as the intersection of discursive and subjective agency, a field of play and labor, rhetorical theorists might find al-Obeidi as narratable in her resistance and consolidations, but also as narratable by inhabiting the norms that first make rape worse than confinement and that renegotiate these norms, privilege community above the individual, and make political freedom the primary human value.

Replay and Reiteration: Eman al-Obeidi's Second Performance

Despite a Facebook page that proclaims our identification with al-Obeidi, "We are all al-Obeidi," in fact we aren't all al-Obeidi. It is a false, co-opting identification, perhaps arising from the desire to cohabitate the discourse and deny our alternative narrations and norms. We can recognize her only in that we narrate her life with care, negotiating conflicting norms, discovering the in-between where we might share agency, and understanding how she labors to constitute mutual inter-ests. False identification haunts the constitutive acts of al-Obeidi, making it too easy to understand her negotiation of cultural norms as resistance and an appeal to our own norms. Instead, interpreters and interlocutors should consider the complexity of discourses she navigates to perform her narratable life. That is, they should not subsume or consume her as inhabiting an ideal. When Butler writes of performativity and "theatrical agency," she warns that the performance of gender is "an assignment which is never quite carried out according to expectations, whose addressee never quite inhabits the ideal s/he is compelled to approximate" (*Bodies* 231). Al-Obeidi's performances, performatives, and performativity are always partial and inexact actions. Performative deliberation depends upon their approximations. In recognizing agential acts, deliberating interlocutors do not know the consequences of acts, either their own or the alien acts they negotiate. Arendt warns of uncontrolled futures and Butler warns of approximations and partiality. Approximate, partial, and uncontrolled describes the deliberate act, as al-Obeidi demonstrates.

If agency is imagined as the performative negotiation of culturally specific norms as well as resistance to those norms, then a comparison of al-Obeidi's initial testimony at the Rixos Hotel and her slightly later CNN testimony demonstrates resistance and engagement in norms as well as the labors of an agent to shift her strategies and placement within norms. At the Rixos, al-Obeidi is more distressed by her sexual assault than by her days of confinement. The Islamic virtue or norm of female modesty (*al-ihtishām, al-hayā'*) was simultaneously upheld by her outrage at its violation and denounced by her international display of its violation. In her first testimony, which she does not identify as a revolutionary moment or event, an assault on female virtue was a greater crime than illegal detention. In her appeal to Western journalists, she seems to tell the colonial narrative of the virtuous woman attacked and injured. Even though there is a partial text of politico-cultural domination and one might want to characterize her as an agent of political resistance, her narratable self, especially as received in the West, is that of a sexually violated woman seeking recognition, protection, and justice. However, if her agency in appearing and speaking in a public space is fully acknowledged, she does more than accept or resist the norms of rape culture. In the Rixos, to create inter-est, she first resists the norms of rape culture (which would silence her), and then she renegotiates the norms as a ground for denouncing the state.

Certainly her initial performance was narrated, voiced over by the media, and Western liberalism held itself out as a court of judgment, interpreting the events as evidence of a savage nation-state's assaulting its victimized citizens, who are in need of saving.[23] Much of her initial appeal to Western journalists was picked up by NGOs and advocates and interpreted within the rape discourse that she had revised. For example, Amnesty International's widely distributed 26 April 2011 email announces, "Despite grave risks . . . [w]omen in the Middle East and North Africa who are fighting for their rights face rape and other abuses." Reinterpreting and narrowing its normally broad frame of human rights, Amnesty focuses on the rape and abuse of women, mixing the heroic with the abject. Praising Eman al-Obeidi because "[s]he dared to speak out about unimaginable abuse," Amnesty's letter draws attention to the daring and the "unimaginable," a curious term in that gang rape is regularly reported in war and is a common pornographic fantasy, an imaginary readily available. Still, Amnesty narrates her rape, *not her unique narratable self*, before it finally connects her event to other forms of gendered abuse such as forced marriages, unequal protection, and inadequate recourse against domestic abuse. Seemingly unequal protection under the law would cover these abuses targeted at women as well as the explicit political rights violations protested in the Middle East and Africa, but Amnesty's donation appeal is expansive on sexual violations (rape, virginity tests, strip searches photographed by male soldiers). In presenting the "entrenched inequality" symptomatically as sexual abuse rather than patriarchal or political power, Amnesty's representations imply that women's rights are limited to sexual rights, as did al-Obeidi herself in her initial appeal. Rape is a norm for interrogating the state of women's rights.

Again, Eman al-Obeidi herself initially framed her attack as rape, barely acknowledging her days of captivity. Her March testimony, though it disrupts the narrative of the silenced and shamed woman, still adheres to cultural traditions that define rape as the worst thing that can happen to a woman, an unimaginable abuse. Her agency was seemingly constrained both by what her body could demonstrate and by the performativity of discourses of gender violence. Although she was able to find a means of resistance in speaking publicly to Western journalists, she was constrained by the discourses of womanhood, which limited the breadth of her outrage and the narratives she could initiate. In effect, she is juxtaposing contradictory norms of womanly modesty with public demands to be heard, and she is refusing norms of feminine silence while she accepts those that define gender violence as the greatest injustice. If this reading supports discursive performativity, in contrast, her bodily presence in the Westernized hotel—her positioned potential—was a powerful part of her agency. In negotiating spatially defined norms of discourse, her body accomplished what words spoken elsewhere might not.

Amnesty's fundraising in late April promoted the traditional narration of woman raped in war, but it lagged behind al-Obeidi, who had repositioned herself. By early April al-Obeidi had redefined the event, moving from a limited, feminized discourse of bodily rights to a robust demand of liberal rights for the Libyan people and a privileging of positive freedoms. She renegotiated the discourses and norms by which she defined events in her life—at least renegotiated them for public performances that would influence the world's deliberations on Libya's fate. In her 4 April CNN phone interview with Anderson Cooper, he describes her as defiant and in danger of her life, with "nothing left to lose." In Tripoli, having been arrested multiple times, speaking through a translator, al-Obeidi no longer speaks for herself alone. The first person is gone: "our life was destroyed, and our dignity tarnished. Our humanity has been taken from us. . . . We are even careful to the air we inhale and exhale in order to regain our freedom." The rights violations are redefined from the events of a lone woman's lost virtue to events concerning a people's freedom. That funny, tainted word of liberalism—freedom—has been taken up as a universal value, a value that will displace gendered rights in her testimony. When she recounts what Gaddafi's brigades did to her, she shifts the focus from rape to abduction: "They abducted me . . . I was bound and tied up; I was beaten and tortured. For two days they violated my freedom." She describes details of bondage, the torture, biting, alcohol in her eyes, death threats, hunger, and thirst, but eight days after her escape and after several more confinements by the regime, the gang rapes take second or third place to the broader issues of abduction, torture, and political oppression. The acts are defined as political, not only in al-Obeidi's shift to involve all Libyans but even in what she reports the brigades saying: "let the men from Eastern Libya come and see what we are doing to their women." Even as the brigades define her as a woman, they are engaging the men in rebellion. Al-Obeidi herself has come to refuse the name of woman, that limit term, and to reclaim her humanity, describing her motive in going to the hotel: "I reached the end of my tolerance for this, as a *human*" (emphasis added).

She has shifted transparently between the normative discourse of violated and outraged woman to the broader discourse of human rights, with all of its liberal, Western, and universal liabilities. If I am tempted to see her shift-ing norms as a straightforward rhetorical (even sophistic) appeal to the CNN West, an importing of alien norms for practical purposes, I must acknowl-edge the force of her agency in extending rights norms to all Libyans, consti-tuting her particular experiences as representative of the inter-ests between all Libyans and conceivably of Western interlocutors. Furthermore, as her speech acts reconstitute the situation, she utilizes her changed position from a battered woman trespassing at the Rixos Hotel to an international source of insider information, sought out by corporate news. From this new position, with all of its potential, she defines the event as not a singular instance of gang rape but as representing the ongoing national terror, daily detentions, and silencings: "The people here live in hell, in detention, and a twenty-four hour state of terror, the same terror that happened to me . . . so I would not speak." Although Cooper is slow to pick up on her move from rape discourse to the broader rights discourse of abduction, torture, and lost freedom, he finally shifts from questions of rape to the broader concept of hurt. Not only has al-Obeidi redefined the normative discourse for her own story, but she has also succeeded in resetting the discursive norms of the interview and making her narratable self no longer the sexualized woman but the hurt citizen, a citizen of rights. Cooper asks, "Did you know any of the fifteen men who hurt you?" "Hurt" is telling here, as it marks physical, psychologi-cal, and rights hurts, creating ambiguity productive for finding inter-ests. If more discourses may describe hurt, then more norms need to be considered and negotiated.

Ultimately al-Obeidi repositions the conversation from past hurts to future desires. As she performs in the present, she imagines and loosely scripts a future. She directly appeals to a liberal in-between and inter-ests shared with her listeners, saying, "Dying is more of an honor than being denied my free-dom, my family, my dignity. . . . To all the people watching us in America, we are a peaceful people . . . we are not asking for anything except for our free-dom, our dignity, and the most basic human rights denied." Even though she performs for unknown, unanswering millions, I resist the concept of audi-ence here, because al-Obeidi seems less concerned with persuasion to take a particular action and more engaged with the labor of gaining recognition for the Libyan people and defining their inter-ests in relationship with CNN watchers. In narrating the lifeworld of Libyans, she undertakes the identity formation of people who desire liberal rights. Those hearing her story on CNN may go beyond textual reception and recognize themselves, telling her tale and their tales in new ways.

To claim and manipulate human rights discourse and norms in the service of performative deliberation, in the negotiation of the in-between, al-Obeidi refuses a woman's body and its experiences in order to speak for a larger citizenry. Although there are clear colonial implications for discarding the resources of Libyan discursive traditions for those of human rights, for masters of agency, such as al-Obeidi, the need to travel through the norms of multiple cultures—and not simply to conform or resist—is part of agential negotiating of in-betweens and inter-ests. Transnational interlocutors traverse a variety of discourses and norms and, in so traveling, create spaces in-between where different participants might imagine inter-ests. If al-Obeidi first presented the colonialist norm of an indigenous woman in need of rescue to riveted world attention, she later performed other "modes of being, responsibility, and effectivity" (Mahmood 14–15). In finding a mode of political being that is responsible and effective, al-Obeidi does more than resist and negotiate norms; she switches discursive tools in an effort to establish spaces for deliberation.

Butler would tell us that al-Obeidi's forging of a future depends on "resources that are inevitably impure" (*Bodies* 241). Arendt would tell us that al-Obeidi's story, told by herself as the actor, is incomplete, rarely "an entirely trustworthy statement of intentions, aims, and motives" (*Human* 192). Al-Obeidi might reflect on her experience and realize the complexity of her days of captivity, and she might narrate in a different discourse next time. Could she tell it "truer" then? In all likelihood, what she said in March in the Rixos had not yet been narrated back to her; then she was concerned with testifying to the deed. Eight days later, on CNN, she already had heard her events told back. With time, a storyteller or historian, perhaps a journalist, will fabricate the story, remake the event, and tell back al-Obeidi's heroic acts, making them more meaningful for her and for others. Discourses and norms are negotiated again and again, away from her body, but not from distinction. Arendt goes so far as to claim that "what the storyteller narrates must necessarily be hidden from the actor himself, at least as long as he is in the act or caught in its consequences." The "meaningfulness" of her own speech and acts *to her* may not be in the current stories. Al-Obeidi will be revealed and her distinctions noticed in history, her agency taught to others.

3

NARRATING RIGHTS, CREATING AGENTS:
MISSING WOMEN IN THE U.S. MEDIA

[T]he sole end for which mankind are warranted, individually or collectively, in interfering with the liberty of action of any of their number, is self-protection. That the only purpose for which power can be rightfully exercised over any member of a civilized community, against his will, is to prevent harm to others. . . . *The only part of the conduct of anyone, for which he is amenable to society, is that which concerns others.* In the part which merely concerns himself, his independence is, of right, absolute. Over himself, over his own body and mind, the individual is sovereign.

—John Stuart Mill, *On Liberty* (emphasis added)

With great efforts we created 7 million additional jobs last year, but more than 10 million new infants have been added at the same time.

—Politburo member Wang Zhen, quoted in Thomas Scharping, *Birth Control in China*

Ur-narratives and local discourses constrain deliberations on human rights. If there exist normative declarations to protect rights, it is unclear how these declarations are made into an international will for enacting rights. Political purposes, more than normative justice, may dominate rights deliberations. In *Human Rights and Gender Violence*, Sally Engle Merry demonstrates how human rights laws need to be respoken in the vernacular in such a way that local agents and advocates can recognize novel claimants and engage their claims. In her analysis, Merry observes that "[h]uman rights documents create the legal categories and legal norms . . . but the dissemination of these norms and categories depends on NGOs seizing the language and using it to generate public support or governmental discomfort" (71). For example, currently women in Saudi Arabia struggle for driving rights within a cultural tradition that historically restricted women's independence. Although one might frame their deliberations in the right of liberty promised in the Universal Declaration of Human Rights, in fact, their focus is economic, involving access to work and the cost of drivers. To deliberate effectively and achieve autonomy, Saudi women engage the local vernacular and engage local restrictions, negotiating their weaknesses. Advocates need the resources of local cultural tensions and practices to negotiate practices of rights, which are neither ideal nor universal in practice. When local practices are examined outside their cultural home, the local practices are subject to international politics. Rather than opening spaces of translation locally and globally, too often rights deliberations become political critiques of foreign nations whose rights norms are judged deficient, creating a "they are wrong and we are righteous" binary in the service of the nation-state.

If the vernaculars of human rights should be more diverse than those of Western liberalism and the UDHR, then interpreting what one sees as a human rights violation, or even as a protection, should be more complex. To recognize human diversity—including a diversity of ethics and rights traditions—critical interpretations and representations of human rights should acknowledge views based in cultural difference, human capacity, and communitarian rights models as well.[1] Feminist theorists, such as Tani Barlow, Inderpal Grewal and Caren Kaplan, and Chandra Talpade Mohanty, criticize international feminism for its representation of women's rights within a supranational, individualist approach; they argue that without a fuller understanding of cultures, nations, and rights, the West will continue to represent women's rights as individual and in conflict with their cultures (often represented as oppressive, deviant cultures). In failing to acknowledge different rights norms, Western human rights discourse becomes victim-centered and retrospective, perhaps compelling because we are all potentially victims (Pendas), but removed from broader frames of analysis, engagement, and deliberative action. Singular approaches to rights may serve to divide and oppose cultures for suspect purposes rather than find an in-between and recognize inter-ests.

Cultures define rights differently. As the epigraph at the start of this chapter demonstrates, John Stuart Mill assumes that one can have a liberty of body, "his own body," which does not affect others. Yet the Chinese official understands differently, conceiving procreation as affecting a national population in profound ways and thus the individual body as inseparable from the collective good. The tension between these two quotations reflects a basic tension within human rights discourse, a tension between individual and collective definitions of rights, which is rarely offered to the U.S. public. As I will demonstrate, U.S. popular media representations of women's rights allow the nation-state to manipulate the divide between an individualist, "universal" standard of rights (negative rights) and rights defined relationally (positive rights). First-generation or negative rights, often connected with liberalism and political liberties, place the individual at the center of human dignity. Alternatively, positive rights, particularly in Confucian cultures, place the people, community, and family at the center of human dignity and so emphasize the health of a whole society in the positive rights to education, health, and work. As Daniel Bell has argued of Confucian rights, positive or communitarian rights are helpful in prioritizing rights, such as those related to economic justice or redistribution, and in justifying particular practices, such as laws strengthening a child's duty to provide for elderly parents. Each of these rights foci are included in the UDHR, but valued differently in different cultures.

Implicit in the media's representations is the promotion of a negative rights model that benefits U.S. alliances with a variety of regimes.[2] In effect, the possibility of deliberation is abrogated by the nation-state's failure to recognize and represent the positions of others. If the current task of the nation-state and its citizens is to recognize a wider, less hostile world, then what can be done, what can the popular press do, to develop a deliberative rhetoric that allows citizens to grasp and respond to the ethical decision making of other countries? Preferably media should help citizens bridge the ethical divides between nations, create an in-between, and define the obligations and responsibilities of citizens and governments. In doing so, the media could work to move audiences from spectators to interlocutors, represent human rights in a context of human actions, show fewer surface images, and narrate more complex portrayals of other cultures.

The deliberative agency of U.S. citizens is curtailed as the press presents only one set of norms without acknowledging alternative norms for negation. Since few U.S. citizens witness rights violations as they occur and—even if they do witness them—interpret them through predetermined interpretive lenses and normative discourses, they are either influenced by or dependent on media representations. Even sophisticated observers may not fully grasp to what degree constructing and iterating interpretations of human rights are speech acts, pregnant with proposed action or inaction. The citizen, however, is not alone in failing to perceive the implicit persuasions. As Stanley Cohen and Bruna Seu note, even human rights scholarship needs more discussions of audience reception and perceptions. Still, there now grows a literature on audience perception and response to suffering, a slow filling of the theoretical chasm between the role of audience and that of interlocutor and advocate.[3] In the following genre analyses of a variety of media pieces on the missing women of Asia and China's one child policy, I show how rarely the U.S. popular press allows its citizens to recognize and understand others and their loses (or gains). Rather, the press pursues lines of inquiry following local, endogenous politics. This chapter considers the kinds of writing necessary to create interspaces or in-betweens and how emotions might move audiences of strategic representations to the deliberative space of interlocutors. Rather than argue for a reasoned procedure, it examines how emotions initiate in-betweens and inter-ests, creating at least a desire for attachments and relationships.

As Elizabeth Spelman reads Plato and Aristotle on tragedy and grief, she notes their suspicion of the bloated and exploitive nature of grief and demonstrates their concern that we be educated in our compassion and not simply wallow in the pleasure of contrasting our fortune with that of unfortunates.[4] Appropriate emotions lead to speech and action. The ancients suggest that the political economy of compassion, an emotional resource, requires that it be spent only on appropriate tragic figures; grief for others may be poorly spent, as entertainment rather than as education or a basis for political action. Long before globalization and mass media, emotion was understood as a political tool, subject to manipulation but also to humanistic use. According to Aristotle, arguments affect audiences through *logos, ethos,* and *pathos* (logical demonstration, the quality of the speaker's character, and appeals to their emotions). In considering emotion as part of rhetoric, Aristotle finds a place for emotion as a piece of deliberation, and he characterizes pity—or, as Nussbaum translates Aristotle's *eleos,* compassion—as a particularly political emotion, necessary to both forensic and deliberative arguments.[5] In the *Poetics,* he sees compassion as based on fear that similar misfortune could befall the viewer; sitting in the audience of a play, the viewer is concerned with the internal state of fear. On the other hand, in the *Rhetoric,* Aristotle separates compassion from fear and describes compassion as "pain at an apparently destructive or painful evil happening to one who does not deserve it and which a person might expect himself or one of his own to suffer, and this when it seems close at hand" (1385b). Aristotelian rhetorical compassion, theorized in the small *polis,* concerns what *might* happen to us and ours, happen *close* at hand. Rhetorical compassion demarcates the space in-between that holds the things that both relate and separate us; moreover, it promises the sharing of being seen and being heard by others, which provides the shared agency of inter-est.

As rich as Aristotelian compassion is in opening up the individual to the events of another's life and thus creating relationships real or imagined, given the distance of global violations, Aristotelian compassion is hard to arouse through contemporary media. Distance, both physical and cultural, raises questions of how an audience might be involved in the scene of suffering, become receptive across difference, and ultimately move to the political actions of interlocutors (NGO membership, petitions, donations, and the like). Furthermore, in the last few centuries the concept of pity, and even compassion, has come to be associated with victimhood, hierarchy, and the distancing moves of charity and sentimentality, all of which emphasize the unfortunate's lack of agency and equality, which diminishes her ability to be seen and heard as a worthy interlocutor. Marjorie Garber notes, "Compassion seems to waver politically between two forms of inequality; the benevolence of those who have (the power of the rich) and the entitlement of those who need (the power of the poor)" (26). If compassion assumed equality within the intimate space of the *polis*, in global times, there is a counterweight to arguments for compassion's ability to raise humanity and create an appropriate response.

Even if rhetorical pity or compassion could facilitate equitable response and recognition for those close at hand, it is not an emotion that easily creates a responsible and responding interlocutor at a distance. That is, many do not believe in its ability to create ongoing political advocacy. Hannah Arendt writes that compassion "abolishes the distance, the worldly space between men where political matters, the whole realm of human affairs, are located" (*On Revolution* 81). That is, compassion destroys distance. Arendt does not see compassion as a political emotion in that it disregards political space and the requirements of changing the world; rather, compassion "lends its voice to suffering itself, which must claim for swift and direct action" (81). Just as one may say "an act of mercy," one may say "an act of compassion." The emotion imparts action, an action directed toward another, and so Arendt argues that compassion demands immediate action, even violent action, not the slow work of deliberation: "Compassion . . . abolishes the distance, the in-between which always exists in human intercourse" (81). Since it is so individual and so action-based, Arendt's compassion is limited for developing visions of performative deliberation, especially human rights deliberations, as rights are negotiated across nation-states. She is wary of it as a political emotion in that it diminishes plurality, shuns "the drawn-out wearisome processes of persuasion, negotiation, and compromise," and, owing to its sentimentality, leads to suspicion of those who differ (82). Even so, as a prepolitical response to human rights violations, compassion is useful to understanding how political acts arise and what might move citizens to action. It epitomizes the emotional force that makes spectators into agents. That is, a modified Arendtian compassion—one that acknowledges and compensates for its removal from explicitly political spaces and its demand of immediate action—would serve contemporary human rights deliberations better than hierarchical pity or propositional reason. To use compassion as a political emotion, a twenty-first-century emotion, one has to understand it as a demand for action, a call to speak and act in the public space. If compassion requires a certain kind of passionate action, action mediated by contemporary cultural and national distances, then the distance of contemporary emergencies may force compassionate action to be mediated, communal, and occasionally deliberative. Distance may be a resource for making compassion, the act of the heart, into political commitment.

Currently, rather than educate emotions and encourage citizens to identify, recognize, and respond to the conditions of others, the popular press repeatedly offers voyeuristic representations that foster sentimentality and charity at best—and more often, simply offers perceptions of abject and debased women, not people worthy of engagement. The media conceive the problem of missing women as a problem of what is missing, not who. They rarely represent someone in similitude (likeness) or as narratable. Rather, she is represented for consumption by a bread-and-circuses audience. Too often citizens are offered a spectacle of misery and abjection, not a politics of pity, let alone a compassionate path to just action.[6] Extending Arendt on stories and agency (*Human* 184), Cavarero argues that the consideration of "who," not "what," conveys a narratable self that necessarily involves recognizing the other as different and valuable, because to recognize another is to recognize her life as different. In narrative desire that is mutual and committed to recognizing the value of each story, Cavarero observes, "this *who* also already comes to us perceptibly as a narratable self with a unique story" (34). Since recognition of the narratable self builds on a mutual desire for narration, it potentially raises the voices of others in the space in-between.

Missing Women

To demonstrate some of the assumptions inherent in representations of women in U.S. media, I turn to the most major human rights crisis in the world today: missing women.[7] In 1990, the Nobel prize–winning economist Amartya Sen published significant work on the ratios between female and male populations in numerous countries. In his research, he found 100 million (100,000,000) missing women, mostly in Asia. For his baseline he did not use the ratios of wealthy Western nations (generally 105 women/100 men), but instead used the ratio found in sub-Saharan Africa (102/100). In his work he found missing women throughout Asia.[8] Here are some recent ratios of women to men, reflecting data from this century: Armenia, 100/116; Georgia, 100/119; India, 100/113 (though in some regions, men are in the 130–150 range); China, 100/120; Vietnam, 100/111 (Guilmoto). Who are these missing women, and where have they gone? While Sen initially described the difference in terms of survival rates and life expectancy, it is now more common to define the difference in the condition of girl children or daughters as well as in ultrasound-based abortion. Missing women become missing girls. Elisabeth Croll's book-length survey of research on missing daughters throughout South and East Asia shows that in most of this region, sons are preferred, and that sex-selection technologies have come to supplement traditions of infanticide and neglect as a means of guaranteeing sons. Researchers repeatedly find that, throughout Asia, rising economies have been counterbalanced with falling birthrates, and falling birth rates correlate with worse sex ratios (Croll 41–45, 46–47, 148–52).

Given pervasive femicide in much of Asia, it is interesting that the United States press focuses on China's missing women and its population control. While it is true that China's ratio is becoming more skewed, parts of Afghanistan, Pakistan, and India continue to have greater percentages of missing daughters than China, and even Taiwan has a high percentage. How does public attention on women's rights become focused on only one country? How are its women represented? To whose advantage? Based on rhetorical analyses, a complex reading of key media sites, I argue that the media focus on China's missing women because the skewed ratio in China is primarily the effect of *centralized (family) planning*.[9] Rather than being given the discourses and representations necessary for informed deliberation on missing women, U.S. citizens are taught to fear China and pity its women. They are offered emotions inappropriate to citizen agency. China's missing women become a focus of American fears—fears of the potential power of China's centralized government, its different religious and philosophical traditions, and its huge and potentially world-dominating population, for which the planning policies are a symptom. The focus on China's so-called one-child policy has served to bypass informed public action and separate the United States from China.[10] These fears are hidden behind the individualistic rhetoric of Western liberalism and a denial of alternative worldviews.[11] By not representing women as fully narratable subjects, but rather as symbols of nation-states, the press focuses on U.S. politics and policy, not on

international women's rights or a world of pluralistic values. Hence, missing women in other Asian countries rarely appear in the American press
because their deaths are not caused by state-sponsored birth control but by
what is characterized as family decision making. This emphasis on choice
takes the American reader away from complex deliberation (such as on
the consequences of overpopulation or the numbers of women missing in
allied countries where the United States already has significant influence).
Implicit in the focus of U.S. publications is a loud condemnation of centralized planning and contraception as a violation of rights and a tacit acceptance
of second-rate health care, nutrition, schooling, and employment for women
and girls.[12] The women's bodies become the transnational site of patriarchal
and national struggle, but the needs of those bodies, their humanity, and
their lives are not represented.

Views of women's rights as human rights—based in material access,
collectivities and communities, or capabilities—are never presented to the
public, and in only focusing on the liberal view of women's rights, the aver-
age U.S. citizen never hears the complex deliberations within rights talk and
among national choices. If citizens in the United States are unfamiliar with
the choices other nations make as they distribute goods, and if they have
never experienced different local, material conditions nor considered a continuum of rights practices, they can neither make reasonable assessments of
the actions of foreign governments nor understand the relationship between
material well-being and commitments to peace. They have little chance of
becoming global citizens, advocating for women in other cultures, or even
voting wisely on issues of security. In effect, U.S. isolation is encouraged as
key global issues are never fully disclosed in the American press, and consequently the U.S. audience remains uneducated in compassion, unaware of
the limits of their positions, and unable to deliberate accurately.

China and the U.S. Press

Representing China—its complex history, diversity, and philosophical and
rhetorical traditions—confounds the best. Building on earlier work that
opposes the Chinese government to its diligent people, in "Big Bad China
and the Good Chinese: An American Fairy Tale," Jeffrey N. Wasserstrom
describes three trends in the distortions of China: (1) the reduction of complex issues into binaries, (2) China bashing, and (3) fantasies of China as
Americanized (13–35).[13] Each of Wasserstrom's distortions has parallels in

the popular representations of women as (1) binary opposites of men, (2) evil witches and abject bodies, and (3) almost men. Couple the tradition of the enigmatic East with that of the unknowable feminine, and Chinese women, let alone missing Chinese women, become fantasies. These are not "Orientalist" fantasies of fragile victims; when they are presented in U.S. popular media, degenerate bodies are the focus. Chinese women are not represented as the pitiable victims of a big, bad government policy, a representation that might solicit a bit of sentimental pity. Contra Mutua's observation that savage-victim-savior is a dominant and distorting narrative within human rights discourse, in discussions of China's population policies, women are exceptional in that they are not represented as sympathetic victims. Rather, they are shown as failed bodies; in this representation, the Chinese government is so evil that it has deformed the human, and women thus do not achieve human status. Through being opposed to men and reduced to extremes with binary thinking, Chinese women can be and are represented in the U.S. press in ways that would be incredible for men.

Given the stature of the *New York Times* as a world-class paper and New York's large Chinese community, it is not surprising that the *Times* covers China in some detail. It offers a relatively complex perspective on China's birth planning, but it does so with minimal representation of women and a vocabulary that leads it away from an accurate representation of China. In a survey between 1998 and 2002, the period surrounding China's 2000 census, there were eight articles dealing with China's birth planning policies beyond a mere mention. Several of these will serve to make my points. Although there are a few later articles similar to the ones discussed, this period is the most active on missing women. It has faded as a concern, perhaps displaced by the world's economic difficulties, the wars in Iraq and Afghanistan, and the Arab Spring.

In "The World: Rethinking Population at a Global Milestone," Barbara Crossette offers us the most complex of newspaper pieces, comparing the burgeoning populations of democratic India and autocratic China and raising such controversial questions as "Could it be that China's draconian population policies, including enforcing abortion and impoverishment for those who don't comply, are paying off in a hurry?" and "Could it be true that democracy is not the most efficient way to bring a country out of poverty?" While she doesn't go so far as to answer her question, she provides ample evidence that China is providing more support to its citizens, including its girls. In China, female primary school enrollment is 99.9 percent; almost one-third of similar Indian girls are not in school. At the time, 16 percent of Chinese children under five were malnourished, but more than half of Indian children under five were. She even quotes the economist Amartya Sen: "China expanded freedom of a different kind." This seems to be a concerned representation of China's policy and a partial representation of the women and children that it benefits, an appeal for communitarian rights and basic needs. Furthermore, framed in Crossette's comparative argument, a binary of complex and competing values invites deliberation. Does a nation-state provide education and nutrition to its citizens, thereby increasing their capabilities as humans, or does one allow reproductive freedom? Which approach better defines human rights, as both are included in the UDHR?

Even so, Crossette presents stereotypical China driven by a one-child household. While the popular media always refer to a one-child policy, over twenty-five years, the rules as written and enforced have fluctuated, accepting between one and two children (Scharping). For China as a whole, the fertility rate (children per woman) has dropped from 6.21 in 1975 to 1.78 in 1995. Estimates for 2011 run between 1.54 and 1.8.[14] Also, there is significant regional difference (if not questions about the accuracy of the official rate). While highly developed and dense urban centers, such as Shanghai and Beijing, have limited family size to 1 child (1.05 and 1.11, respectively), the rural population had been allowed more children, as have ethnic minorities, overseas Chinese, parents of disabled children, and so on. Rural provinces, such as Jiangxi or Guangdong, have higher rates (2.11 and 2.21), and provinces with large minority populations, such as Guizhou, Yunnan, and Tibet, have even higher rates (2.62, 2.39, 3.43). Clearly the one-child policy is a misnomer (Scharping 267).[15]

In representing birth planning as prescribing one child, the press succeeds in literally diminishing the Chinese family, making it smaller than that of the West, when the fertility rate is higher than those in many European nations, such as Italy's 1.38 and Germany's 1.36, and significantly higher than Japan's 1.27 and Singapore's 1.26. The move to differentiate China's family size from the "normal" creates a more authoritarian Chinese government and a more oppressed Chinese people than the numbers reveal, and yet paradoxically it reduces concern about the abortion, abandonment, and neglect of daughters. That is, if parents depend on a son for support in their old age, then one might sympathize with the Chinese people and relegate the moral quandary of growing population and gender balance to their (im)moral government. The government becomes the immoral force, and the parents become pitiable. In such a move, the missing daughter is not seen as the tragic figure here, nor is she narratable. She is absent, while the pitiful parents and authoritarian state are visible. Since the characterization of "one child" does not stress the means of accomplishing this control of fertility, even the mother who is the focus of control is not made visible. We see this clearly in the following articles, which represent birth planning in ways that explicitly ignore the loss of daughters and the role of women in birth. Focusing on one male student, Tony Xu, Nicholas Kristof's "China's Super Kids" details the remarkable accomplishments of Shanghai's kindergartens, which carefully school only children. Similarly focusing on Wang Wu Dong, apprehended on illegal entry into the United States, Celia Dugger's "Sent Back to China, Man Washes Up Again" reports on twenty-three male illegal immigrants claiming persecution under China's "population control policies." Male subjects speak in the papers; they are represented as narratable selves. When one finds a woman present, she is represented as neither super nor persecuted, but as abject. Elisabeth Rosenthal begins a column on the failure of the rural population to register births with a description: "Lin waddles over to dust off her children, two boys ages 5 and 2, and a 3-year-old girl. She is 26, a farmer's wife, and eight months pregnant" (6). Waddle, shamble, lumber: her body fails to function. Her dependent children are dirty, and all she can do is dust them. Her inadequacy and impotence are made clear in one sentence; her position is described through her husband and children. She does speak to say that she can't be fined: "I'm a peasant and I don't really have any income." Her speech, however, only underlines her poverty and lack of position in the society.[16] Her presence is passed over quickly in Rosenthal's demonstrations of noncompliance in many rural counties and her interviews with two male farmers, whose bodies aren't described.

Alongside Lin (one of only two Chinese women quoted in my survey of *Times* articles), one might place Aisha Idris, whose bodily wastes "seep through her vaginal canal and down her legs" (Kristof, "Devastated" 29). A resident of Sudan, Idris was affected by then President Bush's blocking of $34 million for the UN Population Fund; married at thirteen, a mother at fourteen, with no prenatal care or midwife, Idris now has a fistula between her vagina, rectum, and urethra. In "Devastated Women," one of Kristof's articles on UN funding, he argues for the good of the UN Population Fund and for Bush's good intentions while condemning China for its "monstrous" policy.[17] Here the sixty million Chinese women are *mentioned* in a discussion of the Population Fund's successful advocacy of a better-quality IUD, but the focus is on the disgusting bodies of women in other developing countries, the well-intending U.S. leadership, and the unrestrained Chinese government, which bears responsibility not only for its population but also for the suffering of the world's women while the U.S. government withholds 13 percent of the Fund. This can easily be read as China bashing, but most significantly, the missing women of Asia remain missing. That is, rather than discuss China's policies in terms of missing daughters or women's rights, Kristof offers a malodorous body representing Africa and cultivates inappropriate political emotions.

While the *Times*, at least once, offers its readership the rationale behind birth planning in China (Crossette), it offers little to help U.S. citizens negotiate discursive norms or recognize women in other cultures. The subjective distance created by abject bodies isolates citizens from a position of compassion with or without political engagement. A spectator may well be dismayed, but the images of women encourage no sympathetic, let alone reciprocal, connection—pitying, compassionate, political, communitarian—to the women's lives, the Chinese people, and their traditions of human rights. In creating dirty objects rather than competent and compelling agents in need of assistance, the press leaves U.S. citizens without a frame for becoming involved in the scene of tragedy and without a desire for mutually narratable lives. If there is only absence and dirt, how can one become receptive to the needs and rights of others, or create a political course of action? The *Times*, over a series of articles, manages to offer a bit more than Wasserstrom's media characterizations of reductive binaries, China bashing, and Americanization: altogether its coverage provides a complex cocktail of the three and occasionally analyzes the situation of Asian population control. For the most part, however, it fails to represent Chinese women with the kind of consciousness that would encourage Americans to imagine their participation in the formation of a world more just to women. Hence it does not facilitate an in-between space where inter-ests may rise and initiate performance.

Marie Claire

It's June 2001: standing in the supermarket line, you casually pick up a copy of *Marie Claire*. Reading down the list of articles on the cover, you see "Free Nail Polish & Skincare," "Get Your Best Hair Ever New Tips and Tricks," "Men Reveal What Makes a Woman Sexy," "Burn Fat Faster," "Better Sex, Now 10 New Secrets," "Horoscope Your Best Love Match," "Women Addicted to Sex," "7 Ways to Healthy Skin," "Report: Where Babies Are Killed for Being Girls." Between Heather Locklear's right breast and the bar code, in the smallish print, is the tagline for a report on infanticide. Inside, sandwiched between advertisements for pore-refining skin cream and cosmetics for cancer patients, are four pages on "The Baby We Can't Ignore," Abigail Haworth's photo essay with six pictures of an apparently dead baby girl lying in a Hunan street, bypassed by pedestrians, bikes, and buses. The schizophrenia of women's magazines is well analyzed, with articles on diets and fudge recipes, strong women leaders and the mommy track, orgasm and abortion politics.[18] Since women's magazines are one place where women find the specific information they need to make life choices, they offer strange brews of politics, consumerism, and popular feminism. Some mix the brew more potently than others. *Marie Claire* often includes at least one overtly sociopolitical article among the fashion shoots.

Although the *Marie Claire* article can be read simply as China bashing, it is interesting for its attempt, on the one hand, to represent the Chinese government and its people as evil and, on the other, its lack of success in completely distancing the reader from them. In its strange positioning, it raises questions of manipulation and reception. How can we read material that so transparently appeals to the sentimental and yet so eagerly dismisses the humanity of the Chinese? Can we resist being cast as perverse spectators and somehow find a more complex position? In emphasizing *pathos* (pity) in a forum with such limited political *ethos*, can the representation of the dead baby, a synecdoche for missing daughters, achieve the stated political ends with any other than the most naïve reader? That is, what reader would be persuaded to be concerned about missing and endangered daughters in China given the lack of political stature of *Marie Claire*? One wonders whether it is possible for a pathetic appeal to achieve even the ends of pity and outrage, given the transparent manipulation of the piece, where suffering is offered as entertainment. Plato warned us of this, but is it dangerous or banal?

On the first page of "The Baby We Can't Ignore," the title is written large; the red "Baby" alone takes up one-sixteenth of the article. Opposite the title is a picture that covers more than a page. On the following two pages, five small photos and interjecting blocks of large print break up the report, keeping the reading to a minimum. Chronologically arranged, the six pictures show a series of indifferent passersby and then the final placing of the body in a cardboard box. Less the Sino-phobia of the reader be inadequate, large interjections report, "For several hours, people ignored the baby girl" (74), "When one man's second-born was also a girl, he smothered both his daughters" (75), and "Many believe only sons can carry on the family line. Daughters are considered a wasted investment" (75). Each sentence demonizes the Chinese, and the small print is little different. It condemns not just big, bad China, not just the authorities who consider abandoned girls to be "merely worthless trash," but also most of the locals, who didn't "give her a second glance" (74). Nothing indicates why the one-child or population replacement policy might be considered necessary. There is no hint of the economic necessity of having a son, but only a vague discussion of carrying on the line, and no discussion of the lack of old-age benefits that necessitate a son for economic support. In a one-sided report, dismissive of Chinese traditions, economics, and compassion, it is hard to find more than an attempt to create another Cold War with China. That is, when the complexity of family planning in a developing nation is glossed over and economic necessity is reported as moral indifference, we enter into a world divided between the minions of evil empires and those who would not ignore a baby. Rather than negotiating cultural and material difference so that U.S. citizens might respond to the needs of the Chinese, this essay alienates, placing the U.S. citizen on the safe ground of moral indignation, and moral indignation does not lend itself to deliberation.

Even so, the visual rhetoric here is more complex and multivocal than the simple China bashing of the text. Working against the moral divide, and owing to the photographer's limited ability to make the bodies of the Chinese inhuman, the photos—carefully read—do more than simply show the Chinese as cruel. In creating a message about China and the Chinese, none of the photos focuses on the baby. Unlike the large red title "Baby," she always appears in soft focus with people and objects around her; unknowable, her face is never fully seen. Despite lying dead for hours, naked, she is a rosy pink, her head perhaps too flushed and darkened to be healthy, but not with the grey or blue or pallor one might expect of a corpse. We look down upon her, and she looks in need of being swaddled and cuddled. Her smallness is emphasized by her placement at the bottom of the photographs, lying back against the curb, passed by larger people, a bicycle, and a bus wheel. Only in the last picture, where her body is hidden in its cardboard coffin, does the photographer finally center on her. In offering a narrative of women's rights, the image again is the abject body, obviously without critical consciousness. Even so, her dead body is less abject and grotesque than those of women in the *Times*. Like the dead babies of the Victorian age, we are asked to sentimentalize her life and mourn her passing, but not to understand the forces that caused her loss. Readers are offered a familiar and simple narrative of the lost child, not an analysis nor a desire for narratable life.

The smallness of the Hunan baby within the photo frames is part of our feeling of power, but it is also part of the criticism of China. Still, this works paradoxically: her smallness in the history of China is visible in the first photograph, structured to be reminiscent of a travel scene of authentic China, but the beauty of the scene argues against the inhumanity of the tradition. In taking more than one page, the photo shows the dusty street, an extended stretch of sidewalk hand-laid in octagonal bricks backed by the darkened doorways of traditional architecture. The foreground is dominated by the full height of a man passing by, a grey-haired and balding elder. He has walked by her, hands behind his back, showing the details of his suit jacket and the gleam of his clean white shirt. If his trajectory has been straight, he passed within centimeters of her outstretched hand. His head is partially turned away from us, and he is facing in the opposite direction of the baby. Perhaps he is checking for traffic or pointedly ignoring the body, the photographer, and us. Far in the background, leaning against the wooden pillar of a doorway almost as black as the interior of the building, is a school-aged boy, looking toward the camera. Seemingly the man and the boy who ignore the baby represent the indifference of China, but with a careful reading, the embarrassment of the man and the curiosity of the boy raise questions about the photographer's presence and purpose. How is the spectator with a camera different? Is not the photographer's and the reader's spectatorship as problematic as the refused gazes and inaction of the old man and the boy? Why may the voyeuristic reader of *Marie Claire* pay for the perverse pleasure in viewing the child, while the people present are questioned for looking away in discomfort?

In a later photo, the indifferent son reappears, but the effect again is to create ambiguity about Chinese consciousness. On the second page, a boy and girl of similar ages walk side by side. He is on the sidewalk looking up, mouth slightly open in a daydream of childhood. She, on the other hand, walks in the gutter, only just starting to circle the baby. Her eyes are fixed anxiously on the body, not overtly distressed, but conscious of her presence and demise. Her position is perhaps the most moral of the views: present and empathetic. The relationship between the endangered daughter and dead baby represents a position potentially more engaged than that of the voyeur or spectator. She is achieving a consciousness denied to other viewers.

The last two photos show two people attending to the body. We see legs with pink shoes; this person has covered the body with a sheet of wrinkled green paper or cloth, with only the baby's outstretched hand and a bare bit of face showing. The final picture is of a brown-shoed man lifting a box with the green sheet, the sticks he used to lift the body left in the road. The text reads, "Eventually, an old man picked the baby up, put her in a box, and dropped her in a garbage bin" (75). If the article's premise is that no one cares, why then do the two attendants appear? Perhaps to offer a hope of a caring China, but as they are only shown as body parts, it is more likely that they are there to offer closure to an uncomfortable worldview. Certainly that is supported by the last block of large print telling the reader "what you can do." *Marie Claire* advises us to write a letter either to China's ambassador, demanding that the cruelty stop, or to President Bush, telling him that human rights come before trade. These letters are to be sent to *Marie Claire*, which will forward them—almost in a parody of the letter-writing campaigns of Amnesty International. Although the action of speaking and writing may engage spectators more than sending a check and in fact may be a step toward the in-between and the initiation of deliberation, there is an inherent monologic deficit in providing a simple action, such as writing a letter. The magazine encourages its audience to believe that interventions in human rights violations are that simple and that knowledge can be gained from a brief article in a fashion magazine. If deliberation, performative deliberation, is at the heart of constructing a just world, then engaging in imagining and creating that world will require more than speakers and audiences, writers and readers. Performative deliberation needs interlocutors engaged in recognition, creating inter-ests, and sharing agency. Readers are offered no domestic community of activists, no understanding of human rights negotiations, and no transnational connection to agencies that may act beyond letters. *Marie Clare*'s readers are provided with a faux moment of empowerment—no formation of community, not even the real addresses of those in power, and no guidance in how to move from spectator to actor, from audience to agent. The local of the United States and the local of a town in Hunan remain separated without recognition, reciprocity, translation, in-between, or inter-ests.

Deliberation

Neither the *New York Times* nor *Marie Claire* promotes deliberation on women's rights. Rather each, to varying degrees, separates China from the United States and from ethical society, offering a Cold War rhetoric of oppositions and threats. There is nothing in these pieces to prompt self-reflexivity, an educated emotional response, or critical exploration of international human rights discourse. The creation of psychic distance and the representation of abjection do not move citizens to action. To understand the material conditions of other women's lives and the place of rights, to become citizen agents,

readers need studies of multiple patriarchies, international economic conditions, and sufficient connection for compassionate action. If global deliberations can overcome resistance and indifference to women's rights, other
traditions and circumstances should be represented in ways that promote
recognition. As alternatives to dominant narratives of degenerate women
bodies, victimized children, and foreign saviors, transnational feminist narratives should encourage rights deliberations and complex ways of knowing
women who make decisions unlike our own. Rather than seeing representations of bodies (exteriors), interlocutors (not simply readers) should hear
the discourses of and from these women, what might be shorthand for their
interiority, their personhood, their narratable selves. With that beginning,
U.S. citizens might be able to recognize women's rights more complexly. If
it is impossible to represent the interiority of missing daughters—for how
does one represent those who are not there?—what could be the possible risk
of hearing the voices of the women who suffer the losses of children? Given
their lack of voice, there might well be a latent fear that, if the U.S. citizenry
were drawn to compassion for the human rights of women, then political
policies, parties, and administrations would be forced to change.

Instead of insisting on individual or negative human rights, the U.S.
press could more responsibly show how nations negotiate relationships to
a standard of human decency, including those committed to communitarian rights. Although not law, human rights covenants are used to assess
past abuses and normalize future actions. Despite some spectacular trials
of perpetrators of atrocities, the role of the Universal Declaration of Human
Rights might be characterized as deliberative rather than forensic, concerned
with future norms. The document's main work is not to punish violators,
but rather to normalize human rights. When nations and cultures disagree
about human rights norms, there is no law that makes the promotion, development, and (re)definition of rights a given. As Abdullahi Ahmed An-Na'im
argues, instead, it is necessary "to explore the possibilities of cultural rein-
terpretation and reconstruction through *internal cultural discourse and cross
cultural dialogue*" ("Introduction" 3; emphasis in original). That is, to recognize what is a violation of human rights, sometimes we alternately employ
the discourses of individual rights, communal rights, or economic capabilities within particular cultures. Cultural antagonism to other human rights
norms denies rights as deliberative acts, complex inter- and intracultural
deliberation, and recasts them as goal-driven, legitimizing universal norms.
True, son preference is destructive of women's rights, but to achieve familial,

educational, nutritional, and political equality, cultures such as China's have to make changes in psychological, social, economic, and political realities. Still, it is culturally callous to deny the strengths of other traditions. If rights norms are to be translated and renegotiated, on all sides, complex deliberations will need time. Where might that discussion begin? Who will speak? What makes the deliberation move toward action? Just as Arendt's compassion transcends the political sphere, incipient human rights negotiations may also require a realm less limited and finite, a prepolitical space.

To understand the causes underlying violations of human rights (in the case of son preference, say), to develop new human rights within cultures, and to deliberate on what might be universal or at least normative human rights, many people in many cultures will need to be inter-ested in questions such as these:

1. Which principles, norms, and values of the culture are more conducive to which features of contemporary human rights, and which are resistant?
2. What practices, performances, and discourses may have to be modified, developed, or replaced to enhance human rights within the cultural tradition?
3. To what extent can indifference or resistance to aspects of human rights be overcome in ways that reflect cultural tradition and not simply domination by the state apparatus or colonial forces?

In discussions of human rights, given international law, the goal necessarily must be to overcome resistance and indifference to human dignity and rights in ways that are congenial to the traditions under scrutiny. Rhetoric, as traditionally bounded in the media, seems inadequate to answering these questions; the representation of women there is far too bodily defined, too lacking in women's discourse.

Amy Tan's *Joy Luck Club* and Performative Deliberations

There is no popular case of representing missing women that engages the American public in thinking and self-reflecting, not merely seeing, let alone acting. Or is there? Many argue for the significance of the novel in teaching rights, from developing a popular recognition of the individual human (Slaughter) to empathizing with disenfranchised (Hunt).[19] Privileging the speech act, M. M. Bakhtin observes that

[t]he novel can be defined as a diversity of social speech types (sometimes even diversity of languages) and a diversity of individual voices,
artistically organized. The internal stratification of any single national
language into social dialects, characteristic group behavior, professional jargons, generic languages, languages of generations and age
groups, tendentious languages, languages of the authorities, of various
circles and of passing fashions, languages that serve the specific sociopolitical purposes of the day, even of the hour (each day has its own
slogan, its own vocabulary, its own emphases)—this internal stratification present in every language at any given moment of its historical
existence is the indispensable prerequisite for the novel as a genre.
(262–63)

If the heteroglossia of novels represents historical moments in ways richer
in contingency and discursive potentials than journalistic genres, one might
find in the contingencies and discourses, among the stratifications, narratives that represent alternative rights traditions and circumstances in performative ways that aid deliberation. One might hope for narratable selves
and opportunities to recognize the simulacra of concrete others. One might
even hope for representation of what is absent and that the missing become
visible.

Amy Tan's novels are most often interpreted as novels of domesticity,
mother-daughter narratives that are genealogical, rather then social or political. Much as the novels of popular women writers in the nineteenth century are circumscribed by sentimentality, Tan's novels are circumscribed as
sentimental mother-daughter affairs. In the most sympathetic of readings,
they are seen as intergenerational and intercultural dialogues, where the
daughters identify their mothers as China personified and so can proceed to
their own task of Chinese-American subject formation; their mothers' desire
for America is projected onto their daughters, and so the mothers' desire
is vicariously fulfilled. In these readings, Tan's novels are cast as interesting expansions of or variations on American immigration narratives, placing
Asian American literature into an established genre.

In the more critical of readings, her novels are seen as individualistic,
not social, in their explorations of cultural displacements and recuperation
(D. Li). Sometimes their development of mother-daughter communication
is seen as an implicit attempt to enter a community of white female readership by addressing white intergenerational anxieties as well as the readers'
Orientalist tendencies (Wong). Tan's novels are even accused of racializing

Asian sexuality and caricaturing Asian males as evil patriarchs whose forces are countered by Western feminism (Chu).

Alternatively read as too conservative or politically naïve, Tan's work can also be read as more politically engaged in human rights issues than the journalism reviewed above. *The Joy Luck Club*, in particular, provides access to the tensions between liberal, Western human rights and communitarian or local cultural practices; it educates a wide audience in ways of thinking and feeling complexly about human rights and the position of women in China. Tan represents Chinese women during the mid-twentieth century in ways that emphasize their individual and cultural consciousness, but she also links their alien decisions to the decisions a U.S. citizen might recognize through the narratives of their American daughters, their own narratives of American experiences, and their fully developed agency as they negotiate the norms of two patriarchal, authoritarian cultures. The subjectivities of Chinese and Chinese Americans are constituted in their material and cultural locations. Given their strategic performative infelicities and their dramatic performances, Tan's women refuse stereotypes and overdetermination of their lives. Furthermore, readers are taught the appropriate compassion for women who must negotiate norms alien to their own experiences, and in achieving that emotion, they may recognize the women's narratable lives.

The Joy Luck Club was published in 1989, the year of the Tiananmen demonstrations and ten years after the start of China's more stringent birth planning. Amartya Sen's "More than 100 Million Women Are Missing" was published a year later. The novel's timing and content make it an ideal locus for considering the missing women of Asia. *The Joy Luck Club* consists of sixteen intertwining narratives about four mother-daughter pairs. Significantly, the stories of Suyuan and June Woo frame the novel. In the first story, June Woo is invited by her mother's friends, June's aunts, to take her dead mother's place in the mah-jongg club. At the end of the evening, the aunts reveal that "the babies in Kweilin" were found—the daughters that Suyuan was forced to abandon (39). The revelation occasions significant descriptions of both Suyuan and the daughters. The aunts, her peers, judge Suyuan, saying that she is "a very strong woman, a good mother . . . a mother like this could never forget her other daughters." And in response to June's claim of not knowing her mother, not apprehending her life, the aunts list Suyuan's desirable attributes, though they do not narrate her story. Suyuan is marked as an ideal Chinese woman at the novel's outset.

Although the missing daughters are older than thirty-six-year-old June, she first imagines them as babies, "the babies in Kweilin," "lying on the side of the road," "red thumbs popped out of their mouths," "screaming to be reclaimed" (39). The juxtaposition of the good mother and her tiny babies lost and screaming in need is the central tension of the novel, one that is echoed in June's mourning of her mother, in Ying-Ying St. Clair's abortion and in her miscarriage, in the son Bing Hsu's drowning, in Lindo's marriage away from her family at the age of twelve, and in An-mei's mother's suicide. All of these narrations concretely show why good mothers leave their children, but no one mother shows us as well as Suyuan does. The aunts serve as her jury, a collection of distinct individuals representing the larger community: like a jury, they represent institutionalized justice. As a group, their assessment of Suyuan moves beyond friendship and relationship toward one that is of public note. They represent the political potential of compassion, but as well they demonstrate the difficulty of narrating another's life. The list of Suyuan's qualities does not open her complexity or decisions, though it raises the question of child abandonment.

At the novel's end, in Guangzhou, China, June's father tells us how the good mother left "the babies in Kweilin." June's father is not the father of the twins, and because of his gender and his paternity without loss, he is a more neutral and less emotional witness than the aunts, all of whom have experienced loss of a mother or a child. One might see him as representing the objective observer, the neutral judge, but I contend that he also represents the possibility of narrating lives and experiences at a distance. Unlike compassion, which requires immediate response, the narratability of another's life survives time and distance, and as he narrates Suyuan's life to her daughter, his narration fulfills their desire for Suyuan's presence. While he describes Suyuan's difficult physical condition, he does not dwell on her abject body but speaks of her mental state and intentions. In describing the extremity of the Japanese attack and the desperation of Suyuan's flight from Guilin, he says, "she knew she would die of her sickness, or perhaps from thirst, from starvation, or from the Japanese" (282). She *only* left the babies when their *only* hope was to be found by a "kindhearted" person. Abandonment is possible *only* in the mother's "foolish hope" of a "kindhearted" person. Surprised at her survival, Suyuan spends the rest of her life desiring and seeking her lost daughters, because she continues to believe in the acts of the kindhearted person, a person with the right emotions.

Now, it is a long way from babies abandoned by a mother fleeing the Japanese army to the girls ultrasounded and aborted throughout Asia today. Even so, *The Joy Luck Club* puts readers in a place where even a naïve reader can imagine the situated agency of the women characters, learn an appropriate narrative for recognition, and consider justice in an active, alternative world. Readers are asked to understand situations as extreme as an arranged marriage and a mother's suicide and to understand how these acts do not destroy the bond between mother and child, but rather show the strength of family and the power of agency strategically employed in manipulating norms. In repeatedly asking for the acknowledgment of the constraints of culture, the limits and possibility of choice, and the intertwining of luck, fate, and strategy, Tan asks readers to recognize characters who all make difficult choices with careful reason and who all strategize successful lives where there is little hope. She also asks the reader to be Suyuan's "kindhearted person" who will help the twins and so the mother, and although readers are not given explicit directions as to the form of that help, through the farm family and the friends who help Suyuan look for the twins, Tan provides models of continued, ongoing action, not simple spectatorship. Finally, when the aunts discuss Suyuan's character and June's trip to her sisters, they model deliberation within an intimate situation. In making the transnational, political issue of missing girls into a personal issue, Tan implicitly restates that the personal is political. Art and women's lives have political implications.

As a pedagogical instrument, the novel's heteroglossia requires, and even constitutes through the act of reading, what Boltanski calls "an *ideal* and *internalised spectator*," one who desires praise and concord with the other (39–41; emphasis in original). To read as the novel is scripted, a reader must internalize the values of the protagonists. Joseph R. Slaughter argues for the *Bildungsroman*'s ability to teach "human rights literacy" in creating scenes of (self-)recognition for "the emergence and narrative performance of citizen-subjectivity" (254–55). Despite the novel's constituting and positioning of a citizen reader, the internalization of performance, alas, does not require direct action or the agency of the reader. The novel does not create an interlocutor or an advocate; instead, it performs the dialogue of interlocutors within the novel, instructing and constructing the spectator in deliberative fluency. Being constructed in rights recognition and deliberative fluency is not the same as politically enacting recognition and deliberation. Perhaps the crucial difference between rhetoric and hermeneutics is that rhetoric requires the negotiation of cultural norms and offers the dialectical possibility of resistance, while hermeneutics allows one to remain a spectator. That is, journalism and novels create an audience, perhaps an ethical citizen-audience or ideal spectator, but rhetoric, particularly performative deliberation, has the potential to create interlocutors through the act of speaking in the present tense with the positioned potential to effect the world. The speech act constitutes the political moment and event. This symptomatic difference is not absolute, as epideictic rhetoric can celebrate norms and stasis as ideal even as a novel's characters might model inventive political actions. The speech act, however, is the forming act that moves interlocutors.

Even so, political agents and their utterances are constrained as they are constituted in their ability to perform by norms. As Kay Schaffer and Sidonie Smith observed in their study of World War II comfort women, even witnesses to their own violations are constrained by the ur-narratives desired by interlocutors. Constraint and performativity are not the full story of speaking and acting, however. Given the opportunity, Schaffer and Smith write, "former sex prisoners remembered and imagined themselves outside the gendered identities reproduced through local and national gender relations, outside the self-negating horizon of privatized shame" (136). Unlike the characters in novels, their narratable lives have political purpose and accomplishment subject to multiple tellings to and with different interlocutors. The potential for a speaking life exceeds any novel's characters. Novels, however, bring narratable lives from afar, and thus even if novels are internal dialogues and not rhetorical engagements, they still may offer moments when narratable selves speak and rouse our desire for their lives.

Deliberations on justice for women are disproportionately silenced in the U.S. media's narratives of abjection, and too often women's rights are unspoken, their violations unnarrated. *The Joy Luck Club* initiates a moment of recognition when reading or seeing human rights violations positions the reader with the potential to hear and speak of narratable lives within local and global communities. Further, it models the narratability of distinct and different characters. If literature, as a *techne*, does not create activists, it constitutes its reader as a bystander (perhaps frustrated by the inadequacy of bystanding), as desiring to go further. *The Joy Luck Club* creates that potential—not in the individualistic, Eurocentric frame of universal human rights, but within the practices of Confucian family. Tan's women are more than individual, autonomous beings; their family relationships form the identity that is most important to them. Viewing their performances, we understand these women not as victims, but as people with agency that is differently "constructed within formations that are state and nation, geopolitics, economic, sexuality etc." (Grewal, "Global Feminism" 516). They are narrated to us in ways that connect across the cultures of China and the United States.

Readers of *The Joy Luck Club* potentially achieve Aristotelian pity or compassion; they are taught to heed the narratable lives, respect the characters' agency, share the possibilities of their conditions, and achieve the closeness in time and space that is required for an educated, emotional recognition and response. Unlike the disgust created in journalism, an emotion which "draws sharp boundaries around the self," the novel's compassion expands "the boundaries of the self," helping readers evaluate and judge others and recognize their interdependence and inter-ests (Nussbaum, *Upheavals* 300). The recognition, however, follows Arendt's critique of compassion; it is removed from political space and does not lead to deliberation on the nature of human decisions within the negotiated constraints of culture. Despite the potential for action within compassion, readers of novels remain audiences, isolated from the spaces that would allow a productive discussion of human rights. It is not the narrative nor the emotions that isolate the audience; both work well to educate them. Yet the novel's genre does not create a path to deliberative spaces and interlocutors. We cannot map sovereign power or political legitimacy onto the world of a novel. Even as its words are performative and constitutive of a textual world, they do not perform in the nation-state, unless reading citizens move on from hermeneutical explorations of characters, taking what they have learned to more familiar political forums and engaging interlocutors. Arendt would have us in the public realm, the space of appearance, whether that space be agonistic or associative.[20]

If Arendt would criticize the distance of our emotional response and not mistake reading for political action, she does not dismiss Tan's act of storytelling nor my retelling of Tan's stories. She writes, "[a]ction reveals itself fully only to the storyteller, that is, to the backward glance of the historian, who indeed always knows better what it was all about than the participants" (*Human* 192). Human (symbolic) action is revealed fully by the storyteller. The historian who has examined the lifeworld and produced it as a whole knows action best. Yes, the victor writes history, and historians dispute history's events and causes, but for Arendt at least, the storyteller's backward glance sees more than those sitting at different positions in the in-between. Storytelling becomes a means of recognition, but not of political action.

4

THE BEAUTY OF ARENDT'S LIES:
MENCHÚ'S POLITICAL STRATEGY

Therefore there is no absurdity, however strange it may sound, in the saying of the ancient
Father, "I would not tell a willful lie to save the souls of the whole world."
—John Wesley, Sermon 90

Now I feel that a lie that is told for the good of others is not a lie—it is bigger than the truth.
—Garima, quoted in Sangtin Writers and Richa Nagar, *Playing with Fire*

I sit reading Al Franken's *Lies and the Lying Liars Who Tell Them: A Fair and
Balanced Look at the Right*. Written on a fellowship at Harvard's Shorenstein
Center on the Press, Politics, and Public Policy, this book responds to the
lies of the right, exemplified by Ann Coulter's *Slander: Liberal Lies about the
American Right*. As I read, the radio news is discussing lies about health
care reform: Will Obama pull the plug on granny? Perhaps I should check
that claim on the "Truth-O-Meter" of the 2009 Pulitzer Prize–winning website PolitiFact (a project of the *Tampa Bay Times*) or the Annenberg Public
Policy Center's FactCheck.org. We live in a political culture of lies and media
manipulation, one that has the best minds struggling to understand how
citizens can make judgments about political actions, but this is not the first
culture to struggle with the relationships among truth, opinion, lies, hopes,
rhetoric, and politics, nor will it be the last. Lies in politics are a commonplace because just as humans imagine and hope, humans lie and intend to
deceive, and just as political discourse speaks pragmatically, it also speaks
counterfactually, creating alternatives through lies, opinions, and truths. To
be deceitful or imaginative is to change the discourse and unbalance the
scales of the status quo. Symbols, so malleable, facilitate our lies to others
and ourselves.

When Plato promises remembered truth as an ideal external to human
actions and when Confucius promises truth as remembered in rituals from

a better culture preserved in the right actions, they respond to the unstable politics of their times, and they wish for the stable politics of the elite, an imagined nation where cultural consistency creates the shared vision. Habermas, too, argues that deliberation, carefully modulated, comes to consensus, potentially a new and vital truth. In doing so, he reimagines the ancient commonplace of truth in politics, basing it in argument that truth conquers falsehood through open and free speech. Like the truthsayers Plato and Confucius, Habermas's sense of political culture ends with a single vision. In situated and particular politics, however, speech is not about coming to consensus and a tautological peace, but rather about worldly action, finding in-betweens, shared inter-ests, and new discursive regimes. Consequently, when Habermas, for example, argues that utterances should have validity in one of three respects (truth, rightness, or intended truthfulness) (*Moral* 136–37), he is not listing valid criteria for rhetorical or political utterances, strategic utterances that announce position, inter-est, or identity. Indeed, he is creating the dangerous and godlike certainty that Arendt abhors.

Although many may wish the criteria of rhetoric and politics to include truth, rhetorical and political utterances are conceived and spoken in the complexity of contingencies where truth is not to be nailed. Within deliberation, correspondence (constative) truth rarely trumps participatory or constructivist truths, the truths constructed as they impact a community's inter-ests. Truth may not be a realistic criterion for effective political speech, as speech's performativity itself *makes* truth. Whatever the need for fact checking, or perhaps *because of* the need for fact checking, truth is not an innate quality or requirement of political discourse in and of itself. To describe political practices accurately, one well might need a theory of the lie.[1] Or, if not a theory of lies, then a sense of why the criterion of truth is not adequate to deliberations across difference. If truth is understood as contained within the frame of available facts or as tautologically defined within cultural norms, then utterance validity, its truthfulness, varies within and between cultures and situations. For instance, the truths of a geocentric universe and the natural weakness of women were cultural facts that stood without contestation for millennia, but they have increasingly become falsehoods through scientific and political deliberation. Given that the current domestic deliberations of the United States are riddled with accusations of lies (just consider health care rights), how might one deliberate on the extensions and rectifications of rights across cultures without a sensitivity to lies, falsity, and alternative readings of facts? Going even further into the ambiguities of political discourse, if truths are defined by cultural and legal norms, then might not the disenfranchised, the alien, and the constrained have reason to disregard the dominant rules of validity and justice? Should those seeking justice perform whatever speech acts are needed to shift norms?

Recognizing the complexity of telling rational truths, factual truths, and lies, Arendt acknowledges the courage of speaking from "patriotism or some other kind of legitimate group partiality," even in the case of lying ("Truth" 244). She implies that commitments to preserving community and creating relationships and inter-ests may be better criteria for evaluating utterances than truth.[2] That is, rhetorical criteria for an utterance's validity might be based in that utterance's relationship to how a community is constructed, legitimized, maintained, protected, and extended, rather than whether it is empirically true. Although a particular deliberation may contribute to unity, a moment of citizenry and community, and even some sharing of values, in the end, deliberative utterances cannot be committed primarily to reason, institutional procedure, or truth, because they form and are formed in struggles over lifeworlds. Deliberation is not about truths, about a single dimension of assessing utterances, but about how particular forms of life create, transform, and extend the human. The moral force inherent in denouncing political lies, or lies in general, is relatively new. Even the Judeo-Christian tradition has an ambivalent relationship to lies and the requirement of truth. Traditionally, lies are not sins. The Ten Commandments only forbid false witness, a special case of lying. David Hume and Thomas Hobbes see the laws of nature as only forbidding the breaking of covenants and false witness. Particular cases of lying in juridical contexts, of testifying against someone, seem to have moral consequences, but these injunctions against a type of performative utterance do not extend beyond institutional settings that require felicitous circumstances. Outside of the law courts, even God participates in the politics of community preservation; in the Apocrypha, God aids Judith in telling lies (Jth. 9:10, 13; also see Tob. 5:12).

Bracketed by a historical tolerance of lies, traditionally, others question the imperative force of truth. As Cassandra should have taught us, there is no point in being right or true if no one listens, if you cannot convince others, or if the truth is so far from human practices that it doesn't matter. Arendt asks, "is not impotent truth just as despicable as power that gives no heed to truth?" ("Truth" 546). After all, utterances need to meet the performative criteria of being audible and effective more than they need to be true. The project of performative deliberation depends upon an understanding of deliberation as action through felicitous or infelicitous utterance. If the extreme stasis of truth denies performativity, might the study of lies teach us more about the potential and limitations of performative acts? If we approach lies as an extreme of human imagination and forming and not as unethical, despicable, or immoral, we might understand better their performative force and its place in politics. If we imagine lies not as a counterpart of truth, but rather as a human act of creativity separate from truth's criteria of felicity, we might understand the worth of our lies better. In certain deliberative performances, one well might *intend* to deceive others and intend to deceive with good intentions.

The lie is an ideal performative case, a test of Austin's framing vocabulary. Despite tendencies to define and judge utterances as true or false, felicitous or infelicitous, Austin plays with utterances to delineate language's work of locution, illocution, and perlocution, seeking clear examples—such as "I do"—to illustrate performance. Lacking clarity, as counterinstances, lies show a good deal about the instability of criteria and performative language. Like most other utterances, the point of a lie is not to be simply false, untrue, a trick, but to perform a perlocutionary act of achieving something by saying something (Austin, *How* 107–8). The nature of that achievement may be a laugh or a revolution, but lies, by their forming potential, do something of consequence. Hence, it is not simply an untrue constative or a corrupt illocution; its perlocutionary force might, indeed, proceed quite properly from the nature of its illocution. By intending to deceive, a liar may define the truth. My point here is not to prescribe lies or justify them as a means to ends, however evaluated. Rather, I argue that lies perform necessary work in the lifeworld, particularly in politics. They may perform problematically (at least as problematically as fiction, which is also tangential to truth), but lies and fictions are part of the constituting nature of politics. As Franken and Coulter protest, lies are left and right and everywhere. Since lies so flourish, the description of lying is necessary to a theory of democratic politics and deliberation. As truths need delineation, lies need differentiation, acknowledgment, and analysis: misinformation, wishes, denial, counterfactuals, propaganda, hyperbole, compliment, omission, false witness, fantasy, perjury, cover-up, and imagination, so very many types of secrets and deceits, active and inactive. One might protest that my list of terms is too diverse, lacking in criteria and shared situations, but defining lies broadly reveals how our intentions construct new worlds and depend on escaping truth. Wishes and compliments may not be vilified as lies, but the intention to deceive defines them. Although wishes may only begin as self-deception, compliments certainly are utterances that may intend to deceive an interlocutor.

Let me examine a simple case of the complex intention to deceive. A two-year-old is protesting putting on sunscreen. My nine-year-old tells her that it is "princess makeup," and the toddler complies. My sophistic daughter speaks with full intention to deceive through employing misinformation, hyperbole, compliment, fantasy, and imagination. Offering wish fulfillment, she may be employing Disney propaganda. Even as a sophist's audience might ignore the truth for linguistic pleasure, the toddler who knows about sunscreen also ignores the truth for the pleasure of the lie. She wishes to be a princess, an adult wearing makeup, and a person given a choice in what she applies to her skin. The collusive lie is embraced by both the deceiver and the deceived. It does not matter whether a good lie or bad lie was told, for ultimately only the pleasure and utility are of inter-est to the interlocutors. "What justifies a white lie? Any lie?" But I am not concerned with justification and ethics, but rather with how lies perform, and I refuse the question of whether lies have the proper illocutionary force to have the proper perlocutionary effects.[3] If a disciple of Austin might see lies as having a distorted juncture of illocutionary and perlocutionary force, a distortion embraced by the girls enjoying princess makeup, the intentions and effects are negotiated as inter-ests in-between.[4] This chapter will examine how particular lies told by the Nobel Peace Prize winner Rigoberta Menchú facilitated human rights deliberation. There I will touch on ethics, but not so much on the ethics of lying as on the formative performatives of lying and what debates about lies reveal about recognition and cultural hierarchies. This chapter marks off ethical commonplaces to examine how lies work in at least one case of human rights deliberation.

Arendt on Truths and Lies

If Machiavelli praises lies simply for their political expediency, Arendt's discussion of truth and lies offers a more performative perspective on truth, opinion, and lie.[5] To understand the political uses of truth and lies, Arendt examines their political effects. In particular, she analyzes one kind of truth, factual truth, which she sees as having political use, and the types of political lies that harm and help the community. In two essays, she first considers "Truth and Politics" and then "Lying in Politics." Arendt examines lies—many sorts of lies—that have historically been considered legitimate, necessary, and justifiable within politics and diplomacy.[6] Although scholars such as Peg Birmingham and Cathy Caruth tend to emphasize her distress at a "lying world order," which supports totalitarian states and tatters social fabric, Arendt does not write lies out of human action.[7] She observes that "the story of conflict between truth and politics is an old and complicated one, and nothing would be gained by simplification or moral denunciation" ("Truth" 225). According to Arendt, particular lies, as substitutes for more violent means, are relatively harmless when compared to apolitical, "despotic" truth, which is beyond agreement, dispute, opinion, or consent (224). She notes that truth has a "coercive" force outside the "wishes and desires" of citizens and tyrants. That is, truth, like persuasion and lies, has a power to distort.

If Foucault would have us understand truth as the effect of a discursive regime that permeates a social body and regulates its actors, Arendt places truth, for the most part, outside of human action, unlike our lies. Appeals to truth, like those of Plato, Confucius, and Habermas, define the situation outside the work of deliberation and politics. Alternatively, Arendt sees the best humans never as contemplative philosophers, but as acting, creating citizens, always located and responsive ("Lying" 46). Diminishing contemplation, Arendt exalts the *vita activa* for the outward acts of citizens, which create human freedom, distinction, and diversity. Despite her skepticism of contemplative truths, she does acknowledge a limited role for factual truth within politics in forming our political opinions. Factual truths do not arise from structures of the mind nor transcend the world of human affairs. Instead, factual truths arise from contingent events, themselves acts of interpretation conceived in human relationships. In their dependence on human relationships, factual truths are particularly related to deliberation. She writes,

> Factual truth . . . is always related to other people; it concerns events and circumstances in which many are involved; it is established by witnesses and depends upon testimony; it exists only to the extent that it is spoken about, even if it occurs in the domain of privacy. It is political by nature. Facts and opinions, though they must be kept apart, are not antagonistic to each other; they belong to the same realm. ("Truth" 233–34)

As Birmingham aptly explains, factual truth paradoxically possesses both "a stubborn thereness and an absolute contingency that makes it the kind of truth most like *doxa*" (75). Although facts are not independent of opinion and interpretation, in politics and rhetoric, they are "elementary data," forming opinions and answering questions such as whether Belgium invaded Germany or whether Eman al-Obeidi was held in Libya. Factual truths can be the substance of witnesses, the gathered facts in the assessment of human rights, and the counterdiscourse that offers the possibility of a different reality, even a revolution.

Despite the conceptual links between facts and other forms of truth, facts and events are "infinitely more fragile than axioms, discoveries and theories," because, in the flux of human action, facts and events can be forgotten or lied away, never to be rediscovered (Arendt, "Truth" 227). One might reimagine relativity theory or reinvent the wheel, but the facts of history, once lost, are no more. Sufficient denial of genocides, concentration camps, or missing women and the facts of history are lost. Its contingency and its dependence on witnessing and testifying make factual truth open to dispute: the validation of factual truth depends on the evidence of eyewitnesses (reliable and not), texts (subject to forgeries), and material objects and monuments (historic and manufactured). Arendt's concept of factual truth is particularly relevant for human rights deliberation, as political history and the recognition of rights violations both depend on witnessing. Although fragile factual truth is exposed to the enmity of opinion, it is not *created* through deliberation, though it may be sustained through deliberation, and so is not quite political. As its validity does not consider the opinions of others, even as it informs opinions, factual truth is removed from representative politics (237–38). As the *testimonio* of Rigoberta Menchú will show us, the nature of factual truth cannot be definitely separated from opinion and deliberation, but for now, it is fair to acknowledge the strategic importance of factual truth as a fragile type of truth, one founded in human relationship.

Due to the fragility of factual truths and the difficulty of recognizing them (when and where do facts become opinion?), citizens and subjects can be massively deceived by governmental lies: How did a nation of 309 million come to believe in Iraq's weapons of mass destruction? Only in the face of such massive deception does the truth telling become action. According to Arendt, in the face of state and media domination, speaking truth engages and enacts the world order, not through the mere telling of facts, but in speaking against "distorting forces." Then the truth teller, "in the unlikely event that he survives . . . has made a start toward changing the world" (247). In taking a political position and locating himself against another, the truth teller no longer stands alone outside the realm of human affairs, but has entered into deliberative politics and must reconcile opinion with fact. His performative utterances take sheer happenings and make them *humanly comprehensible*, speaking back to a "lying world order" (257). Extending Arendt, speaking truth is action only when the political system has denied factual truths and a new, more real politics needs enactment. One may claim that reality is not performative, but our comprehension of reality requires deliberative utterances on factual truths, sheer happenings made into comprehensible events through strategic truth telling. If one speaks factual "truth to power," then one speaks truth politically and performatively.

If there is at least one performative truth for Arendt, one kind of truth worth telling, there are some very bad lies. In "Lying in Politics," Arendt contrasts the traditional political lie with the modern political lie: a traditional lie is a rhetorical strategy for responding to hostile difference, a modern political lie creates an ideological blanketing to destabilize reality. The traditional lie engages particulars, often in hiding something; it is meant to deceive the enemy only, not the liar, nor his circle. On the other hand, systemic lies, like totalizing or tautological truths, are not based in a contingent situation, and so they become removed from politics. The modern political lie, the destroying lie, seeks to rewrite history and violate and destroy the whole factual texture of the world, observes Arendt. She discusses two versions of the modern lie, the totalitarian lie and the image-making lie. Totalitarian regimes deny facts, intend to deny facts, and work to fix an alternative world. The totalitarian liars' utterances form a world that conforms to the liars' power base. Since this totalitarian world has such a tenuous connection to factual truth, however, it cannot be stable. Liars themselves become lost in the tatters of a lying social order as modern lies lead to self-deception, which further destroys webs of reality and factuality. Total or totalitarian lying cannot stand up to witnesses and testimony, in part, because of the performative nature of all utterances, the excesses that call forth deliberations on the lifeworld. Despite some serious efforts, the killing of all witnesses and destroying of all archives and libraries has proved impossible.[8] Totalitarian systems of lies cannot last forever. It may seem like forever, but contingency always returns.

Arendt's second modern lie, the image-making lie, enters politics through the selling of war in a democracy. Arendt's primary case is the selling of the Vietnam War to U.S. citizens, followed by its imagistic sustaining. As Caruth aptly summarizes Arendt, first, image makers *"make images to sell the war,"* but then "the problem solvers *make war to sustain an image"* (85). The motive shifts from making a change in factual reality to creating an opportunity for performative utterances to confuse a public and continue the images. Unlike Elaine Scarry's account of war as harming to change reality and causing such pain as to force a new construction of borders or alliances, the image-making lie is indifferent to reality and harm. It shifts the goals of war away from the reality of the battlefront and to the reality of the living room. What enters that room loses its dependence on factual truths. Instead, the flickering image becomes the war. If body bags are not shown on televisions, then the U.S. soldiers in Iraq did not die. If Iraqi dead are not reported, then they did not die. Thus, the sustenance of the national image of power disconnects that image from facts and the traditional motives for war. As is typical of image-making lies, it is unclear what reality was changed, and for what purposes, in Iraq. Rather, the war may well have been presented as an image of U.S. imperial power in response to decaying economic power. Obviously the development of image-making lies within a democracy is pernicious, because the lost relationship between fact and political decision disables meaningful deliberation.

Both totalitarian lies and image-making lies depend on *defactualization*, and so they are the lies that citizens should fear most, lies of state power that inherently deny the rights of citizens (to know, to decide, to vote meaningfully in the nation). The performative nature of healthy deliberation is displaced by a tightening system of lies, itself a dramatic performance laboring to construct a symbolic system deaf to other constituting forces. In sum, systemic modern lies seek to stabilize history and create a singular world, a move not unlike some types of truth. According to Arendt, this construct, however, is rendered unstable because it is monolithic without response; even the first to lie have lost access to factual truths and are limited in their knowledge. It would seem that totalitarian systems of lies are innately less stable than performative acts arising in the heteroglossia of factual truths, diverse opinions, and traditional lies. Dissensus proves more viable than the lying world order of totalizing consensus.

In the agonistics and antagonistics of healthy politics, many lies enact wishes, agreements, deceptions, disputes, and consents. Inventive lies, notes Arendt, indicate human natality, a unique, imaginative creativity. The human ability to lie, Arendt's "little miracle," belongs "among the few obvious, demonstrable data that confirm human freedom" ("Truth" 246). By all sorts of lies, citizens can change their circumstances, including the factual truths of existence, because humans are relatively free from factual truths. Arendt's liar is the quintessential "man of action," who "says what is not so because he wants things to be different from what they are—that is, he wants to change the world" (245–46). Lies are connected closely to performance and forming performative acts, the fabrications of word and deed. Although Arendt is sensitive to the dangers of the lie when it extends beyond individual engagements to frameworks of its own creation, the performance of lies in itself does not belong to the forces of totalitarianism and dominant power alone. It is my premise that creative lies also serve the citizen who speaks to power. As speech acts relatively free of constraint and convention, lies may be the most constituting performative of all.

If we think broadly about lies, then constitutions, declarations, and manifestos (along with ideals, utopias, and other fictions), all certainly word and deed, can be called a type of lie. These texts do not abrogate the relationship between opinion and factual truths, but they are not concerned with the factual present. Although the deceptions of such utterances are not foregrounded, their authors and readers know that the documents do not describe the factual world, but are templates invented to reorder the world. Fantasy, myth, and utopia are an extension of what Benedict Anderson calls "imagined communities." When the Declaration of Independence claimed that "[w]e hold these truths to be self-evident," the claim was not self-evident to the world at large. Thus, imagining a cosmopolitan world and constituting its future, the authors of many documents and utterances articulate that future in the now, arguing for a certain way of being and making the wish firm and social, but no more dependent on factual truths than princess makeup or the birthday wish. The primary intention may not be to deceive, but in creating normative documents that do not correspond to factual truths, these texts intentionally create an untruth. Reconfigured from narrative fiction to covenant, ideal imaginings take on presence in legislative and judicial systems.

Even witnessing and testimony—backward-looking, forensic concepts important to Arendt's connection of factual truths to politics—are not immune from the taint of intended deceits. Her connection of witnessing and testimony to factual truths is part of a legal discourse of witnessing, but the genres for witnessing and testifying extend beyond the juridical: a Christian confession, a revelation, testimonio, a "tweet," a memoir, an anonymous sending of documents or photographs, an autobiography.[9] Where to begin with witnessing and testimony? Perhaps we should not begin with the utterance *per se* and its relationship to factual truth, but with the constructed "I" who speaks, the Enlightenment "I" protected by negative human rights. As many have argued, testimonies are rhetorical acts constructed by a speaker facing an audience whose recognition depends on authenticity, legal or political requirements of literal accuracy and facticity, preexisting genres of truth telling, and an authorial need for sympathetic self-representation.[10] Testimony cannot be truth or even just honesty, the intended attempt at truth. Rather, testimony is an act of making a relationship with an audience. It may end as an utterance of factual truth and evidence, but to be heard, testimony begins as a strategic performance, and the felicitous performative must be recognized to be audible, which is especially difficult where the plaintiff represents marginalized and oppressed people, either as a subaltern or as an advocate. Such a speaker must create an authentic persona with an evidential claim of violation; seeking common interests and credentials, she speaks to skeptical or disinterested authorities, censorious citizens, and resisting power. If the witness must create both the in-between and inter-est to be heard and if she must create a performative utterance with internal criteria of felicity, then the performing "I," and even the lying "I" and the fictive "I," is part of that performance of truth, for what use is testimony if it is not recognized and judged appropriately? The effective power of witnessing depends on the speaker's representative force, her claim to a recognizable truth, and her ability to construct interlocutors willing to act. As Lauren Berlant has argued, compassion and, I would add, compassionate acts depend on "social training, emerge at historical moments, are shaped by aesthetic conventions, and take place in scenes that are anxious, volatile, surprising, and contradictory" ("Introduction" 7). Truth is never enough; Cassandra comes to mind again. At the core of advocacy lies the question, Does a witness speak to deliver factual truth or does she speak to initiate inter-est and deliberation and hence to construct a particular recognition among interlocutors and the world?

Refusing Lies and Failing Recognition

Perhaps the human rights testimony most associated with lies is the widely read testimonio or autobiography *I, Rigoberta Menchú: An Indian Woman in Guatemala* (1983). In returning to this much-analyzed work, I show how an acceptance of lies as political tools reveals hidden assumptions about political speech. I argue that recognizing the political intentions and performativity of lies entails acknowledging the political power to create inter-est and transform lifeworlds. Between 1978 and 1984, at the peak of ongoing attacks and oppression, an estimated 150,000 Mayas were massacred or disappeared and at least 450 villages were destroyed. Menchú's testimonio responded to the Guatemalan government's treatment of indigenous people, and it was so effective a response to the genocide as to help win Menchú a Nobel Peace Prize in 1992. Menchú's testimonio represents a rare recognition of the subaltern speaking. Although Venezuelan anthropologist

Elisabeth Burgos-Debray translated and arranged Menchú's memories of the activities of her family, village, and culture, the testimonio itself, Menchú's speaking, created a global readership and a place in history. In the face of what Arendt calls the false politics of totalitarianism, ideology, and government violence, Menchú tells of atrocities promulgated and denied by Guatemala and the U.S. government; she takes sheer happenings and makes them *humanly comprehensible* by narrating lives.

In 1998, the factual accuracy and logical rigor of *I, Rigoberta Menchú* were criticized by anthropologist David Stoll, which was reported on the front page of the *New York Times* by journalist Larry Rohter. Stoll did not offer his observation of minor discrepancies as a critique of the pattern of atrocities including rape, torture, and murder. He fully acknowledges those atrocities, writing, "There is not doubt about [her] most important points: that a dictatorship massacred thousands of indigenous peasants, that the victims included half of Rigoberta's immediate family, that she fled to Mexico to save her life, and that she joined a revolutionary movement to liberate her country" (vii). Perhaps because he understood both the power and normalcy of lies within politics, Stoll never says that she lied, but rather noted omissions and discrepancies that created a "mythic inflation" (232). After years of careful research into the accuracy of her utterances, he never calls them lies but rather presents them as mythic exaggerations, tellingly related to folk tales more than political purpose. Nevertheless, even the hint of dishonesty resulted in his criticism becoming major material for the academic and popular press. Menchú's testimonio (not testimony), her literary utterance (not false witnessing), came to be assessed by juridical standards of accuracy. Among Stoll's accusations—not all of which were substantiated—were that (1) her father's land dispute was not with wealthy landowners, but rather a family fight with in-laws; (2) Menchú did not see her brothers' deaths; (3) she was literate; (4) she did not work as a maid in Guatemala City; and (5) she underplayed her connection to guerrillas and her education in Marxism.[11] These accusations were used to question Menchú's authenticity as a peasant and underscore Menchú's political position and lack of objectivity.

Committed to postmodern theories of agency and the critique of objectivity, literary critics responded to Stoll's accusations with copious tracts detailing the characteristics of testimonio, subaltern agency, cultural differences, editor and translator mediations, rhetorical intentions, and the nature of the public sphere.[12] Seeking criteria to redeem the testimonio as a felicitous utterance, clashing with defenders of the modernist criteria of factual truths, literary critics displayed great sensitivity to divergent language games, while

postcolonial critics listened for subaltern voices. Despite significant deliberations, her partisans have not considered the possibility that Menchú lied.
Certainly some of her political interlocutors on the right labeled her omissions, errors, and misrepresentations as lies,[13] but overall, U.S. scholars are
committed to proving that she did not lie. Despite valuing standpoint epistemologies, opinion, and even intuition over objective truth, critics could not
value lies, even in a just political cause. Lying—in contemporary debates,
academic or political—is not recognized as a legitimate political act, regardless of the efficacy of the lie or the larger truths it serves. Unique among her
sympathizers, Arturo Arias asks, "If Menchú crafted a strategic discourse
to prevent the continued genocide of her people, how can we question the
authenticity of that act?" (83). At the extreme of the academic spectrum, one
might call her act strategic and authentic utterance, but not a lie.

Given his years of work on uncovering omissions and discrepancies,
Stoll must have thought to taint *I, Rigoberta Menchú*, although I do wonder whether he expected the response. As Gillian Whitlock has observed of
other tainted testimony, "[a]ctivists, celebrities, psychologists, sociologists,
lawyers, and academics surround autoethnographies by refugees, indigenes,
and subalterns with benevolent affirmations. These public intellectuals confer authority on the narrator; they both encourage and instruct the reader
to read the text properly" (20). Certainly public intellectuals responded to
Stoll's improper reading, but inherent in their desire to confer authority on
Menchú is a desire to control the interpretation of her text and limit its reception. In effect, potential political readers, potential interlocutors, are remade
into the right kind of audience, hermeneuts committed to fused horizons
mediated by experts. The dismissal of direct engagement depoliticizes the
text's rhetorical power. In effect, the instructions by critics remake the inherently political testimonio into an aesthetic text, to be used in ways similar to
The Joy Luck Club. Aesthetic texts may teach appropriate emotional response,
but they do not demand a performative response in a political space.

My assertion that Menchú's text is performative is not controversial.
Quite a few scholars have discussed it as performative in terms of theater
(Brooks), subject formation (Arias), and speech act (Sommer, "Las Casas's"),
and of course, there is a widespread understanding of autobiography as performance (Anderson; Phelan; S. Smith). To contribute to the extensive academic debates, this chapter will do more than characterize Menchú's writing
as performative. I want to argue that lies, Menchú's lies, are a particular kind
of performative deliberation that destabilizes the present and constitutes the
future. As Arendt promises, "deeds possess such an enormous capacity for

endurance," a frightening endurance that exceeds any individual act (*Human* 233). The speech act can create a past that imposes a new trajectory on the lifeworld. That is, Menchú negotiates the events and reimagines them in agential ways that negotiate the generic norms of testimonio, Western expectation, and justice. She performs all of this to create a future that might bring stability, security, and peace to her community. To this end, she uses her position as witness in Paris to craft a future unimaginable in the village or *finca* (plantation). If we understand lies as *normal political acts*, not moral impurities, then rather than limiting Menchú to being a teller of factual truths and a witness to sheer happening, Menchú could be acknowledged for her ability to make factual truths humanly comprehensible and actionable, even as she lies back to totalitarian lies. More than their danger to factual truths, lies threaten stability, and this may be why lies are abhorrent to many. Sometimes, however, it is necessary to destabilize a regime, and the performative force of lies can destroy as it simultaneously constitutes. Lies can be a strategic part of performative deliberations: utterances where possible futures are imagined and denied.

Strategic lying is part of political discourse. It is also a type of utterance helpful in describing agency in performative deliberation. Lies are defined in the speaker's intention (illocution): Did one intend to deceive by omission, displaced emphasis, or disregard of factual truths? In diverging from facts, acts of lying particularly reveal both an agent's resistance and negotiation. Responses to the lie also demonstrate the resistance and negotiations of interlocutors. To contain and classify the threads of the Menchú disputes, I apply a rhetorical rubric of intention that opens up the question of where intentions reside and how agents find resources for resisting and negotiating cultural norms. Theories of intention vary across fields, from literary prohibitions on knowing authorial purposes to philosophical representations of the mind that present intention as planning informed by desire and belief (Bratman).[14] While hermeneutical approaches to textual interpretation seemingly minimize authorial intention to the benefit of readers' intentions, rhetorical situations are concerned with interlocutors, power differentials, and worldly effects. In rhetorical situations—due to the agonistic nature of politics, the positioning of interlocutors, and the need to establish an in-between with common inter-ests—participants recognize interlocutors and respect and engage their intentions.

To describe how critics understand Menchú's intentional omissions and additions, I utilize a longer argument I made in *Intentions: Negotiated, Contested, and Ignored*. Rhetorical intention does not reside in the mind, but rather infiltrates three culturally specific locations: (1) the form and genre of a speech act, (2) the cultural motives of social or ethnic groups, and (3) the purpose of the speaker. Strategic, agential communication is complexly located, even within the single utterance of a single speaker. Illocution (and perlocution) cannot be located only in the proposition or interlocutor but need to be contextualized, a point that is inherent in Austin's discussion of other minds. In discussing how people recognize that another is angry, Austin argues that people assess symptoms to diagnose the mental state, and anger is recognized "like mumps" or a bittern in the garden. "Being angry" describes "a whole pattern of events, including occasion, symptoms, feelings and manifestation, and possibly other factors besides" (*Philosophical* 109). Ultimately, then, intention is recognized through the contingent clues located in the genre, society's motives, and the speaker's purposes: people will scrutinize and diagnose intentions differently in a eulogy of a hero given by her son than in a critique of a politician given by a rival party.

Critics and a host of others claim to recognize Menchú's intentions, and in doing so, most desire to preserve Menchú's honor. Revealing an unstated concern with intention and the need to control its interpretation, the three locations of intention provide a coherent frame for the copious analyses of Menchú's utterances. If we accept that a speaker has purposes that are delimited by the cultural and historical conditions as well as the discursive structures available, and if most of us have learned to read intention through its symptoms, one has to wonder why public intellectuals feel such obligation to explain Menchú in both positive and negative ways. After all, her testimonio was widely read, translated, and taught. Its vitality creates recognition of Menchú's narratable self, but that narratable self became a site of deliberation on the nature of her narration and who she was.

Literary critics commonly place the misperception of Menchú's utterances as lying in the audience's lack of skill in reading the *genre* of testimonio. The readers do not comprehend the intentions of this alien genre. Not Western autobiography, memoir, or autoethnography but testimonio, the genre of *I, Rigoberta Menchú* requires a special kind of reading, they argue. Although testimonio, autobiography, and memoir share interpretive tensions about memory and fact, rhetoric and aesthetics, subjectivity and objectivity, critics require knowledgeable readers to approach each genre differently. Since testimonios simultaneously represent both the narrating individual and her community—both as the subject, even an agential subject—they present the narrator as a marker of negative rights, of oppression, and the community as a marker of positive rights, of capabilities. Critics argue that the generic structure widens the sources of illocutionary force. Thus, testimonio makes witnessing a complicated act comprising multiple standpoints. For instance, John Beverley notes that testimonio is not just a representation of the single subaltern's life, and he distinguishes testimonio from autobiography by its shift in authorial function, as testimonio affirms the individual subject in relationship to community (*Testimonio* 40–41). North American readers, primarily experienced in autobiography, come to testimonio without understanding the possibility of a communal narrative spoken through the body of one citizen. In keeping with this generic requirement, Menchú herself makes a distinction about how the genre formulates her speech act and the nature of truth, saying, "*I, Rigoberta Menchú* was a testimonial, not an autobiography . . . I have my truth of what I lived for twenty years. The history of the community is my own history" ("Those" 110).

If the genre testimonio narrates a particular life and a community's history, then the nature of evidence shifts, and that shift is marked by the generic intentions, not only those of particular utterances. Given that its generic intentions include an entire community, the witnessing of truth in a testimonio never can be the legal witnessing of courtroom testimony, for more than one person's experience is witnessed. Testimonio's political, literary, and cultural requirements make the genre polyphonic, though somewhat different than the polyphony of a Bakhtinian novel. If Bakhtin would have truth created through the consciousness of the author, characters, and the reader (*Problems* 81), within a testimonio, the author's truth is complicated by her entire culture. Critics like Beverley argue that the creation of narrative truth occurs through the author's narration of her lived experience, which includes the experiences of her community. Hence in reading testimonio, the reader's response is shaped not only through her own consciousness, the voices of multiple characters, and the author, but also through the multiple voices or heteroglossia of the author's culture. The polyphonic discourse within the genre creates a unity that is not monologic (how could that be possible?), but that represents the community's experience as the author's life.

In addition to representing the community as well as the narrator, testimonio has other generic symptoms, symptoms that some say explain Menchú's acts. For example, due to its concern with what Ian Hacking calls "memoro-politics," testimonio legitimizes a unique kind of witnessing. The genres testimonio and autobiography both consider memoro-politics, "a politics of the secret, of the forgotten event that can be turned, if only by strange flashbacks, into something monumental" (214). The memoro-politics of testimonio is distinguished by its strange flashbacks to a Mayan history of oppressed and marginalized witnessing.[15] As a political genre committed to monumental transformations, Beverley claims that "testimonio aspires not only to interpret the world but also to change it" (xvi). Others emphasis testimonio's resistance to state violence, poverty, and degraded living conditions (Warren), its authenticity as well as aesthetics (Brooks), its concern with significance more than veracity (Avant-Mier and Hasian; Taracena), and historical collaborations between an editor and the subaltern (Brooks; Taracena). Together the critiques center the controversy on the genre and away from the political act of witnessing. Authors of testimonios articulate factual truths from a variety of sources, creating a polyphonic discourse including unverifiable facts and what a court might declare as hearsay, but what a community would witness from a variety of positions. By enacting multiple political positions within the polyphonic genre, by narrating the community, Menchú seemingly avoids the legal positions of plaintiff, victim, and witness while representing all three.

Generic descriptions of testimonio respond to Stoll's accusations by avoiding attributing intentions to the author. The performative utterance becomes separated from an individual who might intend to tell either a truth or a lie. Intention, as constructed within the testimonio genre, presents the community's complex truths and multiple intentions simultaneously.[16] Genre, however, is not the only extra-authorial location of intention noted within the Menchú dispute. Critics also consider how *cultural motives* constructed intention. Some significantly argue that Menchú's culture inherently has more communitarian values than those of U.S. culture, and the conventions of speaking for many—for the "we," instead of just the "I"—disrupts Western juridical judgments of truth and the concept of the individual, but are appropriate and normal for Menchú. That is, witnessing in indigenous Guatemala implies witnessing the experiences of the entire community rather than those of a single member. The motives of the community quintessentially include a collective agency and inter-est that overrides individual purposes. Therefore, some argue, Menchú's intentions are not personal purposes but an extension of cultural motives, and they premise a cultural break between Western juridical culture and Menchú's indigenous one. Certainly those who accuse her of inaccuracies—Stoll and others—apply legal definitions to a genre and culture far from the U.S. juridical frame, and as still others point out, those definitions are irrelevant in Guatemala's countryside (Ferman; Lovell and Lutz; Morales; Sommer "Sacred").

In privileging Menchú's genre and her cultural motives, literary critics present and preserve an artificial division between the narratable subject (she who is distinct and concrete) and her culture. Although an initial examination of cultural motives seems to embed an agent in a cultural discourse, in constituting the agent as fully subjected to her culture, critics diminish human distinction within alien cultures, thereby diminishing the significance of located agency and "specific modes of being, responsibility, and effectivity" (Mahmood 14–15). By this means the witnessing subject, Menchú, enters into established conventions and normative discourses in ways that may remake her distinction and her agency; in particular, she who would be the narratable self becomes narrated. The Menchú whom the Left would narrate does not lie, is authentically indigenous, and conforms to a prescribed, (pre)scripted account. Her ability to constitute her story, including its lies, is dismissed when genre and cultural motives overwhelm her individual intentions or purposes. By implying that acts of truth and lie are absent or hazy in the other, critics are not simply claiming that two cultures' motives are incommensurable but that the truths are different, and bridging the truths requires a kind of knowledge and agent not readily recognizable. They inscribe a difference that makes the narration of Menchú's life impossible to many interlocutors, cutting the testimonio off from political effect. Lies, however, are not so hard to diagnose; in discussing honesty, Annette Baier writes, "Learning what counts as a lie is like learning what counts as a debt or a broken promise" (271). Unlike the subtle and sometimes suppressed symptoms of anger, the disconnect between fact and lie is rule bound, varieties of specific language games. When critics describe Menchú's culture as so removed from basic speech rules, like promises, they diminish the obligation to recognize her and proceed to reconstitute her lies (or, as they prefer, her inaccuracies) as symptoms of her authenticity. They construct her as an outsider to Western legal discourse and an insider to indigenous culture. In effect, they ask the nasty identification question—"Is she one of us?"—and they answer, "No." In asking for identification and privileging Menchú's difference, they do not struggle toward a political, deliberative recognition, but cast her as the other.

Although it may have some benefits in creating inter-est, the desire for authentic otherness reduces recognition and in-betweens which, in turn, might build robust inter-ests, inter-ests that are fully deliberative. Leigh Gilmore, concerned with truth telling, makes a similar observation in discussing the autobiography and the public sphere as jurisdictions or forums of judgment that open dominant history to alternative truth tellings. Particularly concerned with differentiating political and legal speech, she writes, "When the claims of the private (or prepolitical) person impinge on dominant cultural narratives, however, or when the 'I' in its witnessing politicizes both the 'I' and the 'we,' memoir and *testimonio* exceed the tolerance they are accorded in liberal discourse and become something much more dangerous" ("Jurisdictions" 700). If prepolitical speech moves to a successful political performance impinging on the dominant liberal culture, then it is recast as dangerous, and recognition of the witness as a political participant is distorted. The resulting deliberation on its utterance becomes subject to judgments of scandal and increased burdens of truth.[17] Although the concept of a prepolitical speech ignores the political and ideological nature of all discourse, Gilmore is useful in discussing how a genre like testimonio quickly becomes imbricated in cultural motives. To extend this, even if the simple act of witnessing atrocity, one to one, Menchú to Burgos-Debray, transcends its private origins and successfully enters the public sphere, it threatens the motives of the dominant culture, including that of liberal intellectuals committed to speaking for the freedom of "prepolitical" others. The testimonio's contingency, here arising in genocide, becomes trivial to outside purposes and motives, and it becomes subject to the reader's response as mediated through the dominant culture's criteria of judgment. The judgments of Menchú may be positive in the case of the left and negative in the case of the right, but the criteria of judgment suit the cultural motives of the interpreter positioned in the West.

Testimonio's political and cultural requirements, as read from the West, create a requirement of authentic ethnicity, but ethnicity is not a stable category. Western critics subsume the individual under her culture; they read Menchú's positioned potential in her genre and her culture (ethnicity). As Arturo Arias observes, ethnicity is constructed "constantly and simultaneously under erasure and reiterated, an irreducible dilemma of representation charged with ironic overtones, hyperbole, broken syntax" ("Authorizing" 80). Despite critical efforts, neither genre nor ethnicity can contain Menchú's distinct intentions once her utterances are labeled lies. Consistently the question of "whose language and whose culture represent the truth" figures in justifying Menchú's discrepancies, though the answers mostly refuse to recognize her distinct purposes. When understanding the testimonio's generic and cultural intentions exceeds the critics' abilities, then the "irreducible dilemma of representation" shifts to the question of whether any single individual can represent her culture. For example, Elisabeth Burgos-Debray's role as editor becomes pivotal for some who argue against Menchú's authorship of lies. In discussing the problem of Burgos-Debray, even Stoll assumes that the text is a hybrid cultural product, a Western-Mayan text created for a Western audience—especially since Menchú's Spanish was basic and her initial, taped story not chronological (Stoll 185). Even so, after hearing the tapes himself, Stoll acknowledges that *I, Rigoberta Menchú* represents Menchú's spoken words (Arias 81). Even if the testimonio is recognized as representing Menchú's words, scholars return to questions of the U.S. and Mayan cultures, asking whether one person's speech can represent Mayan culture (Montejo; Stoll), whether Maya culture can ever be represented to the West (Sommer "Sacred"), and whether judgments of truth and meaning can be made across language games (Sommer "Las Casas's"). When intention is placed within cultural motives, the question of lying seems to be deferred, as the interlocutor is not audible and lacks agency.

Finding intention in the *purposes* of the speaker most concerns judgments of individual integrity.[18] Although genre and cultural motives may constrain discursive production and reception, it is the individual's intention to deceive that marks the speaker as a liar. What was the purpose of Menchú's performance? How did she conceive and reconceive the exigencies of the situation? How did she construct her audience and locate herself to shape their political response? That is, how did she strategically move her readers from audience to interlocutors? When the subaltern speaks to the colonizer, what kinds of political agency can she aspire to and can she achieve? How are the contradictions of her performance, the outsider using the insider's discourse, understood politically? Did she intend to manipulate her audience? In what ways? These questions lie at the heart of political lying; our fear of manipulation fires our anger at political lies. Political lies, however, constitute deliberative directions and productive confusions.

When critics take up Menchú's utterances, her authorship, they sometimes frame her as a subaltern, Gayatri Spivak's unvoiced, or unheard, colonized speaker.[19] By characterizing Menchú as a subaltern, her proponents reframe not just her authorship of lies but even the possibility of her authorship of lies. Critics like Gilmore rightly observe that if the subaltern does speak in politically effective and dangerous ways, she will be marginalized. Although in the end, she might be given some purpose, even some agency, the argument from subalternity has the paradoxical effect of mitigating her agency even as it affords her agency. Rather than characterize her as a gifted narrator and a powerful Nobel Prize winner, the like of Martin Luther King Jr. or Nelson Mandela, critics diminish her power, subsuming it within the history of colonialism, if not her culture. Analyzing the implications of Menchú's speaking, Beverley provides an entry into understanding the intentions involved in lying, especially because of his desire to give Menchú agency without the intention of lying, a deeply problematic undertaking. As Beverley extends Spivak, the question is not simply "Can the subaltern speak?" but rather "Can she speak in a way that matters?" Beverley argues that Stoll seeks inaccuracies within Menchú's narrative because her speaking has come to matter. The book's canonization gives it ideological force, the political capacity to engage a broad audience, and the ability to make a subaltern heard. Beverley argues that Stoll's quarrel is not with Menchú herself; rather, Stoll is concerned with postmodern relativism in the academy and with the question of who has the authority to narrate. In critiquing her testimony, Stoll's purpose is "*resubalternizing* a narrative that aspired to (and achieved) hegemony" (Beverley, *Subalternity* 67).

In recognizing her disruption of hegemony, Beverley is articulate about Menchú as an agent of a transformative historical project as well as an agent who forms strategic alliances, even solidarity, with the professional middle class. He, however, cannot bring himself to say that she lied or manipulated. What he asks for is a special kind of truth claim for testimonios, one that confers a "special kind of epistemological authority as embodying subaltern experience" (77). Granted, elsewhere, in a footnote, he references an anonymous graduate student who remarks, "[T]he question is not Can the subaltern speak? But can the subalterns speak in a way that manipulates or dupes us to serve her interests?" ("Testimonio" 236). A phantom, footnoted graduate student can voice the obvious implications, but it is a position that Beverley cannot quite embrace himself. Rather than consider the subaltern capable of the political lies of the Right (Franken) or the Left (Coulter), Beverley gives Menchú an exotic position that separates her from normal political activity. If she is more political than a "native informer," she is still a subaltern and not a speaking, manipulating, deliberative citizen of the world.

The move to interpret Menchú's individual intentions through a frame of subalternity diminishes her even more than her denunciation as a liar. Subalternity interprets her utterances through a screen that makes her purposes opaque. Recognizing the political act of lying foregrounds her imaginative power in creating a lifeworld; recognizing lies would recognize not just her performative utterances but also her own recognition of her political performativity. When Diana Taylor discusses theatrical aspects of ethnography, she makes a telling observation, easily applied to the Menchú case. I repeat her here: "Insofar as native bodies are invariably presented as not speaking (or not making themselves understood to the defining subject), they give rise to an industry of 'experts' needed to approach and interpret them—language experts, scientists, ethicists, ethnographers, and cartographers" (162).

Although Menchú spoke with profound effect, a global effect that did not need expert interpreters, when she was accused of lies, the industry of experts rushes forward to interpret her. In their interpretations, through a desire to preserve her narration as a (pre)politics, they reinscribe her as a subaltern. Ironically, by interpreting her and explaining her truths, her proponents and defenders both re-create her as an authentic informer. They narrate her life as generically constrained, culturally exotic, and inescapably subaltern. Even so, her existence and exposure in the world continue to reveal her uniqueness, for, as Cavarero writes, "neither exposability nor narratability, which together constitute this peculiarly human uniqueness, can be taken away" (36).

If Menchú is a powerful politician who ran for president of Guatemala in 2007 and 2011, redefining political roles for women in campaigning, the critics fail to recognize her as a narratable self and speak her back in meaningful ways; their possibilities seem constrained by disciplined discursive regimes and narrations. Coco Fusco makes related observations about the reception of her performance piece with Guillermo Gómez-Peña, *Two Undiscovered Amerindians*. Staged internationally at museums and galleries, the two performers lived in a cage as a critique of earlier ethnographic exhibitions of people of color. Responding to charges of dishonesty and moral irresponsibility in her parody, Fusco discusses the mutual lying that takes place in "labeling artifacts from different cultures," arguing that the act of labeling across cultures creates dishonest representations (155). Protesting the extra moral weight placed on artists of color, even by intellectuals on the Left, Fusco describes the lies of her performance as lies for a different story—one might say a different history. They are political lies with political intentions. Similarly, the intellectuals' intentions create dishonesty, though their political intentions may be more hidden, even to themselves. Fusco's observation parallels my claim that lies are traditional political tools and potentially transformative acts. Only when they are powerful and dangerous do they become frightening and potentially decrease recognition.

Rather than refuse Menchú's political status as a liar (even Stoll would not call her a liar), consider instead that lies are a traditional political performative in the face of the enemy. Menchú speaks about enemies to partisans, and she exaggerates, omits, and adds. She lies to partisans. Desiring too simple a solidarity between their professional souls and the speaking subaltern, critics and public intellectuals avoid their usual skeptical critiques in considering her testimonio and read neither as critics nor as citizens but as defenders of a faith in their ability to interpret the margin. Interlocutors who would deliberate prepare for the manipulation and lies within the threats of politics. Seeking shared action, deliberators are open to the threat of recognizing a narratable self who could be speaking back to them, narrating their lives in new ways, but openness may involve strategic responses. In fact, politics may always involve strategic utterances. (Diogenes can continue his search.) In the end, Menchú must lie—not because of the genre testimonio, not because of Mayan culture, but because achieving her purposes is helped by lying about her enemies to those whom she must recognize and constitute in community and act. If she constitutes the liberal West as less than enemy and not quite kin, she recognizes them as an ally necessitated by circumstance. That is politics. She need not trust Western intellectuals any more than she trusts her government. Academics are mistaken in defining their relationship with Menchú as one where they speak for her. There is inter-est, but not a shared form of life.

What is harmed by Menchú's lies? Did not her words stop genocide? Did not factual truths and a few lies speak back to the totalizing lies and rupture their hold? The obsession with the evil of lies may be a response to mass media that work to create systems of lies, lies on which we may act even to our own detriment. Systemic lying—the lying that Arendt abhors—is vile, but harder to see than intentional omissions in the words of an outsider. Systemic lying overwhelms us. Alternatively, when citizens believe Menchú's lies in the service of justice, when governments and NGOs become engaged in response to a human rights crisis, then lies demonstrate the centrality of the speech act in creating a world. Performative deliberation arising from Menchú's lies creates a general will and a shared agency that supports the rights of indigenous people. Furthermore, the acknowledgment of her lies salutes her position as a strategic speaker, a deliberating force, and a sly interlocutor.

Finally, let me respond to those still outraged by lies lest they throw their outrage onto me. My study of the place of lies in deliberation is descriptive, not evaluative or prescriptive. I see lies as strategically prevalent and political, and I resist an ethics to constrain the traditional political lie. Still, if one seeks an ethics, one might assemble an argument that the lies of state power are more damaging to human nature than the lies of human rights activists. It should not be a difficult project. The state's legitimacy relies on its truthful adherence to its laws, but citizen agents must speak back to dishonest states, even with lies. To paraphrase Martin Luther King Jr.'s "Letter from Birmingham Jail," any lie "that uplifts human personality is just." Any lie that "downgrades human personality is unjust." One might conceive an argument similar to that of Judith Butler, following Foucault. She argues that a "regime of truth offers a framework for the scene of recognition, delineating who will qualify as a subject of recognition and offering available norms for the act of recognition" (*Giving* 22). If one does not qualify as a subject of recognition, to break the regime's framework and to be recognized, one must distort or destroy the regime of truth; that is, telling the truth is also problematic if it does not recognize subjects as worthy interlocutors. Menchú's lies serve to challenge the norms of recognition, limited in Guatemala, and to change the regime of truth, forcing it to accommodate her position and inter-ests. Arguments could be made about the ethics of lying to those in oppressive power as a means to share and legitimate power. But that is not my purpose. Rather, I seek to acknowledge lies as inventions sometimes more useful than philosophical counterfactuals and to reclaim them as imaginative speech acts, integral to constituting a citizenry and a just world. Political lies can function as political theory, as counterfactual speech acts seeking to reset norms.

5

VOTING LIKE A GIRL:

DECLARATIONS, PARADOXES OF DELIBERATION,

AND EMBODIED CITIZENS AS A DIFFERENCE IN KIND

[T]he present government of this state has widely departed from the true democratic principles upon which all just governments must be based by denying to the female portion of community the right of suffrage and any participation in forming the government and laws under
which they live . . . and by imposing upon them burdens of taxation . . . without admitting
them the right of representation, thereby striking down the only safeguards of their individual
and personal liberties. . . . In proposing this change, your petitioners ask you to confer upon
them no new right but only to declare and enforce those which they originally inherited, but
which have ungenerously been withheld from them.

—Petition for woman's suffrage, New York State Constitutional Convention, 1846

[O]ne who is entitled to share in the deliberative or judicial office is thereby a citizen.

—Aristotle, *Politics*

In deliberation, there are moments of joint action leading to cultural change,
and these moments are part of why "procedure" and "process" are controlling metaphors within much of deliberative theory. The metaphors appeal
with their spatiotemporal implications, i.e., a linear timeline, which give one
kind of narrative power to descriptions of deliberative events, sequences, and
endings. Even so, on close examination, historical moments of joint action
and cultural change may be as tricky to own or identify as origins and ends.
When and where a process starts or ends is not clear. Speakers may also
resist acknowledging the perlocutionary force of their utterances. Remember
Arendt's warning that humans are afraid of the consequences of their acts,
trembling at "the burden of irreversibility and unpredictability" (*Human*
233). The consequences of human acts are not predictable, despite our desire
to construct timelines and histories of events and to identify patterns and
paradigms throughout history, assembling stability from a plurality of phenomena. When Alpheus S. Greene presented his neighbors' petition at the

1846 New York State Constitutional Convention and initiated public deliberation on women's suffrage, he could have had no idea that the 1846 deliberations might be setting the stage for the world's first convention on women's rights two years later in Seneca Falls, and the seventy-three years of feminist performative deliberation that followed.[1] Nor, in all likelihood, could he have named the cultural sources that led to the beginning of women's suffrage in rural New York. Did he recognize the burden of irreversibility and unpredictability in his actions?

Deliberations over new rights or extensions of existing rights—gay marriage, universal health care, and protection from hate speech—represent transformative potentials in how a nation and its citizens conceive and enact themselves. In defining new rights, interlocutors must define new violations, rename citizens of rights, and substantiate legal approaches. Rather then examining ongoing, contemporary struggles that are too close to see, "Voting Like a Girl" looks back at deliberations over U.S. women's suffrage. First it demonstrates how the *paradoxical* nature of rights generates deliberation; that is, performative utterances themselves in their *internal* and *iterative* nature can create occasions of performative deliberation. The success of new rights depends on recognition, in-betweens, and inter-ests, but the utterances themselves may create the terms of resolving disputes. The chapter then proceeds to demonstrate that the physical performance of citizenship is a deliberative act important for the development of the subject of human rights, the citizen's agent, and the culture that supports the rights. The act of performing citizenship, i.e., voting or running for president, might be deemed infelicitous or illegal, but the performance has force beyond its acceptance. Citizens' normative, physical actions define the subject of rights and are more than merely persuasive or remonstrative: they enact the imagined world. The chapter explicates how performative deliberations worked at two points in the early history of U.S. women's suffrage and then briefly considers how the performative deliberations of gaining women's rights are different from those granted or imposed by a nation-state for its own purposes.

Performative Paradoxes

Let's begin with the premise that paradoxes, more so than ambiguities and resistance, defeat consensus models, which implicitly value monologue, and that paradoxes themselves, textual paradoxes, make performative deliberation basic to politics exactly because a deliberative speech act, both controlled and destabilized by the paradox, inherently takes interpretive turns as it reveals the culture's contradictory values.[2] Not only in strategic utterances, but even in founding documents, paradoxes generate deliberation, granting a promise of agency as interpreters make claims upon the documents. Ever since Rousseau defined democracy's paradox of origins, politics has been characterized by any number of other paradoxes. Rousseau specifically puzzled over the paradox that democracy needs good men to make good laws, but needs good laws to make good men. Political paradoxes, however, are copious; most relevant to this project are the paradoxes of human rights discourses.[3] Some scholars see rights paradoxes exploited to maintain hegemonies. Julietta Hua tellingly critiques modernity's project of universalizing not just the human subject, as she analyzes the extension of universals into human rights. In the European construct of rights universalism, she argues, the mythic ideal of universals becomes "a real and discoverable object" (16), and particular "cultural values, economic relations, and legal institutes" (7)— the differences—are rendered in need of reform. In effect, rights universalism erases the rights of difference, implicitly the right to difference, and universalism paradoxically allows it to become a tool for Westernization.

Other scholars, including myself, find the resources of paradoxes potentially productive of both new rights claims and committed citizens. For example, Chantal Mouffe sees the liberal promise of universal equality as contradicted by the division between who rules and who is ruled (as exemplified in current deliberations on immigrants, felons, children). Defining this paradox as a tension, not a fatal flaw, she sees the contradiction as creating the opportunity for challenges to exclusion, "though references to 'humanity' and the polemical use of 'human rights'" (*Democratic* 45). In *Emergency Politics*, Bonnie Honig also provides an argument for paradoxes as productive in considering the politics of emergencies. Imagining new rights claims as inhabiting "a world not yet built" (47), she responds to deliberative democracy's redefinition of the paradox of origins as the paradox of democratic legitimation. Rather than seeing democratic legitimation as the work of politics, she argues that the paradox of origins, Rousseau's paradox, is a feature of democratic life that constantly (re)interpellates citizens into being. Good citizens are called upon to make good laws as good politics infuse citizens with commitments to ideals, such as universal rights.

Following Mouffe and Honig in characterizing paradoxes as productive, this chapter develops the deliberative dynamics of paradoxes within the particular politics of human rights propositions. Rather then advance paradoxes as epistemic problems or intricate puzzles, I argue that they can be seen as discursive resources, linguistic opportunities to reiterate and restructure discourses. As Roy Sorensen writes, "[p]aradoxes are questions (or in some cases, pseudoquestions) that suspend us between too many good answers" (xii). In creating a suspension between good—and even bad—answers, paradoxes have particular potential to create in-between spaces; since no single answer is adequate, paradoxes push interlocutors to define inter-ests that will resolve the clausal conflict. Paradoxical utterances do not hold the answer or argument to create consensus. Rather, they disrupt the stability of answers, arguments, consensus, and so they define the work of human deliberators. Through paradoxes (and ambiguities, oppositions, and infelicitous performatives), utterances can escape both their context and citational histories, offering opportune moments for renegotiating social tensions and redefining cultural practices.

For the purposes of analyzing the embodiment of citizen agents engaging in gaining suffrage, we need four classes of paradoxes: one that reflects a historical tension between old and new ideas; a second concerned with the irresolvable contradiction between rights as norms and the effectiveness of those norms; a third concerned with political origins; and a fourth definitional paradox, which is irresolvable. As an example of a paradoxical clash between old and new beliefs, Joan Wallach Scott quotes Olympe de Gouges, a French revolutionary, on the paradoxes of rights. De Gouges, who wrote the 1791 Declaration of the Rights of Woman and Citizen, describes herself as "a woman who has only paradoxes to offer and not problems easy to resolve" (qtd. in Scott 4). Scott observes that de Gouges uses paradox in a nontechnical sense, not as indicating an irresolvable proposition but as indicating a set of radical claims about women that challenge traditional beliefs and doxa. That is, this kind of paradox puts into play two sets of conflicting ideas that may be resolvable or not. Another example of the new idea challenging doxa can be seen in this 1919 interpretation of First Amendment law by Justice Oliver Wendell Holmes. In tension are the new idea of absolutely free speech and the traditional view of free speech modified by legal concerns. Holmes argued that

> the First Amendment, while prohibiting legislation against free speech as such, cannot have been, and obviously was not, intended to give immunity for every possible use of language. . . . We venture to believe that neither Hamilton nor Madison, nor any other competent person then or later, ever supposed that to make criminal the counselling of

a murder within the jurisdiction of Congress would be an unconstitu-
tional interference with free speech. (*Frohwerk v. United States*)

Holmes claims that the framers of the Bill of Rights, the traditionalists
who wrote something as direct as "no law," could not have intended to make
legal the counsel of murder. He appeals to the distant intentions of the
founders, attempting to abrogate two interpretations of the First Amendment, a relatively new, absolutist one and his own traditional view, for the
amendment offers too many good answers. In this, he follows de Gouges's
pattern of placing two views in play, one orthodox and the other challenging.
This type of paradox is highly contextual and evident in types of change.
The clash between old and new ideas, however, is a normative condition in
modernity and the common condition of deliberation, evaluating the new
against the old.

The second type of paradox specifically concerns human rights covenants
as normative statements that generate irresolvable paradoxes that reveal cultural conflicts and create deliberative moments. There are close connections
between this paradox and the fourth, which is a broadening and founding
theory of this pattern, but to begin a discussion of irresolvable paradoxes, let
us start with a narrower set of utterances, statements such as the promise
of equality for all men in the Declaration of Independence. Wendy Brown
discusses similar, irresolvable paradoxes within rights norms, noting how
rights mark a designation as they protect the marked individual ("Suffering"). For example, both my religion and my speech become marked, and
they mark me, as I am free to practice them.[4] One might say that one is free
only to be marked or identified (as religious or speaking), and so one's freedom is limited by its labeling and its interpellation of identity. Brown further
observes that rights are paradoxical in that, while they are guaranteed to all,
they empower differently. In the ideal, the poor can speak freely, but in the
real, those with material and social resources are more likely to be heard. In
summing up the paradoxes of rights, she argues,

> Rights function to articulate a need, a condition of lack or injury, that
> cannot be fully redressed or transformed by rights, yet within exist-
> ing political discourse can be signified in no other way. Thus rights
> for the systemically subordinated tend to rewrite injuries, inequalities,
> and impediments to freedom that are consequent to social stratifica-
> tion as matters of individual violations and rarely articulate or address

the conditions producing or fomenting that violation. Yet the absence
of rights in these domains leaves fully intact these same conditions.
(431–32)

Rights propositions, in and of themselves, are of limited effect in helping
the marginalized escape the label of their subordination. In fact, they reiterate the violation. Hence, al-Obeidi's witnessing creates sympathetic spectators exactly because she represents an individual in need of redress and not
an entire society in need of change. Societal change, even the initiation of
societal change, demands meaningful response and sacrifice on the part of
others, while the rights of an individual might be met more easily. Yet despite
the limits of individual rights, if al-Obeidi did not speak, the social order
would remain intact.[5]

As a form of naming and norming, rights demarcate and paradoxically
preserve a site of injury, creating a contradiction between what they promise
and what they norm. Even so, I differ with Brown's claim that rights rarely
address the conditions producing rights violations; the definitional marking of a site of injury, the revelation of paradox, generates deliberation. The
marking of violation is a performative utterance in that it makes public and
impacts the violation, the normative criteria of equality, and the forum for
redress. Although the individual redress is more common (al-Obeidi has
been flown to the United States), there are social and political forces in reiterations. Since human rights utterances have the potential to generate deliberation, their validity may not be in their truth claims but in their ability to
generate deliberation on what it means to be human. Rather then reading
them as "despotic" truths insensitive to culture, citizens should understand
them as opinions requesting and requiring deliberation.

A third paradox concerns the difficulty of political origins, a chicken-and-
egg paradox relevant to the later discussion of women's suffrage. The paradox of chickens and eggs animates a significant discourse. Although in the
Politics Aristotle notes the difficulty of defining citizens by parentage for the
founding citizens of a city, within political circles, the paradox of founding
or political origins begins with Rousseau. As he defines the problem of the
general will within democracy,

For a young people to be able to relish sound principles of political
theory and follow the fundamental rules of statecraft, the effect would
have to become the cause; the social spirit, which should be created by
these institutions, would have to preside over their very foundation;

and men would have to be before law what they should become by means of law. (*Social Contract* bk. II, chap. 7)

The impossible question: How do democratic citizens exist within the democracy (prior to democracy) to create the democracy? The paradox assumes linear time in a distant past with both clear causality and ideal, singular commitments to democratic norms. That is, it is only a paradox if one imagines the need for founding U.S. citizens to spring forth, full-grown, without earlier experiences with governance and the ability to be constituted as they proceed. Even so, it is a productive lens for thinking about national origins and legitimacy. Deliberative democrats Habermas and Benhabib move the paradox to present tense, where it defines the tensions within democratic legitimation: How can the general will (collective good) of the people be equally in the interests of all? How can the interests of eighteenth-century men be integrated with universal suffrage? Honig argues that neither theorist offers an adequate solution. Neither the ideals of the right procedure (Habermas) nor the finest moral standpoint (Benhabib) can resolve the tension. No escape: a democratic people must always generate, through their acts, what is supposed to motivate their acts, and within their contingent practices, the general will "can never be really equally in everyone's interest nor really equally willed by everyone" (*Emergency* 19). Theories will not undo the paradox. To extend Honig, despite a desire to idealize deliberation and evade the finitude of decision through focusing on its procedures or its initial moments, deliberative theory must acknowledge deliberation's outcomes, which can never be always in the interest of all, but rather reflect at best an ongoing politics to minimize violence, mob rule, and ends. Productively, the paradox of democratic origins forces contestation and deliberation, and it reminds thoughtful citizens that a general good may slip into mob rule.

The fourth paradox—irresolvable definitional paradoxes, internal even within individual words—is exemplified in Burke's work on substance and constitution.[6] Burke's difficult discussion of paradoxical constitutions is enhanced through his work on definition and the concept of substance.[7] He writes, "a thing's substance is what whereof it is constituted" (*Grammar* 337), and he identifies "constitution" as a member of the "stance" family, words rooted in the Sanskrit *stha*.[8] Building on John Locke's insight that substance, "standing under," is related to understanding, Burke describes substance's key work as being "to designate what a thing *is* . . . from designating what a thing *is not*" (23). For "substance," "constitution," and definitions in general, their essence (or substance) is defined by what is around them. Burke asserts, "linguistic behavior here reflects real paradoxes in the nature of the world itself—antinomies that could be resolved only if men were able . . . to create an entire universe" (56). The necessary definition of words by terms outside of themselves creates paradoxes in understanding the universe. Although Burke acknowledges a range of constitution's denotations and connotations, from "the action of enacting" to "authoritative ordinance," he focuses on constitutions as "fundamental, organic laws or principles of government" (341). In Burke, constitutions are covenants referring outside of themselves to motives and wishes, and they structure, merge, and balance contrary wishes into unstable manifestos and promises. As "an enactment of human wills," Burke might argue, a constitution's clauses and paradoxes mark our anxiety about deliberating, translating, and understanding politics (323). A constitution, like human rights declarations and other covenants, records a moment in cultural production and a strategic, unstable utterance that captures the possibility of a moment's agreement, shared inter-est, or compromise, certainly not consensus. In capturing the moment, a constitution internalizes both the instability of summation and the conflict of wishes, desires, beliefs, intentions, and motives.

Thinking of the United States, "the *United* States" or "the United *States*," Burke demonstrates how a plurality of wishes acts as a unity (375), how the united whole is composed of states that are conflicted in how they understand rights, identities, and freedoms, and yet they are merged into a single nation-state. The United States of America exemplifies the paradox of designating something by referring to what is extrinsic to it. Not only is continental North America more than one nation-state, but the single nation is defined by its fifty parts and its international relationships. The paradoxical form is productive as it fulfills the wish for a singular nation, a wish that results in a merger and balance that allows for difference and unfolding, and so the structure's instability is part of its constituting power as well as the force of constraint. One cannot have a United States without the constraint of engaging fifty states and the constituting acts of the states' multiple motives. One cannot have a nation-state without unity across difference. Given the instability of the mergers, they are potentially a device for the transformation of traditions and norms.

Burke, however, may be overly dialectical in claiming that "[c]onstitutions are agonistic instruments. They involve an enemy, implicitly or explicitly" (357). Although some constitutions arise as revolutionary instruments and others as guarantees of negative rights, the means by which citizens extracted promises from sovereigns to protect themselves from "abuses of authority," this agonistic definition skirts the fusions and solidarities of constitutions and the complexity of their normativity. As speech acts, they create a simple norm ("thank you") and norms to modify abuse ("don't hit"). In a more balanced moment, Burke writes, "For what a Constitution would do primarily is *substantiate an ought* (to base a statement as to *what should be* upon a statement as to *what is*). And in our 'agonistic' world, such substantiation derives point and poignancy by contrast with notions of what should not be" (358). Within the deliberative formation of a constitution, speech acts or constitutional clauses must find *"merger* or *balance* or *equilibrium"*; that is, from the contrasting stances of what-should-be and what-should-not-be come a structure, a scale that balances motives and wishes. Ultimately, in the finished text or act, there remains "conflict among the clauses" (357, 349), but the conflict is embedded in and controlled by the formal structure.

Constitutional paradoxes preserve disputes. Consider the case of a conflict between clauses or within a clause. Then interpreters cannot simply repeat the Constitution, for reiterations, citations, and rituals are all trapped within the paradox. To resolve the conflict, interpreters must become interlocutors, inventing arguments, appealing to discourses and material conditions beyond the text and its cultural history so that they can create in-betweens and inter-ests. For example, current free speech issues include hate speech, pornography, campaign finance, and the media's profitable manipulation of facts, all of which set liberalism's value of liberty in conflict with its value of equality. Two wishes, freedom and equality, are embedded differently in the Constitution: The First Amendment, which resists government control, is balanced against the Fourteenth Amendment, which broadens the definition of citizen and provides equal protection under the law to all citizens. Faced with conflicting clauses, some, such as antipornography lawyer Catharine MacKinnon, value equality over freedom; others, such as Judith Butler (*Excitable*) and Drucilla Cornell, privilege freedom over equality. In discussing what might be an "impasse," Owen Fiss analyzes the limits of reconceptions that make both clauses conform to either the value of freedom (freedom of marginalized groups to participate through speech) or equality (equal protection for speech) (15–18). Synthesized reconceptions do not remove the paradox, however. If we accept the impasse, rather than throwing up our hands, we might instead acknowledge that the clausal conflict creates ongoing and useful deliberation on what counts as equality and freedom and how they might be formed in the future.[9]

The irresolvably paradoxical nature of constitutions and rights declarations are embedded more deeply than in conflicting clauses reflecting different moments in their historical development or the positions of different negotiators. Internal paradoxes *within* clauses also initiate deliberation, as demonstrated by the phrase "freedom of speech." The paradoxical utterance of even such a basic right suggests that the deep structure of language generates dispute and potential deliberative acts, and it does so despite a tradition that characterizes open speech as leading to truth.[10] While the first amendment is written as an absolute, "make no law . . . abridging the freedom of speech," what "freedom of speech" entails is ambiguous, controversial, and impossibly paradoxical.[11] Even freedom of speech "absolutists," such as U.S. Supreme Court justice Hugo Black and the American Civil Liberties Union, do not believe that one can commit perjury or parade the midnight streets with a bullhorn. Faced with the paradox, many have struggled to present coherent pictures of freedom of speech.[12] The mid-twentieth-century public intellectual Alexander Meiklejohn, himself a modest absolutist, accepts some conformation to community standards of time, place, and procedure. Even so, he would allow no suppression of political speech. Addressing the restrictions of the McCarthy era, he would not balance free speech against clear and present danger or recognize political or seditious libel as free speech. Meiklejohn argues that only political speech is protected, writing that protected speech encompasses "the activities of thought and communication by which we govern," claiming further that "[p]olitical freedom is not the absence of government. It is self-government" ("First" 245, 254).

In Meiklejohn's historicist interpretation, democratic freedom is not freedom from control but rather the freedom of self-control, that is, not freedom as much as self-determination. He claims that the paradoxical tension between freedom and responsibility is at the heart of discussions of democratic speech.[13] Responsibility here implies both *response to* and *accountability for* the speech of the community, for Meiklejohn characterizes the U.S. Constitution as a fundamental political development with which people became self-governing. He conceives speech as "human action . . . subject to regulation . . . in exactly the same sense as is . . . shooting a gun" (232). With these conditions, Meiklejohn makes his argument for free political speech by examining the First Amendment in the context of three other passages of the Constitution: the Preamble, the Tenth Amendment, and Section 2 of Article I. Attending to their historical setting and the demands made by the Constitution, he reads these passages as presenting a coherent description of the Rights and Powers of the governing citizens. In the service of understanding the First Amendment, he describes the distinction between the clause *"the freedom of speech"* (thought and communication as public powers) and *a freedom to speak* (a private right), and his reasoning is compelling, if inadequately fleshed out as rhetorical analysis (*Political Freedom* 20–21; "First" 255). Inherent in "the freedom of speech" is a grammar of freedom, a grammar committed to democratic values and engagement (255).[14] I want to extend Meiklejohn's distinction by looking at the implications of writing "freedom of speech" versus "freedom to speak," arguing that the paradoxes and calculus of intention, even at the clausal level, move deliberation forward. Constitutional utterance is fully deliberative in its paradoxical performance of citizens' wills.

To make this point, I approach the First Amendment through ordinary language philosophy, arguing that too often the preposition "of" is imagined as the genitive case, simply a matter of possession. Speech possesses the freedom—speech's freedom. The *Oxford English Dictionary*, however, provides a different orientation to "of," one where it functions as an adverb as well as a preposition. In its original sense, "of" expressed movement: removal from, origin, derivation, cause. If one examines the *OED*'s first seven broad categories of meanings for "of," four of which will be discussed here, one finds that possession is not a dominant relationship between freedom and speech. First, "of" represents "motion, direction, or distance" (I), most clearly movement away from, out of, "indicating the place, situation, or *source from which action is directed or moves*" (I.1.a.3; emphasis added). Thus, one might imagine drawing the blood of another or freedom as action coming out of speech. The freedom moves out from speech; speech is the place that directs the action and the movement toward freedom. Speaking constitutes the freedom, and so speech is responsible for freedom rather than the gift of freedom. The second broad meaning also suggests an ousting, a fromness or offness. Stripped of clothes, free of guilt, freedom of speech. Here freedom is separated and removed from the speech. If the second meaning stresses absence and loss, the state of not having clothes or guilt, then one has speech potential first and then is free of it. Speech preexists freedom. Their relationship is not unitary; rather, freedom is one possible relationship for speech. Their separateness rather then their unity is emphasized. Obviously "free of speech" is not the same as "freedom of speech," but this definition shows the complicated nature of the relationships demarcated by "of" and the potential for a paradoxically driven rupture between freedom and speech even within a defining term of the relationship.

Perhaps the meaning of "of" will seem less dichotomous and paradoxical if we consider its third broad meaning, "Of origin or source. Indicating the thing, place, or person from which or whom something originates, comes, or is acquired or sought" (III). Alas, in this sense, too, freedom is separated from speech in ways echoing the earlier meanings. Just as an infant is born of a mother or technology is bred of science, freedom is born and bred of the speech act. It is implied that citizens have responsibility for creating a type of speech as a source of freedom. Here is the grammatical evidence for Meiklejohn's argument that our freedom originates in our speech acts, and citizens have responsibility for a certain quality or kind of speech. So, too, the fourth meaning of "of" is "a starting point of action," though in respect to "motive, cause, reason, or ground" (IV). Speech is then the motive, cause, reason, and/or ground of freedom. Freedom does not cause or enable speech, but speech acts cause freedom. Rather than continue with the *OED*, which would only belabor my point, let's conclude that simple possession is not the relationship between speech and freedom.[15]

The relationship between speech and freedom is dynamic—of motion, momentum, and motive—and the source of the motion is speech's creating freedom. It is harder to follow Meiklejohn to conclude that protected speech is educational, scientific, philosophical, aesthetic, or political. "Of's" grammar does not authorize speaking in a simple taxonomy. The grammar within "freedom of speech," however, does suggest that one speaks with the motive of creating freedom, but there is no clarity about what speech genre brings freedom, though perhaps there is a bit more regarding the genres that do not.[16] In search of precision, one might compare "freedom of speech" to "freedom to speak," using Meiklejohn's opposition. Here "to speak" tends to function as an infinitive—as a verb without a predicate or an adjective expressing purpose—and not as a preposition. Still I can't help but compare the prepositional meanings "of" and "to." Returning to the *OED*, I find that "to" as a preposition signifies simple location or movement *toward*. If one imagines freedom as moving toward speech, then in that simpler relationship, one might see freedom as going forward to speech; that is, freedom is the origin of speech. We are free for the purpose of speech. This is the more common interpretation of the First Amendment, but not the one signified by "of." The single paradoxical word "of" defines speech as the source of the political value—freedom.

Interrogating "of" reveals the deliberative resources inherent in the clause "freedom of speech." At stake is not just what is meant by "speech," or what is meant by "freedom," but even what is meant by "of."[17] The tiny preposition works to destabilize any easy understanding of freedom of speech, as it merges perspectives on what speech and freedom mean. Even so it does suggest that speech is the basis from which freedom arises. Freedom does not guarantee speech, but speech guarantees freedom. The ability of a clause to generate arguments, which represent simultaneously the perspectives of multiple interlocutors, demonstrates an ability to initiate and maintain disputes that might have been lost in a different wording, such as "freedom to speak." The generative, performative dimension of clauses underlines the place of performative deliberation internal to declarations, constitutions, and covenants. Their words do something in a formal, structural sense. The context and contours of U.S. history may strengthen their ability to function as Austin's performatives, but their internal paradox generates a deliberative moment and has an impact on history, too.

If this discussion seems a bit removed from nineteenth-century deliberations on voting, let me bring the deliberative potential of definitional paradoxes to a specific moment in the history of suffrage. In the week prior to the world's first convention on women's rights at Seneca Falls, the founding document of the women's suffrage movement, the "Declaration of Sentiments," was composed. It played on the felicity of an earlier utterance, the Declaration of Independence, working with the paradox internal to just one word—"man"—to reorient the balance of the document. In their pursuit of a resolution, the authors of the *History of Woman Suffrage* reported "the humiliating fact" that the ladies of Seneca Falls depended on "masculine productions" to form their demands (Stanton, Anthony, and Gage 68). Performativity, fully here in Butler's sense, depends on reiteration—and the women's humiliation, in depending on the oppressor's tongue, reflects the linguistic entrapment that silence people's experience as they try to frame their grievances. Yet within their entrapment, the paradoxes of rights offered women an avenue for negotiating their agency and a means for claiming their rights. Having scant feminine productions, they found an appropriate constitution, a merger and balance that allowed them to enter political discourse.

In all probability, the writers of the Declaration of Sentiments had heard the Declaration of Independence read on 4 July 1848 and listened once again to the universal claim: "We hold these truths to be self-evident, that all men are created equal, that they are endowed by their Creator with certain unalienable Rights, that among these are Life, Liberty, and the pursuit of Happiness." This single sentence offers all the paradoxical tension a radical would desire, but for purposes of understanding all four types of paradox, examining two words, "we" and "man," should work. Obviously the familiar ideas of the Declaration provided the doxa that would need to be reexamined; in the most familiar of deliberative moves, the familiar placed against the new—but, tellingly, because the framers of the Declaration of Independence once faced the paradox of political origins—the Declaration itself struggles with its solution. For the framers to be the citizens representing a general will, not mob rule, they must legitimize their action. When they claim "[w]e hold these truths to be self-evident," the "we" creates an inclusion, a social contract, but the nature of that inclusion is unstable, forcing truths upon all auditors, universalizing the holding of truths, all the while not referencing an established citizenry. "We" is both universal and without reference.

Arendt examines declarations of truth and reads the founding fathers as attempting to place the "truths" beyond their own will (to extend Arendt, endowed by a creator as an external to their internal, inalienable rights), and yet as having to claim the truths as a "we hold." Based on an unstable we, they make the claim of truth into a matter of opinion and belief rather then apolitical fact. That is, the political effectiveness of the proposition is in the "we" rather than "truth," because even factual truths are outside the political realm and not part of the negations of opinions, which are human and political. Thus the self-evident truths do not provide principles for action in and of themselves. Only within a felicitous context, a context that demonstrates oppression by an outsider, do they gain political significance, for factual reality is disturbingly contingent. Although not directly concerned with the Declaration of Independence, Mouffe also focuses on the political significance of a "we," often a nonconsensual "we," and connects it to the conception of citizenship as both free and equal. Envisioning radical democracy to include many different enterprises, but all in the service of the core values of liberty and equality, Mouffe conceives citizenship as more than a single identity; rather the concept of citizenship references a multiplicity of positions. Mouffe describes citizenship as "an articulating principle that affects the different subject positions of the social agent (*Return* 84). Even as citizenship inflects multiple positions or standpoints, it allows "for a plurality of specific allegiances and for the respect of individual liberty" (70). Since citizenship represents more than any single identity (liberalism) and less than a defining identity (civic republicanism), Mouffe's social agent, the citizen body, has responsibility for interpreting liberty and equality within private and public across social movements. When the citizens of a democracy construct a "we," they stress equivalence and not a consensus or identification. The "we" is part of "the 'grammar' of the citizen's conduct" (72). Ultimately she argues that "we" marks democratic equivalence without erasing difference. To extend Mouffe, unlike the "we" of consensus or identification, a political "we" would allow the disenfranchised women of the nineteenth century to partake in the grammar of citizen conduct, because they are rendered as equivalent. The exclusionary function of "we" is muted by its tolerance of difference. In their grammatical participation, Mouffe might argue, every "we" "implies the delimitation of a 'frontier' and the designation of a 'them'" (84). Within a "we," diversity, conflict, and competing interpretations of liberty and equality create an outside "them." Even a nonconsensual "we" creates an outside, an exclusion, a division. How interlocutors place themselves in relationship to the "we" is significant for initiating broader communities. How do those outside and excluded find a way into "we"?

When the few women planning the Seneca Falls convention considered the Declaration's Preamble, less than two weeks after Independence Day, they felt that exclusion as well as the inclusion. The "we" incorporated them, promised inalienable rights, and placed them in citizenship, all the while denying their inalienable rights and marking them as a frontier. The single word with great interpellative force set for them the grammatical difficulty of suffrage, and so the word became a site of performative deliberation. If we framed the difficulty of merger and agonism, the word "man" is where they acted. Into this utterance, both promise and refusal, they inserted only two words: the addition of "and women" both acknowledged their membership in the "we" and broke the declaration's ritual form, breaking open the speech act and making evident its deepest paradox. As Butler would characterize the utterance, the reiteration of the Preamble held the possibility of contamination and displacement. The contamination of the universal with the specific and the displacement from men to women together reconstructed the political imaginary, and new rights claims emerged from the paradox of declaration.

The Declaration of Sentiments itself would have a similar effect upon interlocutors, calling them into a paradox with many answers. Brown's paradox of marking is useful here. In adding the words "and women," Stanton and her fellow founders both mark their difference as they claim their rights of equality and liberty; they claim the symbolic right before they can perform rights acts. Although the Seneca Falls adaptation of the Declaration presented later grievances, which reflected a more radical departure from the initiating speech act, in its first revision it transformed the nature of demands for women's citizenship and political agency by placing the demands fully in reiteration.[18] The paradoxes within words and propositions cannot rewrite the conditions or system that caused the injury, as Brown has noted in discussing rights paradoxes. Rather, they historicize and preserve the injury as a merger, balance, or equilibrium. Their interpreters may make claims against norms of equality and freedom, but the human capacity for political growth depends upon embodied performances, performatives, and discourse's performativity. In addition to human rights declarations, the achievement of political rights requires material conditions, historical contexts, constituencies, deliberation, and citizen agents. Early suffragists in the United States exploited the clausal paradoxes to define disputes and create inter-est, but they used their bodies as well.

Voting like a Girl

This chapter, including its title, is indebted to Iris Marion Young's essay "Throwing Like a Girl: A Phenomenology of Feminine Body Comportment, Motility, and Spatiality" (1980), a very early essay on the performativity of gender. Responding to de Beauvoir's essentialist reading of women's bodies, Young argues that women's historical circumstances, despite individual differences, has unity specific to "a particular social formation during a particular epoch" (142). She argues that women's bodily comportment, motility, and spatiality, like their minds, are caught in the tension between achieving transcendent subjectivity and remaining immanent objects. She observes that "[t]he more a girl assumes her status as feminine . . . the more she actively enacts her own body inhibition" (154). In this early examination of gender as performative, Young suggest that bodily comportment may be connected to timidity, fragility, and a lack of confidence. If Young can write this of women in the late twentieth century, I cannot help but consider the effects of bodily comportment, motility, and spatiality on women in the middle of the nineteenth century. Consider the changes in comportment required to take a podium, to vote, and to run for national office. The right to vote as a symbolic right would have seemed far from the right to vote as an act; the transcendence and universalism of the symbolic right would remove it from a woman's embodied existence and feminine acts. The struggle to vote as an embodied woman, not as a universal claimant symbolically engaging in voting, has played out in slow time. Although "throwing like a girl" has become an anachronism, at least in the United States, voting like a girl is a relatively new phenomenon. Women only began a pattern of voting differently from men in 1980, sixty years after women achieved suffrage.[19] The example of Susan B. Anthony will show that women first learned to vote like men, their only models, and only decades later did they come to vote like girls, with a gender gap and identified women's issues.

Certainly comportment, performativity, practice, and act have been extended to the concept of citizenship. In *Acts of Citizenship*, Engin F. Isin and Greg M. Nielsen analyze the differences between citizenship as formal legal status and as substantive cultural, political, and symbolic practices, such as voting and learning a language. These embodied and located acts of citizenship go beyond legal status to construct the citizens' identity performatively. Observing that substantive practices provide the supporting basis for formal status, they identify the possibility that "acts of citizenship" break the historic routine and rituals and argue that citizens' acts "disrupt habitus, create new possibilities, claim rights and impose obligations" (10). The acts of citizenship may be ritualistic at first, but they are also formative, as they are "answerable acts" that require interlocutors and constitute citizens, constituents, and rights bearers (9). In being answerable acts, they request dialogue requiring interlocutors and engagement, which both sustains and changes the nature of citizenship.

In arguing for the bodily necessity of voting, I depend on Mahmood's concept of embodied negotiation of norms. Her discussion of embodied virtue among Egyptian women in the mosque movement can be extended to embodied citizenship. Paraphrasing her, I argue that the effective citizen agent does not precede the performance of normative political acts; both her agency and the norms of citizenship depend upon her performances (163). Mahmood characterizes her difference from Butler's insistence on reiterated norms in her understanding of subject formation, arguing that reiterative performances build on previous performances and participants scrutinize the performances to see if, in fact, the acts do take hold and constitute a new disposition, both of character and body. Evading the true difficulty of founding a relationship between the speech act and the body, a relationship Butler calls "chiasmus" (Butler and Connolly), Mahmood pragmatically follows the lead of the women whom she studies, women who treat the body as a medium rather than an object or an identity. Mahmood argues that women in Egypt's mosque movement literally re-tutor their bodies rather than depend on destabilizing signification practices. Similarly, I observe that with such reeducation, U.S. women deal deeply with their comportment, motility, and spatiality to create a new lifeworld. Changing the significance of the vote was not only a change in performative utterance as in we and man, but also a change in acts of deportment and performance.

Again, women's suffrage demanded changing citizenship both in formal legal status and in cultural, political, and symbolic practices. For the marginalized citizen agent to achieve rights denied by the state, she must create both rights covenants and herself as a subject of rights, working through the paradoxical acts within original documents to reiterate and negotiate new arguments. Her ability to participate and perform speech and physical acts of citizenship alters her subjectivity and that of her interlocutors. From the first twenty-four years of the suffrage campaign, let's analyze two moments that demonstrate the nature of performativity, the place of bodies, and the initiating of rights practices in deliberations. In *Feminism and Suffrage*, Ellen DuBois argues that demands for votes made by nineteenth-century women in the United States and their massive organizing efforts—women's suffrage—were radical, even more so than abolition, arising on a world stage where women had not spoken in public, owned property after marriage, or voted. If, by the mid-nineteenth century, women achieved recognition for a few civil and moral rights, they still were denied political rights and agency, unrecognized as independent political subjects or citizens, and even deemed incapable of self-ownership.[20] The radicalism of suffrage renamed male authority as tyranny and required women to demand self-ownership by developing political skills and sensibilities through the performance of political acts, from conventions, speeches, legal changes, running for office (from Congress to the presidency), and voting, illegally and legally. The seventy-three-year-long U.S. suffrage movement supported these acts as women developed political rhetorics, networks, public forums, and subjectivities that enabled them to shape the nation's understanding of women's rights.

Although this chapter emphasizes *action and agitation* over *organization*, organization and friendship networks dominate the scholarly discussion of suffrage perhaps because they are in keeping with feminized visions of talking and nurturing social networks, but they also can be seen as significant in developing the in-between and inter-est as the shared agency among a people who had given only limited form and voice of their oppression prior to the middle of the nineteenth century. Certainly individuals, such as Abigail Adams and Abraham Lincoln, had identified a need for U.S. women's political rights, in keeping with the liberal logic of the American Revolution and the Constitution, but individuals and writings, no matter how analytically or rhetorically astute, do not by themselves create political movements and international changes.[21] As we saw in the discussion of the Declaration of Sentiments, declarations may initiate freedoms beyond the understandings of the initial composers, but their reception and transformation of existing discourses depend on the symbolic work of future agents. When women first organized, they could not speak on their own behalf, but "shrank" from leading the meeting and leading its deliberations, depending on a man to lead

(Stanton, Anthony, and Gage 69). Even so, once women's rights were set in motion—that is, *enacted*—women described the effects of hearing their inter-ests defined, made public, and offered for further action. Western New Yorker Emily Collins narrates what might be described as her finding of an in-between at Seneca Falls and defining her inter-est: "from the earliest dawn of reason, I pined for that freedom of thought and action. . . . But not until that meeting at Seneca Falls in 1848, of the pioneers in the cause, gave this feeling of unrest form and voice, did I take action" (qtd. in DuBois, *Feminism* 48). Inter-est marks the sharedness that shifts pinings to form and voice, and form and voice perform the acts and speech that Arendt defines as political. Collins desires freedom of thought and action, but without a political space to shape form and voice, the desire was prepolitical. Only by finding inter-locutors and inter-ests does Collins enter into action.

Women's political agency, as a public agency in their own interest, comes with the first women's conventions, which created the in-between necessary for the multiple ties of inter-est.[22] Lucretia Mott and Elizabeth Cady Stanton first met at the World Anti-Slavery Convention in London in 1840. Women delegates were not to be seated at this convention, but the political decision of women's participation was debated publicly and recorded. The debate over women as representatives gave a form and voice to the silenced Mott and Stanton. Although Mott and Stanton privately spoke of a women's con-vention there—"we resolved to hold a convention" (Stanton, Anthony, and Gage 68)—it took some eight years of letter writing to find an in-between, a physical and conceptual space where sufficient women might participate in defining inter-ests and developing shared agency. Perhaps encouraged by the passage of New York's Married Women's Property Act and a debated pro-posal for women's suffrage at the New York State Constitutional Convention, both in 1846, they put together a convention in one week in 1848, a revolu-tion initiated by "four ladies, sitting round the tea-table" (68). Approximately ten days later, three hundred met at church in Seneca Falls, New York.

The women at Seneca Falls avoided any drive to consensus, as they were finding the grievances that would create solidarity. They also avoided identifi-cation, that co-opting, controlling gesture. In fact it was repudiated in favor of empathy, an emotion that they understood as necessary for recognition and critical to deliberation. Considering matters of difference, the convention's conveners understood the limits of their standpoint. They wrote in critique of their position, writing that "they had not in their own experience endured the coarser forms of tyranny resulting from unjust laws, or association with immoral and unscrupulous men, but they had souls large enough to feel the wrongs of others, without being scarified in their own flesh" (68). Rather than deny their own material and educational privilege and thus claim to represent the experience of all women—women in factories, in widowed poverty, or embattled with drunken husbands—the women of Seneca Falls make clear that the movement will be founded on shared inter-ests in justice and that its recognition would have unequal reciprocity. They valued differences and did not picture a single image of women's oppression. Although in the list of grievances they assumed the narratable lives of other women, they refused simple identification as a means by which to found a movement. The open convention format was part of this strategy of finding what would create the in-between necessary to a political movement.

The conveners resisted structures that might have precluded what the convention could offer, though of course the convention reiterated earlier structures. Just as the Declaration of Independence informed the Declaration of Sentiments, the "realities of choice and location" limited what could be said, and yet with an open agenda, the convention cracked open a space, what bell hooks has called "a space of radical openness," that radical standpoint on the margin which determines "our response to existing cultural practice and our capacity to envision new, alternative, oppositional aesthetic acts" (145). At the earliest stage of the woman's suffrage movement, as spaces for recognition, response, and deliberative acts, conventions were essential for negotiating the new ideologies of woman's rights (Flexner), training women in public performance, and developing articulate arguments and beliefs to address critics and sway bystanders. Moving beyond the movement's early dependence on Quaker women—women such as the Grimké sisters, Lucretia Mott, and Susan B. Anthony, who were practiced at speaking in meetings—conventions created new leadership, mentorship, and participants where few had dared to stand and speak. The acts of political women called forth further recognition of their narratable selves in new performances of grievance, oppression, politics, and rights.

In the first convention's initial propositions, only one resolution was not unanimously ratified. Suffrage was seen as too radical, and many feared that it would "make the whole movement ridiculous" (Stanton, Anthony, and Gage 73). The response to suffrage in the many ridiculing and denouncing publications, however, had political uses in constituting deliberative engagement. If some of the original hundred signers (sixty-eight women, thirty-two men) withdrew their names in the storm of repudiation and ridicule, the tension between ridicule and support created a national political discourse on suffrage.[23] If the ridicule was mostly vehement response, not all of the response was ridicule, for not even a majority found the convention a farce. Historian Timothy Terpstra examined fifty-eight newspaper articles on Seneca Falls and found that 42 percent opposed, 29 percent responded favorably, and 28 percent reported neutrally (in Wellman 210). Deliberation over women's suffrage had started. If some chose to narrate women as ridiculous, dependent, or gentle, narrations lacking in recognition, reciprocity, and respect, those narrations served the purpose of eliciting a response. As Stanton recorded in her diary much later, on 20 August 1888, "Do all you can, *no matter what*, to get people to think on your reform, and then, if the reform is good, it will come about in due season" (Stanton, Stanton, and Blatch 252). In this backward glance, Stanton presents her acts as outwardly aimed at engaging interlocutors in the consideration of reform (although it is unclear that that was her earliest or only purpose). In the first utterances of suffrage advocates, doing was deemed more important than persuading. In effect, the short-term goal of creating dispute exceeded an elusive goal of persuasion.

Although rhetorical critics sometimes describe Stanton's speeches as persuasive acts addressed to a resisting audience, this was not the nature of the address at Seneca Falls.[24] Later address and declarations often seemed aimed at persuasion. However, to create deliberation—let alone rights and the subjects of rights—where none existed required multiple performative strategies and also required the finding of form, voice, and positions for deliberation. Over time, the textual task shifted from developing ideology, discourses, and arguments. Then the nature of performance shifted from utterance and convention to performing the acts of citizenship, practices beyond public meeting and speaking. The changes coincided with other changes in advocacy, one of which occurred with the passage of the Fourteenth and Fifteenth Amendments, the securing of voting rights for black men and the creation of "a strategic dead end for woman's suffrage" (DuBois, "Women's" 247). These amendments clarified the failure of shared interests between the movements of abolition and woman's suffrage. Prior to the passage of the Fourteenth and Fifteenth Amendments, the movements seemingly had political alliances that benefited both parties at certain spatiotemporal locations, but the sharedness of action and agency implicit within inter-est proved insufficient when one group might move forward without the other. In response to this strategic failure, significant changes in suffrage strategies were required to redefine women's inter-ests, and disagreement about those strategies resulted in a split suffrage movement. Two woman's suffrage organizations formed: the National Women's Suffrage Association, committed to national suffrage, and the American Woman's Suffrage Association, committed to petitioning for suffrage state by state.

Just as the woman's suffrage movement split and changed strategy, this chapter changes strategy, moving from the analysis of paradoxes and interests to the examination of what it means to embody citizenship and rights. It argues that acts of citizens, even if they are illegal and denied, are performances that create the subjects of rights. As women struggled to find new strategies after the Reconstruction amendments' passage, they began to perform acts reserved for citizens. In part, I follow Jules Lobel's argument that legal cases can have success without victory, for "[s]uccess inheres in the creation of a tradition, of a commitment to struggle, of a narrative of resistance that can inspire others similarly to resist" (7). Although the cases discussed here are legal cases (that is, many of them go to court), it is less clear that appearance in court is necessary to their impact. Even press coverage is a success for marginalized voices and minority perspectives. Just as Carol Moseley Braun depended on emotional arguments to formulate a space for legislative action, the acts of running for office and illegal voting formulated a deliberative space from which to visualize legal voting. I further depart from Lobel as I do not consider the political acts of women as resistance, but as normative acts of running for national office and voting. Rather than marking a symbolic right, their acts demonstrated a change in physical and symbolic behavior: more than an infelicitous performance and more than an imaginatively or wrongly executed iteration, women who voted and ran for office performed roles significant to the constituting of events and new practices. In sum, the acts themselves and their publicity created new norms and citizens in dresses, not just for the voters, but for all those who witnessed, aided, and obstructed voting.

Voting begins at the same juncture of women's candidacies for national office. Although the election of women to national office required more generations and involved fewer women, it was another aspect of performing citizen rights even as they were unjustly denied. In 1866 Stanton ran for Congress and received twenty-four votes. Representing the Equal Rights Party, with Fredrick Douglass nominated as her vice president (he refused), Victoria Woodhull announced her candidacy for president in 1870. Though she did not mount a full campaign, she did a year later call for a new constitutional convention if Congress did not grant women full citizen rights, promising treason and revolution to "overthrow this bogus Republic" (qtd. in Lutz 184). With a more developed platform, Belva Lockwood fully ran in

1884, collecting a few thousand votes, and again in 1888, when no votes appear to be recorded.[25] Due to electoral changes, these presidential candidates were the last women to receive votes until 1964, when Margaret Chase Smith ran, but the early performances normalized women's candidacies, leading women to school committees in the 1870s and state legislatures in the 1890s.

Just as running for office was a strategy responding to the Reconstruction amendments, so too is "voting like a girl." Beginning in Vineland, New Jersey, in 1866, almost 200 women cast ballots into voting boxes set aside for women, and the following year, 40 women in Hyde Park, Massachusetts, also voted with symbolic ballots.[26] By 1869, the same year women received the vote in the Wyoming Territory, the married couple Francis and Virginia Minor fully argued that rather than seeking a new constitutional amendment, women should assert their right to vote under the gender-neutral language of the Fourteenth Amendment, claiming voting as a privilege of U.S. citizenship, an argument that Anthony and Stanton distributed in ten thousand copies (Lobel 79). Although the Fifteenth Amendment prohibited denying citizens the right to vote based on "race, color, or previous condition of servitude" (negative rights not including women), the Fourteenth presents a generalized citizen, proven by birth or naturalization, and declares that individual states may not "abridge the privileges or immunities of citizens" without due process. Using the promised rights of the general or universal citizen, a subjectivity to which they were entitled, suffrage advocates argued that they already had the vote, and they proceeded to vote, demonstrating simultaneously both their disenfranchisement and enfranchisement as true citizens and becoming active at the polls and in the courts. Emboldened by earlier performances of symbolic voting, between 1871 and 1872, 150 women in seven states and the District of Columbia attempted to vote. In response to direct voting action, a number of court cases were brought, but the internationally publicized case of Susan B. Anthony provides excellent evidence of how changes in comportment initiated deliberation. Anthony's action, the most embodied of performative deliberation, forced women's issues into the public debate, much as the ridicule of suffrage had twenty-five years earlier. The act demanded deliberative space.

In 1872, Anthony, her three sisters, and 46 other women registered to vote in Rochester, New York. Although many did not vote, worried by the $500 fine, Anthony, her sisters, and 11 other women did (Gurko 251). They successfully exercised the franchise in part because Anthony had promised to pay the legal expenses to the election inspectors if they were charged. In making that most classic performative utterance, the promise, Anthony was able to build on the political rituals of registering and voting to extend appropriate citizenship acts to women. In effect, she refused gendered citizenship, and in doing so, she engaged the inspectors in denying gendered citizenship. With their physical acceptance of registrations and votes, together the inspectors too redefined normal political acts, demonstrated that the ideals of woman's suffrage were viable (or at least not cataclysmic), and forced the consideration of both prior denials and future possibilities.

The cumulative effect of all these voting women normalized women's votes. Although Anthony had not expected to vote and had planned to bring suit against inspectors for their failure to register women or their failure to accept women's votes, the positive actions of the inspectors demonstrated the possibility of women's suffrage, broadened public awareness of and commitments to suffrage, and constituted the inspectors as advocates of women's suffrage. When they were fined $25, money which Anthony had promised to front, two inspectors refused to pay and went to jail, where they were visited by hundreds of neighbors. After a week in jail, President Grant pardoned them (Gurko 254). Inherent in the jailing, visitation, and pardon, citizens performed commitments to suffrage; in addition, their actions, initially radical, became reconstituted as a kind of normal. In becoming normal, these acts engaged others in considering new norms. The in-between broadened from the fifty radical women who initially registered to include officials of the government. In connecting the radicals and the U.S. president in similar abrogation of the law, the relationship between the law and governance was destabilized, opening possibilities for new laws.

Much has been noted about Anthony's case: how she spoke with conviction throughout a sympathetic county, causing a change of venue; how unfairly Justice Hunt conducted the proceedings; how his opinion was written before the trial; how eloquently Anthony spoke in court; how widely covered the case was. What is not widely discussed is how Anthony used her body as a means to make manifest the relationship between citizenship and the vote. By her physical presence in the registry and the voting booth, she constituted and reconstituted the citizen as genderless. Her act of voting became the touchstone of her citizenship and personhood, but it also performed citizenship in a new way. Even before the trial, she argued for a direct correlation within the United States between being a person, being a citizen, and being a voter (Anthony 165). During the trial of the inspectors, she testified, "I presented myself not as a female at all, sir; I presented myself as a citizen of the United States. I was called to the United States ballot box by the

14th amendment, not as a female, but as a citizen, and I went there" (127). In this sentence, she emphasizes the political interpellation to her as a voter and a citizen. In denying her female self twice, she betrays gender performativity, its comportment, motility, and space, constructing herself as citizen whose duty to vote exceeds other forms of identity. Earlier women negotiated political activism and appropriate comportment, often balancing the ethical call to action against the religious definition of women; for example, Alisse Portnoy describes Catharine Beecher's feminine dilemma in participating in the Indian and slave debates. Aided by her articulate Quakerism, Anthony refuses the dilemma and negotiates her agency to vote, not as resistance to religious or state-mandated comportment but as a manipulation of the paradoxes and ambiguities of the Constitution to find an embodied presence with which to act. She fully sees herself as the citizen of civic republicanism, denying any other identity than citizen of the general will, and of course, as she constitutes herself as citizen, she reconstitutes the concept of citizen.

Although it is now a theoretical commonplace to argue that the universal citizen is gendered in the white, male body, in Anthony's time, this was explicitly recognized, not a trope hidden behind the back.[27] Her constitutive move to vote negotiated the world and word as it was figured around her. She manipulated her most contingent of votes into universal suffrage. In effect, she extended specificity and defined position into the universalism—the once strategic, paradoxically composed universalism of the U.S. Constitution re-spoken and re-strategized to attain a new form of citizenship, seemingly consistent in symbol, but radically different in act. To vote, she must be recognized as a citizen, and she could only negotiate that identity through the strategic dismissal of her female body. Discarding the body that carried her to the polls and the courtroom, Anthony gained her legal recognition (if only to appear in the courts). Although it required that she become the generalized other and deny the contingencies of her position, Anthony found that to vote like a girl, she must vote like a citizen. To enter into public deliberation, to act, she performed, to the best of her ability, universalist citizenship, one historically and deeply male. Her willing subjection to gender hierarchy may offend today's ethics, but universalist language created the in-between that in turn created the potential for recognition, although in this case sanction without victory.

In the courtroom, employing a traditional U.S. response to injustice, she spoke of the need to violate wicked laws and the expediency of civil disobedience, pronouncing, "As then, the slaves who got their freedom must take it over, or under, or through the unjust forms of law, precisely so now, must women, to get their right to a voice in this government, take it" (Anthony 84). In this single utterance, she makes three arguments. First, in relating the freedom of escaping slaves to women's votes, she intertwines the familiar value of freedom with the newer value of political equality. Instead of contrasting the values of freedom and equality as contemporary theorists do in hate speech discussions, rather than putting them in dispute, she allies them in their call for the act of taking rights. Second, since the Civil War, slavery had been ruled unjust and illegal, and in allying freedom and equality, slaves and women, she predicts a voting future as well. Justice will prevail, she strategically claims. Third, in violating unjust forms of laws, she emphasizes the forming aspects of legal utterance, even as the law's form is ritualized and seemingly static; she reconceptualizes a forming and reforming resistance, a word she later uses not in negating or reversing a law but in finding a way to exploit its limits. Her act of voting is not to resist or oppose within a binary relationship, but rather to change the discourse from a refusal of suffrage to engagement with the act of suffrage. Although she does resist injustice, rather than finding her agency in resistance, she defines her agency in exploiting the limits of laws. By taking over, under, and through normative laws that unjustly deny voice, Anthony finds voice, demonstrates voice, and achieves a political voice, enacting a new subject position and agency potential, much as Emily Collins had twenty-three years before. As Anthony emphasizes the voice of voting, she simultaneously emphasizes the physical nature of acquiring that voice, first in her example of the running slave and then in the very physical taking of rights in ways that circle and cut through the unjust forms of law.

The strategy of direct action failed to give women immediate suffrage, but between1870 and 1900, women gained the vote in four states and two territories. By 1888, twenty-five thousand women registered to vote in local school elections (Norgren 167). One might understand the wide acceptance of women's right to vote in school elections as both many women's initiation into legal voting and a further expansion of women's private sphere into the public, opening private mothering into political, public mothering. Even though sixty years earlier, the education of women to be teachers had been controversial, by 1888 women's public role in educating children had become integrated into their gendered citizenship.[28] The extension of rights to include employment in elementary education marked women as women, but employment rights and the inherent gender marking were later used to extend rights to include suffrage, though, paradoxically, the limited voting rights still marked women as humans in need of voting rights. Still, in offering ingress into the voting booth, school elections extended the performance of citizenship, and in doing so, they negotiated norms, creating more women as voting citizens and extending their role in the public sphere while giving the appearance of containing them to issues of the private sphere. The movement exploited paradoxes—old-new, rights labeling, political origins, and definitional—to force established discourse and rituals into disputes and finally new permutations. For women and other marginalized citizens, political agency depends on negotiating existing norms as well as creating and transforming public spaces. Women's political agency depended on the interruption of male hegemony. Except for a few, both privileged and exploited, citizenship is not achieved by the bestowal of statutory status but in acts of political participation, the struggle for a particular identity, the performances of civic acts such as voting, paying taxes, partaking in education, and speaking in the public sphere. "Citizen" marks a legal status and a practice (Isin and Nielsen).

A Difference in Kind

The woman's suffrage movement was and is a large, diverse rights movement, and certainly by the 1890s, advocates worldwide understood suffrage as part of an international campaign (Edwards and Roces 1).[29] Although the paths to suffrage, rights, and political voice are multiple, to evaluate the concept of performative deliberation, I want to draw attention to an alternative method of gaining women's rights. In the cases of newly formed Uzbekistan (1924), Communist China (1949), and occupied Japan (1945–52), political space opened for women, but more in the service of authoritarian and/or colonizing states. Women's rights were achieved without performative deliberation, making their achievement a different kind of politics. Yes, justice and literacy, for example, increased dramatically under the rule of rights-mandating states, and literacy fosters economic development and reflective thinking. Still, the meaning of rights and citizen agency are more problematic. Suffrage, or other rights, may be granted by a state or colonial power in ways that bypass indigenous movements, local translations, and what An-Na'im calls *"internal cultural discourse and cross-cultural dialogue"* ("Introduction" 3; emphasis in original). Unlike governmental decree, local deliberative rights work is slow, but it constitutes a subject and culture of rights, building from the national culture and historical contingencies toward sustainable futures. As Adam Przeworski summates, "[i]n a democracy all forces must struggle repeatedly for the realization of their interests. None are protected by virtue of their position" (14). When the state or occupying power grants rights, it is not forming rights or struggle. Rather, it is reforming and reformulating its own interests in ways that bypass the transformative power of performative deliberation. Furthermore, when states grant rights as part of colonialism or a larger political strategy of nation building, they distort or even lie about the significance of rights, molding them to create an illusion of citizen power to the benefit of national sovereignty. The granting of rights may have positive aspects—how enormously difficult to argue against rights!—but when nations grant rights in the service of hegemony, the recognition of the "human" within "human rights" is subsumed under the nation and political coordination. In such a granting, rights may represent illegitimate power enacted without any meaningful reconstitution of the state in relationship to its people, which is the deep concern of theories of deliberative democracy.

State legitimacy depends on performatives, performances, and performativity to defeat monological authoritarianism, which may use rights talk to silence oppositional voices. In the historical examples of Uzbekistan, China, and Japan, in raising the value of women's rights the authoritarian or colonizing state dismissed culturally significant traditions. At least in part, women in newly created Uzbekistan received rights as Communist Russia moved to hinder local Islamic religious forces and develop a national identity where there was none.[30] In China, Mao Zedong proclaimed that women "held up half the sky," and the Communist Party extended women's rights as it diminished Confucianism and traditional family relationships.[31] In Japan, at the end of World War II, Douglas MacArthur gave Japanese women the right to vote in the U.S. effort to sweep out imperial rule.[32] In all of these nations, women's rights advocates had previously been jailed as they struggled to make women into citizens, but it was not the decades of feminist activism that constituted their rights.[33] All three state actions effectively privileged nation building as a self-authorizing act over citizen performance or communicative acts, and although it makes little sense to argue that the state actions were wrong in extending women's rights, they functioned as acts of flawed legitimation and mechanisms to deny citizen agency.[34] First, in granting rights, the nation-state artificially creates for itself a benevolent legitimacy, hiding and belying the authoritarian power implicit in dictating rights. Rather than recognizing citizen initiative and indigenous traditions, the state avoids acts of deliberation over its nature and its sovereignty. Second, in denying dispute and deliberation, it minimizes structures of citizen participation, structures that cultivate agency, making citizen positions irrelevant to governance. In addition to the large structural problem of bypassing citizens and indigenous rights movements, however marginalized, to dictate rights in the service of its own rule, authority, and legitimation, a government's dictation of rights disrupts the formative potential of deliberation itself and denies constituting agency to citizens. When decreed by autocrats or external powers, the vote can represent an imposition of a universal right under a universal rule of democratic law, cloaking a modern strategy of power; in such cases, suffrage stipulates a citizenry committed to the values and legal institutions of the Enlightenment, and in doing so, it transforms the right to resist and dissent into anti-rights. Rights decreed from above and outside fail to recognize citizens as constitutive participants in the struggle for rights, the writing of law, and the legitimacy of deliberation, and thus the state denies the subject of rights as an agent with a narratable life. Instead of creating narratable citizenship, the dictating state creates and sustains a "national fantasy," but not one experienced through time and space (Berlant, *Anatomy* 21). Certainly fantasies are part of the national narratives as ideals and performances necessary for the formation and transformation of national identity. Shifting the balance to fantasy, however, denies citizen agents and their deliberative rights.

As I have argued, along with others who understand the deliberative nature of rights, human rights are not universal, nor are they simply a matter of writing laws; they need local translation and cultural imprint to be enacted by citizens who are agents, capable of navigating as well as resisting norms. Their agency formed in the interplay of their speech acts and their strategic acts, even unto their fictions, lies, and illegal acts, constitutes their political membership. Benhabib rightly notes that political membership "is meaningful only when accompanied by rituals of entry, access, belonging, and privilege" (*Rights* 1). One can practice the rituals infelicitously, as Anthony did, but to be recognized as a member of the political community and to practice politics, one must be embedded in narratives, speeches, lies, rituals, and even physical movements of the culture. Mandated rights—through daily performances and practices—might eventually become culturally embedded rights through repeated performative deliberations, copious with strategy, infelicity, resistance, and paradox, all of which allow the reworking of symbolic rights into rights practices.

Deliberation Without End

The act of voting marks an end to persuasion, reasoned argument, procedure, and deliberation, or so some would say. Anthony's vote clarifies that voting itself is not an end; her case demonstrates that even the ritual act of voting can push at the edges of performance, performatives, and performativity, showing the vote as simply one act in a series of deliberative acts, constituting the citizen in deliberative snapshots. Similarly, at least one critic has called performative deliberation a narrative theory of deliberation, but narration too implies end. Humans like endings. Tragic or happy, endings call to us because ends are partially descriptive of human concerns. Humans have ambitions, motives, desires, wants, needs, and goals leading us forward, but as the accomplishment of our plans repeatedly shows, accomplishment is only a point on the way to more extensive plans. Humans meet even their deaths with visions of paradise and ongoing action.

Deliberative utterances are performed in a moment, but the perlocution of a deliberative act exceeds its locutionary moment, constituting inbetweens, identity, inter-ests, agency, and the event itself. As Oliver Wendell Holmes wrote, "when we are dealing with words that also are a constituent act, like the Constitution of the United States, we must realize that they have called into life a being the development of which could not have been foreseen completely by the most gifted of its begetters" (*Missouri v. Holland*). Even as human acts performed in the present tense, deliberative acts have future consequences as they simultaneously revise our prior understandings of the past. Historical understanding is remade in deliberation. Deliberative time is not sequential, but rather incessant; performative deliberation simultaneously is, will, and was. The deliberative act in the present opens felicitous and infelicitous possibilities of the many becoming action. Although it would not be false to imagine performative deliberation as sharing openness with the nostalgic terms "happening" or "be-in" from the 1960s, the power of its political positions heightens its transformative potential. Looking forward, at action's "burden of irreversibility and unpredictability," Arendt tells us, action has no end; "the process of a single deed can quite literally endure throughout time until mankind itself has come to an end" (*Human* 233). Looking back, performative deliberation strengthens earlier iterations, silences others, causes critical reassessments of historical facts, or ruptures the storyline.

The infinite progression and regression of deliberative acts is alarming, even frightening. It is not just constitutions, public policies, or ideologies that restrain arguments and deliberations; citizens fear the transfiguring power of their actions. If some few do not place their lamps under baskets and deny the burden of action, at least some others anxiously write procedural limits, diminish volatile language, sanctify consensus, demand shared ends (endings), subscribe to ur-narratives, decry political lies, and reduce paradoxes to singularities. Anxiety about the openness and ambiguity of each utterance works against robust and daring performances of deliberative acts and the full embrace of human dignity inherent in rights talk. Through singling out the dynamic nexus of recognition, utterance, and constituting action, performative deliberation presumes to face that anxiety and to examine the burdens and bounties of utterances' irreversibility and unpredictability. In doing so, performative deliberation privileges acts of advocacy while reclaiming the repressed potential of each deliberative utterance. It celebrates the world-making and -remaking force of deliberation. Deliberation without end.

NOTES

INTRODUCTION

1. Moyn dates the increase in journalistic usage from the 1960s, with a surge in 1977 (231).

2. A historical orientation to the Cold War evolution of rights may be found in Baxi; Glendon; Hunt; Koshy; and Moyn.

3. For a larger discussion of representing Afghan women's rights, one might begin with Brodsky as well as Farrell and McDermott.

4. For an initial orientation to the problematic representation of human rights, see Baxi; Bradley and Petro; Cheah; Cubilié; Goldberg; Hesford and Kozol; Keenan; Kiss; Lyon and Olson; Merry; Moeller; Mutua; and Schaffer and Smith.

5. In her treatment of rights traditions, Singer identifies four traditional foundations of rights: individualism, a priorism, essentialism, and adversarialism (claims against another). Singer defines rights as entailing a relationship between an entitlement to a right and an obligation to respect it. By this definition, she rejects earlier traditions.

6. The critique of rights universalism is tellingly massive. One might see An-Na'im; Baxi; Butler (*Precarious Life*); Donnelly; Hua; Kennedy; Koshy; Mahbubani; Mutua; Narayan; Spivak; and Whitlock. Some scholars attempt to modify universalism in mitigating ways. Consider Mailloux's concept of "contingent universals" (*Disciplinary Identities*) or Badiou's discussion of universalism.

7. Korsgaard's *Sources of Normativity*, particularly the introduction, provides a useful discussion of the conceptual history of norms.

8. Mutua argues that the West has framed the discourse of rights in the metaphors of savior, savage, and victim.

9. The Harvard sociologist Steven Pinker has documented a decreasingly violent world and Peter Singer has documented a decrease in world poverty. Pinker posits six trends contributing to the decline in violence: the Pacification Process of transition to agricultural civilization; the Civilizing Process of forming larger kingdoms with centralized authority and commercial infrastructures; the Humanitarian Revolution of the Enlightenment; the Long Peace following World War II, a peace among great powers; a following New Peace of declining war in general; and the Rights Revolution following on the heels of the UDHR. Although all these trends are transformative, both the Enlightenment's Humanitarian Revolution and the Human Rights Revolution require specific changes in how whole societies of humans view each other and come to treat each other as competently human, if not as equals. Beyond political change, they mark changes in relationships and attachments.

10. Despite many humanistic analyses of how human rights are represented and interpreted, extended inquiries into human rights deliberation are limited, though growing. Although none of these examples is directly concerned with deliberative theory, their concern with public discourse and rights rhetoric has varying implications for

deliberative rhetoric. A brief survey of rhetorically oriented work includes publications by Doxtader; Hasian; Hauser; Hesford; Hua; Merry; Lyon and Olson; Patton; Payne; and Royster and Cochran.

11. J. Cohen, Habermas, and Rawls are recognized as laying the core arguments, but deliberative democracy informs much of democratic theory today. For introductions, see Benhabib ("Toward") and Bohman. Also see Barber; Fishkin; and Gutmann and Thompson (*Democracy*).There is a broad range of theorists characterizing themselves as deliberative democrats; some are more inflected by rhetoric or postmodernism. For example, Payne frames her work in deliberative democracy, but she is articulate on the benefits of "contentious coexistence" as a frame for democracy-building practices.

12. Responding to the political limits of epistemic and hermeneutical rhetorics, which dominated the twentieth century, rhetoricians are looking for more contentious forms of rhetorical theory, ones that might rehabilitate contestation. Lynch, George, and Cooper make a compelling argument for a historic response to the academic rhetorics that dominated the twentieth century.

13. Even if Hauser, Eberly, and Wells are more concerned with the public sphere than deliberative democracy, their books represent the depth of Habermas's penetration into rhetoric.

14. For example, Nino examined rights in connection to constitutions and deliberative democracy, but inherent in his connection is a definition of human rights as civil rights guaranteed by constitutional definitions of legitimate state power. Against the failed states, exemplified by Rwanda, Afghanistan, Haiti, or Yugoslavia, deliberative democracy and constitutionalism promote an important stable political and economic order. See also Dworkin; Fox; Franck; Holmes; and Koh and Slye's anthology *Deliberative Democracy and Human Rights*.

15. This book attempts to avoid repeating the arguments between philosophers and rhetoricians, as they are well known and often proceed in caricatures. For some balanced discussions, see Hariman; Kimball; Vickers; and the essays in Connors, Ede, and Lunsford's *Essays on Classical Rhetoric and Modern Discourse*.

16. See Habermas ("Three").

17. Deliberative democracy is criticized as being less concerned with justice and rights and more concerned with deliberation in celebration of democratic process. After all, deliberation can result in unjust action, and while supporters argue that deliberation opens injustice, history, the advantage of elites, and strategies of interest groups to critique (Gutmann and Thompson, *Why* 42), a focus on minority views, identity, historical frames, power differentials, and inequality is missing from discussions of process. Benhabib is an exception (*Situating*).

18. For a lengthy clarification, see Baynes, as well as Hamlin and Pettit's introduction to *The Good Polity*.

19. Gaus provides a robust critique of two of these three.

20. For introductions to his work, see Fultner (*Jürgen Habermas*) and Ingram.

21. His seven-step procedure begins, "Processes of deliberation take place in argumentative form, that is, through the regulated exchange of information and reasons among parties who introduce and critically test proposals." It proceeds to "the interpretation of needs and wants and the change of prepolitical attitudes and preferences" (*Facts* 305–6).

22. The attempt to limit acceptable speech within the *polis* goes back to Plato, who did at least allow allegory and myth (Fontana, Nederman, and Remer 18). The desire for limits asks the question of whether we want an ideal that critiques reality or a model that describes reality.

23. In the last decade, Habermas has recognized embodiment and religious pluralism, writing toward a cosmopolitan democracy. See *Between Naturalism and Religion*.

24. For extended critiques of reason as a means of silencing the margins, see Fraser; Warnke; and Young ("Communication").

25. Given all the contemporary devices of mass appeal and education, it seems strange to try to limit deliberation to reasoning. The move replays the question of whether we want an ideal that critiques reality or a model that describes reality.

26. That is, following Austin, he separates illocutionary effects—what language does—from the perlocutionary effects it has on the hearer. For a fuller description, see Habermas's *Theory of Communicative Action*. Warnke explicates his theory well, as does Fultner.

27. Benhabib repudiates the transcendental nature of Habermas's claim of reason in favor of an "interactive universalism" (*Situating* 30). McCarthy (*Ideals*) argues that rational consensus is not a viable presupposition within practical discourse. Gutmann and Thompson provide for a limited role for rhetoric. J. Cohen, Mansbridge, and Young all argue that deliberation should take place in a wider range of civic and political institutions.

28. In political theory, Chambers carefully extends Habermas's sense of reason. There is more critique in collections such as those by Bohman and Rehg; Fontana, Nederman, and Remer; and Schomberg and Baynes.

29. Madison (62–90) makes this argument in analyzing claims of truth, more fully demonstrating Habermas's line of thinking in *Moral Consciousness and Communicative Action*. In *Situating*, Benhabib responds to Habermas's universalism and offers an alternative of ongoing moral conversation (34–38).

30. Warren makes the telling point that consensus is cognitive, not political, within discourse ethics.

31. There is a long history of trusting popular judgment and diversity within the state. Saxonhouse discusses fear of diversity within classical Athenian texts, but too optimistically concludes that the fear ends with Aristotle. See D. Cohen for an alternative view of Aristotle, where Aristotle too fears diversity and seeks to contain it as well as the popular will.

32. Benhabib ("Sexual"), Gardner, Heller, Madison, McCarthy, Moon, and Wellmer also argue against the value of consensus. See Markell for a more positive reading of Habermas and consensus, although in the end he is dismissive of contemporary concerns with dissensus.

33. McCarthy's "On Reconciling" lucidly draws out the implications of convergence in Charles Taylor, Immanuel Kant, and Habermas.

34. See Madison for an extended discussion. Deveaux also makes this argument more fully (150–54).

35. Seyla Benhabib and Nancy Fraser articulate this critique more fully in Benhabib et al., *Feminist Contentions*. See also Young (*Justice*).

36. McCarthy makes a similar point.

37. Ober and Saxonhouse separately develop the work of dissent within Athenian democracy.

38. See also "Social Difference as a Political Resource" in her *Inclusion and Democracy*.

39. In "Democracy and Foreignness," Honig discusses tensions around contradictory myths of the U.S. immigrant, who is both a danger and a source of renewal. With less particularity we can see the tension in discussions of difference.

CHAPTER I

1. Certainly there are other translations of Aristotle, even more rhetorically based translations. Roberts's translation of *Rhetoric*, a very common translation, was chosen

for its succinct emphasis on action itself rather than the more focused acts of exhorting and dissuading.

2. If one returns to the first recorded dialogues of Athenian deliberators, be they the reasonable soldiers or dogmatic elites in *Antigone* or Socrates and his unsuccessful interlocutors, one can see how their performances exceed a description based only in persuasion: single speakers are rarely so powerful as to convince others, a hopeful future is not guaranteed in winning an argument or achieving an end, and even cultural commonplaces are not a given. In *The Fragility of Goodness*, Nussbaum's interpretation of *Antigone* highlights many of the problems with deliberative theory as it exists and suggests some of the limitations of persuasion. If Creon is flawed in his refusal to deliberate, recognize opposition's side, and negotiate the conflicting values of familial piety and civic obedience, Antigone too refuses to deliberate, to open herself up to deliberating by any definition, even with her sister. They are tragic not because they do not persuade each other, and not because their strategies are inadequate, but because they consider only their own ends, because they refuse to think on both sides, because they righteously rant at an unyielding audience and do not engage each other as interlocutors. They fail to recognize.

Nussbaum draws our attention to successful deliberators, too. As she writes the common soldier, "cowardly, crudely egoistic," models "ordinary practical deliberation," pacing back and forth as he considers two sides, "two unpleasant alternatives" (53). She also discusses Tiresias and Haemon on the significance of responsiveness to others and the world.

3. For discussion of the difference between classical and modern democracy, one might start with Arendt (*Human*); Robinson; and Yunis.

4. This is not unlike Protagoras's position in Plato's *Protagoras*, a position only slightly modified by Socrates. Yunis argues this sensibility was widely accepted in Athens; see 28–32.

5. Wardy discusses Aristotle's "epistemological optimism," but he notes textual contradictions.

6. Garver provides a good example of a contemporary Aristotelian who sees deliberation as concerned with means.

7. In the early efforts to recover the rhetorical theory of classical China, scholars struggled with translating "rhetoric." From a very early focus on *bian* (argue, debate) as the term that most closely approximates "rhetoric" between 500 and 200 B.C.E., through the acceptance of multiple terms including *shuo* (explain, speak), *shui* (speak effectively, convince), *quan* (urge), *jian* (remonstrate), *ming* (name, dialectics), *yue* (speak), *ci* (speech), and *yan* (say, language), comparative rhetorical studies has been concerned with identifying the Chinese words that approximate Western concerns and developing "a language of ambiguous similarity" (Lu 91–93). A language of similarity, however, focuses on cultural commonality and does not access what lies beyond similitude.

8. Han Feizi addresses persuasion explicitly, though as a very dangerous undertaking. See Lyon ("Rhetorical Authority").

9. See Lyon ("Confucian Silence") for further discussion on the deliberative implications of Confucius.

10. I make this point at length in "Confucian Silence."

11. For connections between feminist care ethics and Confucius, see C. Li's "Confucian Concept of Jen" and responses by Star, Yuan, and Li in *Hypatia*. Consider Luo for a recent discussion of their relationship.

12. Lynch, George, and Cooper protest argumentative theory's move to epistemic and hermeneutical concerns rather than full engagement in arenas where writers have stakes, and they provide an argument for "agonistic inquiry and confrontational

cooperation," which have demonstrable pedagogical use. It is unclear that their model offers a significantly better approach in the political realm.

13. Among the many positive readers of Confucius on democracy are Hall and Ames; Kent; and Tu.

14. Ames, Jullien, Lyon ("'Why'"), and Yu have written about the philological evolution of *shi* in ways helpful to thinking about deliberation.

15. Saussy criticizes Jullien's attention to differentiate as a Western tendency to transform "'the other' into 'our other'" and draws attention to the difficulty of ever dealing adequately with another culture's vocabulary (112). In my use here, I am careful to outline related Western concepts to minimize the othering inherent in comparative work.

16. Butler (*Giving*); hooks; Jarratt; Lynch, George, and Cooper; Mouffe; and Weir also are quite clear on the necessity and constituting force of conflict. Jarratt, in particular, emphasizes how disputation, not wrangling, is constitutive because it depends on the "ability to move into different positions" (120).

17. For a few examples that include rights and recognition in their titles, see Düttmann's *Between Cultures: Tensions in the Struggles for Recognition*; Schaffer and Smith's *Human Rights and Narrated Lives: The Ethics of Recognition*; Hesford's *Spectacular Rhetorics: Human Rights Visions, Recognitions, Feminisms*; and Fiore and Nelson's *Recognition, Responsibility, and Rights: Feminist Ethics and Social Theory*. Oliver's work also follows this line of inquiry.

18. See Baxi; Boltanski; Butler (*Giving*); Fanon; Foucault; Fraser; Honneth; and Mutua.

19. I thank an anonymous reviewer for the distinction between recognition as a condition of possibility and actual performance. Although s/he asked it of my later discussion of Arendt, I decided to develop the significance of recognition as act earlier in the discussion.

20. For more nuanced discussions of intersectionality as it pertains to rhetoric and communication, see Chávez and Griffin's edited volume *Standing in the Intersection*.

21. Oliver discusses the reflexive nature of subjectivity/identity specifically in relationship to rights, as does Butler (*Giving*) and Hesford. Recognition of another is commonly considered part of recognizing oneself in a Hegelian dialectic of same and different.

22. Space, described through the metaphor of the inclusive, diverse city, becomes a defining term in Young's political theory; it is where citizens meet and know each other.

23. Connolly mourns how the time of democracy is out of synchronization with the contemporary pace of transportation, entertainment, culture, and communication. Although he does not directly address deliberation, the issues of fragile democracy and the politics of becoming are indirectly part of understanding what happens in the deliberative present. Democracy cannot progress quickly because its deliberating citizens are required to change, a complex and rarely rapid evolution.

24. Arendt writes that power and violence are distinct. Absolute power needs no violence; absolute violence needs no power (*Violence* 52–53).

25. Consensus is criticized specifically by Arendt in *Men* (31) and *Jew* (182).

26. In her redefining of identification as reciprocal and transformative, Weir argues that identification ("our solidarities") shapes the identities in which we participate. Identification so understood implies agency in constituting our identity (111).

27. What it explains may be the negative, controlling, monolithic side of identity politics and not the productive and inescapable capacity within identity politics. As Appiah writes, "I count seven different ways in which I've said that you might speak of 'identity politics.' (1) There are political conflicts about who's in and who's out. (2) Politicians can mobilize identities. (3) States can treat people of distinct identities differently. (4) People can pursue a politics of recognition. (5) There can be a social micropolitics enforcing

norms of identification. (6) There are inherently political identities like party identifications. And (7) social groups can mobilize to respond collectively to all of the above.
Maybe it's not so surprising then that, as I said at the start, I'm never quite sure what
people mean when they talk about identity politics" (22). In the end all politics are identity politics.

28. Hesford warns of the power of identification to promote and maintain the monologue of the powerful, observing that "those in positions of privilege need to be careful
not simply to celebrate difference in a way that recenters themselves" (*Spectacular* 199).
Her particular instance is the 2001 unveiling of the Afghan feminist Zoya by Oprah
Winfrey, a performance that recenters Western values and performers—tellingly, before
a performance of Eve Ensler's *Vagina Monologues*.

29. Any number of theorists (Weir and Mouffe come to mind) have discussed the
relationship between identity and identification, arguing that identity is constituted
through acts or practices of identification. Burke does not make such a simple connection, and he does not end there, as so well exemplified in Anderson's significant exploration of constitutive rhetoric, *Identity's Strategy*. Despite a fair amount of writing on both
identification and identity, Burke only speculates about identity. I will return to this topic
in the next chapter.

30. For a discussion of the dialectical nature of Burke's inquiries, see Brummett;
Crusius; Wess; and Zappen.

31. In critique of his glib binary, Davis aptly argues that identification precedes division biologically, emotionally, and socially (24–27), but within Burke's political and rhetorical realms, they function dialectically.

32. At one point, Burke echoes an Aristotelian optimism about the powerful ends of
deliberation, seeking a means by which "the various voices, in mutually correcting one
another, will lead toward a position better than any one singly" (qtd. in Zappen 296).

33. As Wess wryly observes, Burke dissolves the ideological individual into the complexity of identifications (189–90). Political uniqueness falls to the side, and agency,
even motive, is hard to separate from forces of identification. In *Regulating Aversion*,
Brown critiques Freud's concept of identification, arguing that Freud places identification in love and desire, conceiving of group enthrallment (identification) as regressive
from rationality and conscience, and hence dangerous. Davis differentiates Burke's and
Freud's conceptions of identification. She approves of Burke's response to Freud; rather
than seeing identification as Oedipal, Burke understands identification as social and
persuasive.

CHAPTER 2

1. In conversation, Carine Mardorossian pointed out that when Neda Agha-Soltan
died in Iran, many women made claims that "I am Neda." With even more pathology
than identification with rape, these women identified with death, clearly even further
from their experiences. In both cases, the claim of identification obscures any real recognition of difference.

2. Ebert provides a telling materialist critique of the limits of postmodernist feminists. Both Noland and Mahmood extend postmodern theory to address the limits of
agency.

3. Miller provides an overview of some of the extensions.

4. Many scholars have used Burke to address the limits of postmodernism. For a
range of approaches, consider Blakesley; Crusius; Gunn; Henderson; Lentricchia; Lyon
(*Intentions*); Southwell; and Wess.

5. The difficulty of poems and jokes, even his own, troubles Austin; he later writes, "If the poet says 'Go and catch a falling star' or whatever it may be, he doesn't seriously issue an order" (*Philosophical* 241). Of course, Austin is criticized for finding so much of language lacking in seriousness. A poet (John Donne?) might respond that he does issue an order, but given the rarity and heat of falling stars, the nature of that order is provocative, upsetting, and richly ambiguous, but deeply serious.

6. "Performative Utterances" and several of the other essays in Austin's *Philosophical Papers* provide a richer sense of his pragmatism, his disinterest in cracking the "crib of reality" (241), and his chagrin at the simplicity of philosophers, their "occupational disease" (252).

7. Another example of his earliest structuralism: in *Counter-Statement* (1931), his chapter "Lexicon Rhetoricae" attempts to codify effectiveness in literature.

8. Hawhee is particularly helpful on Burke's multiple approaches to the body as she examines Burke's quest to conceive the body as more than reason's other. She examines Burke's reading of other theorists in his quest to understand the body in physical and symbolic space.

9. Burke does not make significant statements about identity. He even goes so far as to write, "Identity itself is a 'mystification'" (*Philosophy* 308).

10. I must note here that Charles Taylor approaches the identity problem differently, reconceiving what as a where and returning to the arguments of position. Of the question "Who am I?" he writes, "this can't necessarily be answered by giving name and genealogy. What does answer this question for us is an understanding of what is of crucial importance to us. To know who I am is a species of knowing where I stand" (27). His argument could effectively be included in the last chapter's discussion of position, and it bolsters the argument against what questions, but beyond those two additions, it does not further performative deliberation across difference.

11. Moruzzi makes telling connections between Arendt's fear of bodily need and Kristeva's concept of abjection. Even so, Arendt fully acknowledges the body as part of thinking and acting (*Life* 32, 34).

12. Birmingham is quite detailed on the relationship between natality and human rights. This particular relationship is not the primary direction of my argument, but she is useful in framing a perspective with some parallel implications.

13. Burke offers us a citizen agent, but one whose agency is shared by the forces of the other dramatic terms, act, purpose, and scene. In a particularly clear moment of exposition, Burke argues that "men are capable of but *partial* acts, acts that but partially represent themselves and but partially conform to their scenes" (*Grammar* 83).

14. Cavarero uses this concept rather than that of "the individual," in part, as a critique of individualistic theory, which is either competitive or concerned with equality and individual rights. Cavarero's project, like Arendt's, is concerned with preserving communitarian aspects of politics as identity and agency are preserved.

15. Schaffer and Smith, focusing particularly on Korean comfort women, are articulate on the force of ur-narratives in human rights witnessing.

16. Noland carefully follows Butler's ambiguities in discussing the relationship between body and discourse, particularly interrogating the tension between discursive acts and physical acts ("acts, gestures and behaviors"); see particularly 175–78. Magnus reads the development of Butler's theory of subject and restricted agency more sympathetically. Although later Butler acknowledges the possibility of bodies and explores more ground for agency, she remains wedded to discursive formations in ways that deny physical experience and offer a subjected subject.

17. In her 2003 Adorno Lectures, Butler rejects Arendt's and Cavarero's theories of distinction and argues that recognition entails social and linguistic laws, laws overarching

and framing two consciousnesses, and so exchanges are mediated by discourses, conventions, and norms (see also *Giving* 34–35). I do not find her argument compelling, as the existence of discourses, conventions, and norms does not preclude two located and temporal consciousnesses negotiating among these limits. See Magnus for an extended discussion.

18. Kottman explicitly critiques this position in his introduction to Cavarero (xii–xiii) and, as discussed later, Butler clarifies her position (*Giving* 53).

19. For fuller discussion of the paradox of subjection, see Burke (*Grammar* 40–41), Foucault (*Power/Knowledge*), and Butler (*Bodies*).

20. Invention here is rhetorical invention, finding the available means of forming new discourses to sway others.

21. Nelson argues that personal identity, a conception formed through self and other interactions, informs one's ability to act. Oppression damages identity through the harms of deprivation of opportunity and infiltrated consciousness. Hence it reduces moral agency.

22. See my articles on Han Feizi and Daoism for discussions of alternative rhetorics.

23. Mutua sees the savage, victim, savior metaphor as benefiting the West, but on occasion, its assumptions pragmatically benefit the victims in soliciting support. Advocacy is not ethically pure, as it solicits advocates, resources, and recognitions.

CHAPTER 3

1. The literature on alternative approaches to human rights is massive. Here are some starting points: An-Na'im ("Introduction"); Nussbaum; Sen; and Walzer.

2. See Zoelle for a discussion of U.S. self-image and its resistance to signing the International Convention on the Elimination of All Forms of Discrimination Against Women.

3. See Arendt (*On Revolution*); Boltanski; Nussbaum (*Upheavals*); and Spelman.

4. When Plato banishes the poets to control the disruption of emotion and Aristotle describes the benefits of catharsis (refinement of emotions), they reveal their relationship to diversity within Athens. Plato desires sameness, while Aristotle rejects such foolish unity and acknowledges diversity as necessary if in need of structuring (Saxonhouse).

5. In *Upheavals*, Nussbaum carefully delineates the origins and implications of pity, compassion, and sympathy. She does not engage empathy, a recent word, though Garber does in her discussion of the relationships among these affects.

6. I come to differentiate the spectacle of suffering, the politics of pity, and the politics of justice through Boltanski's interpretation of Arendt (*Distant Suffering* 3–5).

7. Some might argue for the primacy of other cases, such as genocide or the AIDS pandemic. I would say in response that genocide is a general term, like femicide, and as such is not parallel to the situation of women and girls in particular Asian cultures. AIDS is a disease, not a human rights violation. Certainly there are human rights violations around AIDS (many more socioeconomic than political violations), but the horrible deaths from the disease are not in themselves human rights violations.

8. In the literature on the demographics of missing women, Coale offers a low-end estimate; focusing on specific countries in Asia, he estimates 56.8 million missing in East and South Asia, an enormous problem even by his analysis. Klasen and Wink suggest that, while the absolute number of missing women has increased, the number has fallen as a share of living women ("Missing"). For a full, current discussion of Sen's work on missing women, see *Feminist Economics* 9 (2003).

9. For most of history, China was pronatalist; the cultural emphasis on family, the empire's need for taxes, and the need to fight foreign encroachment created a culture of

early marriage and large families. Discussions of the problems of development and over-population began in the fifties, but only in the seventies did birth control become linked to food and economic policies. Concern for economic development, universal education, nutrition, and environmental degradation argued for controlled population growth, a push that contradicted tradition. In the effort to control fertility, there has been violence, but to understand the policy, one needs context.

10. Presidents Reagan, George H. W. Bush, and George W. Bush used China's human rights violations around birth planning to withdraw from the UN Population Fund. See Crane and Finkle.

11. It is beyond the scope of this chapter to provide an introduction to Chinese traditions of human rights and rhetoric. Good orientation materials are Lu's *Rhetoric in Ancient China*, de Bary and Tu's *Confucianism and Human Rights*, and Lyon's "Confucian Silence."

12. Some see these representations as part of the agenda of conservative antiabortion forces who certainly affect our international policies; Kristof discusses this, though he doesn't blame them. I see the focus on China's one-child policy as benefiting the religious right without being caused by the religious right. After all, female fetuses are aborted throughout Asia.

13. For a discussion of the limits of American visions of China, see Mann. Tien and Nathan offer an overview of why we have such ambivalence in envisioning China.

14. The earlier rates are from Scharping; the 2011 rate of 1.5 is a common estimate, lower than that of China's National Population and Family Planning Commission's rate of 1.7–1.8.

15. The United Nations Economic and Social Commission of Asia and the Pacific has an excellent website that demonstrates the different demographics by province (www.unescap.org/pop/database/chinadata/intro.htm). Lavely provides an analysis of China's 2000 census.

16. I have to wonder at the translation "peasant" here. Sinologists usually refer to "farmers"; the term "peasants" describes people under European feudalism, not China's tradition, and is not used for current agricultural workers. According to the article, the woman stands next to "an imposing government office building," selling soda and toys from a stand. This is just another misrepresentation of China by the West, but it is outside the purview of my chapter.

17. In another article, "Bush vs. Women," Kristof describes the conditions of Aisha Idris in Sudan; Mariam Karega, nursing her dying baby in Tanzania; and Sriy, a thirteen-year-old Cambodian prostitute dying of AIDS. Again their lives are linked to China's policies, and indirectly, China becomes responsible.

18. See Modleski and Walker for good discussions of women's magazines and popular culture.

19. Even beyond the novel, some argue that narrative is the basis of emotion and our compassion for others. In *Upheavals*, Nussbaum would have us understand the historical, experiential, and social development of our emotions and emotional responses. She argues that tragedies hone emotions toward characters, implied authors, and one's own possibilities, as they provide emotional delight at understanding something new about the world or oneself (272). Aristotle would have us learn proper responses and social norms from tragedy, but Nussbaum sees art, particularly diachronic art, as shaping human possibility.

20. Arendt has two views of the public realm. It can be a space of amoral and political greatness where heroism and preeminence are revealed, displayed, shared with others (*Human* 22–78) or associational public space where "men act together in concert" and "where freedom can appear" (*Past and Future* 4) .

CHAPTER 4

1. Truth, of course, has been a conceptual problem at least since the beginning of the twentieth century. Long before its critique by figures such as Foucault and Derrida, science struggled with Heisenberg's uncertainty principle and Einstein's theory of relativity.

2. Unlike a moral rule that requires adherence to truth, I am gesturing toward Confucian and feminist care evidence, more fully discussed in chapter 1, particularly in note 12. See Luo for a recent discussion of their relationship. If, within rhetoric and politics, the morality of lies is not rule bound but concerned the preservation of community values and cultural, gender, and personal identity, then the criteria for assessing utterances shift to affiliation and association.

3. The literature on the ethics of lying is large. One might begin with Bailey's sophistic *The Prevalence of Deceit*, continue on to Bok's practical ethics in *Lying*, and finish with Carson's *Lying and Deception*, which holds honesty as a cardinal virtue.

4. Ken Dauber reminded me to consider Austin in understanding the felicity of lies.

5. Any number of scholars have turned to Arendt to understand lies. In addition to my discussion, one might consider Derrida's "'Parjune'" or Jay's "Ambivalent Virtues."

6. Burke wrote, "rhetoric is par excellence the region of the Scramble, of insult and injury, bickering, squabbling, malice and the lie, cloaked malice and the subsidized lie" as well as "evangelical love" (*Rhetoric of Motives* 19).

7. Arendt uses "a lying world order" in "Truth" (257), but she first used it in "Seeds" (145).

8. As Arendt writes, total lying can only happen if one can "kill all of his contemporaries and wield power over the libraries and archives of all countries of the earth" ("Lying" 13).

9. For an orientation to rhetorical witnessing, see Arabella Lyon and Lester Olson's special issue of *Rhetoric Society Quarterly*.

10. For a basic orientation to this claim as made in rhetoric, see Gilmore (*Autobiographies* and *Limits*); Hesford; Merry; and Schaffer and Smith.

11. Carey-Webb provides a detailed account of what Stoll found inaccurate, what Menchú replied, and what the final assessment was.

12. Avant-Mier and Hasian provide an extensive review of the controversy.

13. Arias's *Rigoberta Menchú Controversy* documents a handful of Latino journalists and a very few Western academics who say that she lied.

14. While I developed a book-length rhetorical theory of intention, *Intentions: Negotiated, Contested, and Ignored*, there are other complex, social approaches to intentionality within the humanities. Hancher considers authorial intentions as consisting of a generic or *programmatic* intention to use a particular form, an *active* intention to be understood by an audience to be acting in a particular way, and a *final* or perlocutionary intention to achieve an effect. Though it is helpful to understand the triadic nature of authorial intention, Hancher's focus on the author is too reductive for our contemporary understanding of speech acts and the subject. That is, Hancher is not dialogic enough to inform deliberative theory,

15. Lovell and Lutz discuss four sixteenth-century modes of testimony, classifying Menchú's work as *memorias*, which seek to draw attention to broad claims of grievance.

16. Ferman usefully distinguishes between textual truth, historical truth, and media truth. Although I do not make use of her taxonomy, I do find it an interesting way to approach life writing through different truth criteria than history or the media.

17. Gilmore's "Jurisdictions" examines the requirements of some courtrooms that would judge Menchú's narrative inadequate, but notes that the International Court of the Hague allowed similar information to be admitted (704).

18. Stoll seems to be alone in considering her agency. Some of his accusations consider details disconnected from a communal "we"—details such as whether Menchú was literate, a Marxist, or a maid—and these raise more questions. How far do her culturally based motives limit her discursive possibilities? Are her culture's assumptions about witnessing inadequate to and uncontaminated by legal requirements established in the developed world? I think a case could be made for Stoll alone recognizing her political purpose, integrity, and agency, but in fact a number of scholars question Stoll's purpose and integrity in exposing Menchú (Sklodowska; C. Smith; Sommer, "Las Casas's"). His agency is not in question.

19. Beverley (*Subalternity*), Sklodowska, and Sommer ("Sacred") all reference Spivak and connect a Nobel Peace Prize winner to the silenced subaltern.

CHAPTER 5

1. Little is known about the farmwives who drafted the petition, but Cogan and Ginzberg contextualize the document, suggesting the sources that informed middle-aged women at the kitchen table.

2. A number of scholars have discussed political paradoxes. In addition to in-text citations, this project was influenced particularly by the concerns of Altman; Fiss; Hunt; Meiklejohn ("First"); and Slaughter.

3. In addition to Honig and Mouffe, see Hauser; Hesford; Ignatieff; and Slaughter.

4. Others, such as Arendt (*Origins*) and Žižek, discuss the paradox as it relates to the refugee, whose paradox is that human rights are denied to the human stripped of a nation. Donnelly discusses the paradox of a right being most valuable when a subject doesn't have that right.

5. Although a discussion of what particulars were and are needed for Libyan liberation is beyond this inquiry, it still is worth noting the significance of the concrete other as a political force. Whether the concrete other is an advocate, like al-Obeidi, or a character in a novel, like Tan's Suyuan, has implications for the construction of audience or interlocutor, but in either case, the articulation of a need or injury rewrites the injuries.

6. Honig discusses the paradox of constitutional democracy, where the constitution represents a law-rule that, by means of the concept of self-rule, constrains the people and their democracy. In brief, it encapsulates "the conflict between freedom and rule" (*Emergency* 28). Burke considers the linguistic paradox of "constitution," a paradox not particularly useful to the analysis at hand.

7. Holmes discusses a less definitional paradox within democratic constitutions: They guarantee the freedom of democratic decisions as they precommit citizens to certain procedures, rules, and boundaries.

8. Burke's analysis of "constitution" has been receiving more attention in recent years; Wess provides the most extensive reading. Anderson and Clark have also engaged the last third of the *Grammar*.

9. MacKinnon's privileging of equality in defining the limits of speech and representations has withstood court challenges in Canada and India, unlike the U.S. cases in Indiana and Minnesota.

10. Aristotle's *Rhetoric* argues that truth and justice are stronger than other forces and will win out. John Milton's *Areopagitica* (1644) and John Stuart Mill's *On Liberty* (1859) are early advocates of freedom of press in the service of truth and justice's victory. Meiklejohn articulated the relationship between citizenry and freedom of speech in the 1950s. Shiffman is quite telling in his critique of speech's eventually leading to justice, a position implicit in the work of Barber; Fishkin; and Gutmann and Thompson (*Democracy*). Speech alone does not eradicate evil.

11. The UDHR also has a free speech clause. Article 19 reads, "Everyone has the right to freedom of opinion and expression; the right includes freedom to hold opinions without interference and to seek, receive and impart information and ideas through any media and regardless of frontiers." While the clause avoids the First Amendment's difficulty with defining speech, as this essay's argument will show, there are aspects of this clause as open to deliberation through internal paradox.

12. Meiklejohn provides a continuum of interpretations from absolutists (though none are close to absolute) and balancers (though what is being balanced remains unclear) ("First").

13. This argument is in Rousseau's *Social Contract*. The "we" of the Declaration of Independence and the first paragraph of the Constitution discuss responsibilities for self-control. Certainly this is Martin Luther King Jr.'s argument in "Letter from Birmingham Jail."

14. Meiklejohn is also concerned with the paradoxical nature of the amendment. He describes the tension between statements regarding the Congress's ability to regulate citizens and statements demanding no abridgment of freedom ("First" 257–63).

15. The fifth broad meaning sees "of" as "indicating the agent or doer." "Eaten of worms," "warned of God" (Acts 12:23/Matt. 2:12). Freedom of speech. Yes, of course, "freedom" is not a passive verb like "eaten" or "warned." What a horrid slip to mix freedom with passivity! Still, the agency inherent in "of" should be obvious by now. Increasingly, from this perspective, speech bears and bares the weight of freedom, and freedom becomes the responsibility of speech. Speech is not guaranteed as a freedom, but is responsible, a guarantor for freedom, even indicating its "means" (VI), what freedom feeds off (VI.17.b), or what it is made of (VII).

16. Candidates for speech genres not creating freedom include hate speech, obscenity, fighting words, and pornography.

17. Speech is sometimes differentiated from conduct, perhaps most tellingly in Hugo Black's absolutist approach. Lists of what does not count as speech are sometimes developed (calling fire in a crowded theater, fighting words, lying under oath, inciting riot, libel, obscenity, and so on).

18. Wellman provides a good overview of the eighteen grievances (199–201). Although the number of grievances was the same, the nature of those grievances was different. Wellman breaks them into four categories: civil and political rights; legal discrimination; rights in work, education, and the church; and the values that supported woman's oppression.

19. The gender gap, the difference in the percentage of men and women supporting a candidate, is about 10 percent nationally in the United States. It is worth noting as well that women have voted in greater numbers than men in every election since 1964 and in higher rates since 1980 (see Center for American Women and Politics).

20. McMillen provides a careful analysis of the material and political context that fostered the rise of suffrage.

21. Wellman provides excellent background materials.

22. Women had created movements and engaged in politics in a number of ways that did not directly address their status earlier. See Portnoy and Wellman for histories of protofeminism in the new republic.

23. Stanton is quite clear about the backlash against suffrage. Even her own father worried about her sanity (*Eighty Years*).

24. See Campbell, Engbers, and Skinnell for discussions of Stanton's rhetoric.

25. For more details on their candidacies and exceptional lives, I recommend Goldsmith's biography of Woodhull and Norgren's biography of Lockwood.

26. New Jersey had allowed women to vote from 1776 to 1806, closing suffrage to women in response to a particular case but also in response to less revolutionary times.

Still, this is an important footnote as we consider the possibility of women's voting. Its early practice was meaningful in imagining later demands.

27. One might examine Benhabib (*Rights; Cosmopolitanism*); Berlant (*Cruel*); Grewal and Kaplan; Hesford; Hua; and Ong for elaborated discussions of the gendered and raced citizen.

28. Although focusing primarily on Catharine Beecher's work, Portnoy discusses the movement to educate women in the 1830s (186–93).

29. Good surveys that examine global issues of suffrage include Edwards and Roces; Fletcher, Mayhall, and Levine; Rupp; and a special issue of *Pacific Historical Review*, edited by DuBois and Cherny.

30. See Kamp.

31. See Edwards, "Chinese Women's Campaigns" and "Woman's Suffrage."

32. See Molony.

33. The routes to suffrage are many. As Edwards demonstrates so well, Chinese women's fight for the vote was linked closely to movements for modernization and nationalism, sometimes overlapping competing visions, such as the Communist and Nationalist ideologies. This path is different from that of the United States; despite the threat to modernism and the nation state played out in the Civil War, the seventy-year movement to suffrage was often opposed to the national state. Since Uzbekistan was a state created by the Soviet Union, the women's movement was involved in imagining a state, part of creating the "national fantasy" (Berlant).

34. In this discussion, I bypass developing the particulars of each culture's earlier rights histories. Certainly early struggle affected the ability and success of the state to decree rights. For instance, Chinese feminists were active decades before Mao Zedong asserted that women "held up half the sky." They stormed the Republic of China's parliament in 1912, demanding women's suffrage; in 1921, women who staged a similar protest in a provincial parliament in Guangdong were attacked and wounded (Edwards and Roces 1). Although his granting of legal rights, such as to education and marriage choice, helped women, they did not end ongoing struggles into this century over these rights, as the culture had not deliberatedand decided.

WORKS CITED

Abizadeh, Arash. "The Passions of the Wise: *Phronêsis*, Rhetoric, and Aristotle's Passion-ate Practical Deliberation." *The Review of Metaphysics* 56 (2002): 267–96. Print.

Alcoff, Linda. "Cultural Feminism Versus Poststructuralism: The Identity Crisis in Fem-inist Theory." *Signs: Journal of Women in Culture and Society* 13.3 (1988): 405–36. Print.

———. "The Problem of Speaking for Others." *Cultural Critique* 20 (1991): 5–32. Print.

al-Obeidi, Eman. "Eman al-Obeidi to Anderson Cooper (Complete)." [CNN interview from 4 April 2011.] *YouTube*. Web. 27 April 2011.

Altman, Andrew. "Equality and Expression: The Radical Paradox." *Social Philosophy and Policy* 21.2 (2004): 1–22. Web. 3 May 2009.

Ames, Roger T. *The Art of Rulership: A Study of Ancient Chinese Political Thought*. Hono-lulu: U of Hawai'i P, 1983. Print.

Anderson, Benedict. *Imagined Communities: Reflections on the Origin and Spread of Nationalism*. London: Verso, 2006. Print.

Anderson, Dana. *Identity's Strategy: Rhetorical Selves in Conversion*. Columbia: U of South Carolina P, 2007. Print.

An-Na'im, Abdullahi Ahmed. "Introduction." *Human Rights in Cross-Cultural Perspec-tives: A Quest for Consensus*. Ed. Abdullahi Ahmed An-Na'im. Philadelphia: U of Pennsylvania P, 1992. 1–18. Print.

———. "Toward a Cross-Cultural Approach to Defining International Standards of Human Rights: The Meaning of Cruel, Inhuman, or Degrading Treatment or Punishment." *Human Rights in Cross-Cultural Perspectives: A Quest for Consensus*. Ed. Abdullahi Ahmed An-Na'im. Philadelphia: U of Pennsylvania P, 1992. 19–43. Print.

Anthony, Susan B. *An Account of the Proceedings on the Trial of Susan B. Anthony, on the Charge of Illegal Voting, at the Presidential Election in Nov., 1892, and on the Trial of Beverly W. Jones, Edwin T. Marsh and William B. Hall, the Inspectors of Election by Whom Her Vote Was Received*. Rochester, N.Y.: Daily Democrat and Chronicle Book Print, 1874. Reprint, New York: Arno, 1974. Print.

The Apocrypha; or, Non-canonical Books of the Bible: The King James Version. Ed. Manuel Komroff. New York: Tudor, 1936. Print.

Appiah, Kwame Anthony. "The Politics of Identity." *Daedalus* 135.4 (2006): 15–22. Web. 26 April 2011.

Arendt, Hannah. *Between Past and Future: Eight Exercises in Political Thought*. New York: Penguin, 1954. Print.

———. "The Ex-Communists." *Commonweal* 20 March 1953: 599. Print.

———. *The Human Condition*. Chicago: U of Chicago P, 1958. Print.

———. *The Jew as Pariah: Jewish Identity and Politics in the Modern Age*. Ed. Ron Feld-man. New York: Grove, 1978. Print.

———. *The Life of the Mind*. Vol. 1, *Thinking*. New York: Harcourt Brace Jovanovich, 1971. Print.

———. "Lying in Politics: Reflections on the Pentagon Papers." *Crises of the Republic.* New York: Harcourt Brace Jovanovich, 1972. 1–47. Print.

———. *Men in Dark Times.* New York: Harcourt, Brace and World. 1955. Print.

———. *On Revolution.* New York: Viking, 1963. Print.

———. *The Origins of Totalitarianism.* New York: Harcourt, Brace and World, 1966. Print.

———. "The Seeds of a Fascist International." *Essays in Understanding, 1930–1954.* Ed. Jerome Kohn. New York: Harcourt Brace, 1994. 145. Print.

———. "Truth and Politics." *Between Past and Future: Eight Exercises in Political Thought.* New York: Penguin, 1954. 223–59. Print.

Arias, Arturo. "Authoring Ethnicized Subjects: Rigoberta Menchú and the Performative Production of the Subaltern Self." *PMLA* 116.1 (2001): 75–88. Print.

———, ed. *The Rigoberta Menchú Controversy.* Minneapolis: U of Minnesota P, 2001. Print.

Aristotle. *The Ethics of Aristotle: The Nicomachean Ethics.* Trans. J. A. K. Thomson. New York: Penguin, 1953. Print.

———. *The Politics of Aristotle.* Trans. Ernest Barker. New York: Oxford UP, 1995. Print.

———. *Rhetoric.* Trans. W. Rhys Roberts. New York: Modern Library, 1984. Print.

Atwill, Janet. *Rhetoric Reclaimed: Aristotle and the Liberal Arts Tradition.* Ithaca: Cornell UP, 1998. Print.

Austin, J. L. *How to Do Things with Words.* Cambridge: Harvard UP, 1962. Print.

———. *Philosophical Papers.* New York: Oxford UP, 1961. Print.

Avant-Mier, Roberto, and Marouf A. Hasian, Jr. "Communicating 'Truth': Testimonio, Vernacular Voices, and the Rigoberta Menchú Controversy." *The Communication Review* 11.4 (2008): 323–45. Web. 7 July 2010.

Badiou, Alain. *Saint Paul: The Foundations of Universalism.* Stanford: Stanford UP, 2003 Print.

Baier, Annette. "Why Honesty Is a Hard Virtue." *Identity, Character, and Morality: Essays in Moral Psychology.* Ed. Owen Flanagan and Amélie Oksenberg Rorty. Cambridge: MIT Press, 1990. 259–62. Print.

Bailey, F. G. *The Prevalence of Deceit.* Ithaca: Cornell UP, 1991. Print.

Bakhtin, Mikhail. "Discourse in the Novel." *The Dialogic Imagination: Four Essays.* Ed. Michael Holquist. Trans. Caryl Emerson and Michael Holquist. Austin: U of Texas P, 1981. 259–422. Print.

———. *Problems of Dostoyevsky's Poetics.* Minneapolis: U of Minnesota P, 1984. Print.

Barber, Benjamin. *Strong Democracy: Participatory Politics for a New Age.* Berkeley: U of California P, 1984. Print.

Barlow, Tani. "International Feminism of the Future." *Signs: A Journal of Women in Culture and Society* 25.4 (2000): 1099–105. Print.

Baxi, Upendra. *The Future of Human Rights.* New Delhi: Oxford UP, 2002. Print.

Baynes, Kenneth. *The Normative Grounds of Social Criticism: Kant, Rawls, and Habermas.* Albany: SUNY P, 1992. Print.

Bell, Daniel. *East Meets West: Human Rights and Democracy in East Asia.* Princeton: Princeton UP, 2000. Print.

Benhabib, Seyla. *Another Cosmopolitanism: Hospitality, Sovereignty, and Democratic Iterations.* Ed. Robert Post. New York: Oxford UP, 2006. Print.

———. *Critique, Norm, and Utopia: A Study of the Foundations of Critical Theory.* New York: Columbia UP, 1986. Print.

———. *The Rights of Others: Aliens, Residents, and Citizens.* Cambridge: Cambridge UP, 2004. Print.

———. "Sexual Difference and Collective Identities: The New Global Constellation." *Signs: A Journal of Women in Culture and Society* 24.2 (1999): 335–61. Print.

———. *Situating the Self: Gender, Community, and Postmodernism in Contemporary Ethics.* New York: Routledge, 1992. Print.

———. "Toward a Deliberative Model of Democratic Legitimacy." *Democracy and Difference: Contesting the Boundaries of the Political.* Ed. Seyla Benhabib. Princeton: Princeton UP, 1996. 67–94. Print.

Benhabib, Seyla, et al., eds. *Feminist Contentions: A Philosophical Exchange.* New York: Routledge, 1995. Print.

Bentley, Russell. "Rhetorical Democracy." *Talking Democracy: Historical Perspectives on Rhetoric and Democracy.* Ed. Benedetto Fontana, Cary J. Nederman, and Gary Remer. University Park: Penn State UP, 2004. 115–34. Print.

Berlant, Lauren. *The Anatomy of National Fantasy: Hawthorne, Utopia, and Everyday Life.* Chicago: U of Chicago P, 1991. Print.

———. *Cruel Optimism.* Durham: Duke UP, 2010. Print.

———. "Introduction." *Compassion: The Culture and Politics of an Emotion.* Ed. Lauren Berlant. 1–15. New York: Routledge, 2004. Print.

Bernstein, Richard J. "The Retrieval of the Democratic Ethos." *Habermas on Law and Democracy: Critical Exchanges.* Ed. Michael Rosenfeld and Andrew Arato. Berkeley: U of California P, 1998. 287–303. Print.

Beverley, John. *Subalternity and Representation: Arguments in Cultural Theory.* Durham: Duke UP, 1999. Print.

———. *Testimonio: On the Politics of Truth.* Minneapolis: U of Minnesota P, 2004. Print.

Biesecker, Barbara. "Rethinking the Rhetorical Situation from Within the Thematic of *Différance.*" *Philosophy and Rhetoric* 22 (1989): 110–30. Web. 12 May 2007.

Birmingham, Peg. "A Lying World Order: Political Deception and the Threat of Totalitarianism." *Thinking in Dark Times: Hannah Arendt on Ethics and Politics.* Ed. Roger Berkowitz, Thomas Keenan, and Jeffrey Katz. New York: Fordham UP, 2010. 75–77. Print.

Blakesley, David. "Kenneth Burke's Pragmatism—Old and New." *Kenneth Burke and the 21st Century.* Ed. Bernard L. Brock. Albany: SUNY P, 1999. 71–95. Print.

Bohman, James. "Survey Article: The Coming of Age of Deliberative Democracy." *Journal of Political Philosophy* 6.4 (1998): 400–425. Web. 28 December 2008.

Bohman, James, and William Rehg, eds. *Deliberative Democracy: Essays on Reason and Politics.* Cambridge: MIT P, 1997. Print.

Bok, Sissela. *Lying: Moral Choice in Public and Private Life.* New York: Pantheon, 1978. Print.

Boltanski, Luc. *Distant Suffering: Morality, Media, and Politics.* Trans. Graham Burchell. New York: Cambridge UP, 1999. Print.

Bradley, Mark Philip, and Patrice Petro, eds. *Truth Claims: Representation and Human Rights.* New Brunswick: Rutgers UP, 2002. Print.

Bratman, Michael E. *Intention, Plans, and Practical Reason.* Cambridge: Harvard UP, 1987. Print.

Brodsky, Anne E. *With All Our Strength: The Revolutionary Association of the Women of Afghanistan.* New York: Routledge, 2003. Print.

Brooks, Linda Marie. "*Testimonio*'s Poetics of Performance." *Comparative Literature Studies* 42.2 (2005): 181–222. Print.

Brown, Wendy. *Regulating Aversion: Tolerance in the Age of Identity and Empire.* Princeton: Princeton UP, 2006. Print.

———. "Suffering the Paradoxes of Rights." *Left Legalism/Left Critique.* Ed. Wendy Brown and Janet Halley. Durham: Duke UP, 2002. 420–34. Print.

Brummett, Barry. "Kenneth Burke's Symbolic Trinity." *Philosophy and Rhetoric* 28.3 (1995): 234–51. Print.

Burke, Kenneth. *Counter-Statement.* Berkeley: U of California P, 1968. Print.

————. *A Grammar of Motives.* Berkeley: U of California P, 1945. Print.

————. "On Persuasion, Identification, and Dialectical Symmetry." Ed. and intro. James Zappen. *Philosophy and Rhetoric* 39.4 (2006): 333–39. Web. 1 Aug. 2011.

————. *Permanence and Change: An Anatomy of Purpose.* 3rd ed. Berkeley: U of California P, 1984. Print.

————. *The Philosophy of Literary Form.* 3rd ed. Berkeley: U of California P, 1973. Print.

————. "Rhetoric—Old and New." *Journal of General Education* 5.3 (1951): 202–9. Print.

————. *A Rhetoric of Motives.* Berkeley: U of California P, 1962. Print.

————. *Rhetoric of Religion: Studies in Logology.* Berkeley: U of California P, 1970. Print.

————. "Words as Deeds." *Centrum* 3 (1975): 147–68. Print.

Butler, Judith. *Bodies that Matter: On the Discursive Limits of "Sex."* New York: Routledge, 1993. Print.

————. "Critically Queer." *GLQ* 1.1 (1993): 17–32. Web. 16 June 2007.

————. *Excitable Speech: A Politics of the Performative.* New York: Routledge, 1997. Print.

————. *Gender Trouble: Feminism and the Subversion of Identity.* 2nd ed. New York: Routledge, 2006. Print.

————. *Giving an Account of Oneself.* New York: Fordham UP, 2005. Print.

————. *Precarious Life: The Powers of Mourning and Violence.* London: Verso, 2006. Print.

————. *Undoing Gender.* New York: Routledge, 2004. Print.

Butler, Judith, and William Connolly. "Politics, Power, and Ethics: A Discussion Between Judith Butler and William Connolly." *Theory and Event* 4.2 (2000): 40 pars. *Project MUSE.* Web. 28 Dec. 2010.

Campbell, Karlyn Kohrs. *A Critical Study of Early Feminist Rhetoric.* Vol. 1 of *Man Cannot Speak for Her.* New York: Greenwood P, 1989. Print.

Card, Claudia. "Gender and Moral Luck." *Identity, Character, and Morality.* Ed. Owen Flanagan and Amélie Oksenberg Rorty. Cambridge: MIT P, 1990. 199–218. Print.

Carey, Christopher. "Rhetorical Means of Persuasion." *Essays on Aristotle's Rhetoric.* Ed. Amélie Oksenberg Rorty. Berkeley: U of California P, 1996. 399–415. Print.

Carey-Webb, Allen. "Teaching, Testimony, and Truth: Rigoberta Menchú's Credibility in the North American Classroom." *The Rigoberta Menchú Controversy.* Ed. Arturo Arias. Minneapolis: U of Minnesota P, 2001. 309–31. Print.

Carson, Thomas L. *Lying and Deception: Theory and Practice.* New York: Oxford UP, 2010. Print.

Cartwright, Lisa. *Moral Spectatorship: Technologies of Voice and Affect in Postwar Representations of the Child.* Durham: Duke UP, 2008. Print.

Caruth, Cathy. "Lying and History." *Thinking in Dark Times: Hannah Arendt on Ethics and Politics.* Ed. Roger Berkowitz, Thomas Keenan, and Jeffrey Katz. New York: Fordham UP, 2010. 79–92. Print.

Cavarero, Adriana. *For More than One Voice: Toward a Philosophy of Vocal Expression.* Trans. Paul A. Kottman. Stanford: Stanford UP, 2005. Print.

————. *Relating Narratives: Storytelling and Selfhood.* Trans. Paul A. Kottman. New York: Routledge, 1997. Print.

Center for American Women and Politics. "The Gender Gap and the 2004 Women's Vote: Setting the Record Straight." Center for American Women and Politics, Eagleton Institute of Politics, Rutgers University. Web. 28 Dec. 2010.

Chambers, Simone. *Reasonable Democracy: Jürgen Habermas and the Politics of Discourse.* Ithaca: Cornell UP, 1996. Print.

Charland, Maurice. "Constitutive Rhetoric: The Case of the *Peuple Québécois.*" *Quarterly Journal of Speech* 73.2 (1987): 133–50. Web. 7 July 2006.

Chávez, Karma R., and Cindy L. Griffin, eds. *Standing in the Intersection: Feminist Voices, Feminist Practices in Communication Studies.* Albany: SUNY P, 2012. Print.

Cheah, Pheng. *Inhuman Conditions: On Cosmopolitanism and Human Rights*. Cambridge: Harvard UP, 2006. Print.

Chu, Patricia P. *Assimilating Asians: Gendered Strategies of Authorship in Asian America*. Durham: Duke UP, 2000. Print.

Clark, Gregory. *Rhetorical Landscapes in America: Variations on a Theme from Kenneth Burke*. Columbia: U of South Carolina P, 2004. Print.

Coale, Ansley. "Excess Female Mortality and the Balance of Sexes in the Population: An Estimated Number of Missing Females." *Population and Development Review* 17.3 (1991): 517–23. Web. 19 June 2004.

Code, Lorraine. *Rhetorical Spaces: Essays on Gendered Locations*. New York: Routledge, 1995. Print.

Cogan, Jacob Katz, and Lori D. Ginzberg. "1846 Petition for Woman's Suffrage, New York State Constitutional Convention." *Signs: Journal of Women in Culture and Society* 22.2 (1997): 427–39. Web. 24 May 2011.

Cohen, David. *Law, Violence, and Community in Classical Athens*. New York: Cambridge UP, 1995. Print.

Cohen, Joshua. "Deliberation and Democratic Legitimacy." *The Good Polity: Normative Analysis of the State*. Ed. Alan Hamlin and Philip Pettit. New York: Blackwell, 1989. 17–34. Print.

Cohen, Stanley, and Bruna Seu. "Knowing Enough Not to Feel Too Much: Emotional Thinking About Human Rights Appeals." *Truth Claims: Representation and Human Rights*. Ed. Mark Philip Bradley and Patrice Petro. New Brunswick: Rutgers UP, 2002. 187–201. Print.

Condit, Celeste Michelle. "Post-Burke: Transcending the Sub-stance of Dramatism." *Quarterly Journal of Speech* 78.3 (1992): 49–55. Print.

Connolly, William E. "Democracy and Time." *Neuropolitics: Thinking, Culture, Speed*. Minneapolis: U of Minnesota P, 2002. 140–73. Print.

Connors, Robert J., Lisa S. Ede, and Andrea A. Lunsford, eds. *Essays on Classical Rhetoric and Modern Discourse*. Carbondale: Southern Illinois UP, 1984. Print.

Cornell, Drucilla. "Introduction." *Feminism and Pornography*. Ed. Drucilla Cornell. New York: Oxford UP, 2000. 1–18. Print.

Coulter, Ann. *Slander: Liberal Lies About the American Right*. Foreword Rush Limbaugh. New York: Three Rivers Press, 2003. Print.

Crane, Barbara B., and Jason L. Finkle. "The United States, China, and the United Nations Population Fund: Dynamics of U.S. Policymaking." *Population and Development Review* 15.1 (1989): 23–59. Web. 19 June 2004.

Croll, Elisabeth. *Endangered Daughters: Discrimination and Development in Asia*. New York: Routledge, 2000. Print.

Crossette, Barbara. "The World: Rethinking Population at a Global Milestone." *New York Times* 19 Sept. 1999, sec. 4: 1. Web. 26 Dec. 2004.

Crusius, Timothy W. *Kenneth Burke and the Conversation After Philosophy*. Carbondale: Southern Illinois UP, 1999. Print.

Cubilié, Anne. *Women Witnessing Terror: Testimony and the Cultural Politics of Human Rights*. New York: Fordham UP, 2005. Print.

Culler, Jonathan. "Philosophy and Literature: The Fortunes of the Performative." *Poetics Today* 21.3 (2000): 503–19. Print.

Davis, Diane. *Inessential Solidarity: Rhetoric and Foreigner Relations*. Pittsburgh: U of Pittsburgh P, 2010. Print.

de Bary, Wm. Theodore, and Tu Weiming, eds. *Confucianism and Human Rights*. New York: Columbia UP, 1998. Print.

de Lauretis, Teresa. *Technologies of Gender: Essays on Theory, Film, and Fiction*. Bloomington: U of Indiana P, 1987. Print.

Derrida, Jacques. "'Le Parjure,' *Perhaps*: Storytelling and Lying." *Without Alibi*. Ed. and trans. Peggy Kamuf. Stanford: Stanford UP, 2002. 161–201. Print.

Deveaux, Monique. *Cultural Pluralism and Dilemmas of Justice*. Ithaca: Cornell UP, 2000. Print.

Donnelly, Jack. *Universal Human Rights in Theory and Practice*. 2nd edition. Ithaca: Cornell UP, 2003. Print.

Doxtader, Erik. *With Faith in the Works of Words: The Beginnings of Reconciliation in South Africa, 1985–1995*. East Lansing: Michigan State UP, 2009. Print.

Dryzek, John S. *Deliberative Democracy and Beyond: Liberals, Critics, Contestations*. New York: Oxford UP, 2000. Print.

DuBois, Ellen Carol. *Feminism and Suffrage: The Emergence of the Independent Women's Movement*. Ithaca: Cornell UP, 1999. Print.

———. "Women's Rights and Abolition: The Nature of the Connection." *Antislavery Reconsidered: New Perspectives on the Abolitionists*. Ed. Lewis Perry and Michael Fellman. Baton Rouge: Louisiana State UP, 1979. 238–51. Print.

DuBois, Ellen, and Robert W. Cherny, eds. *Women's Suffrage: The View from the Pacific*. Spec. issue of *Pacific Historical Review* 69.4 (2000). Web. 28 Dec. 2010.

Dugger, Celia W. "Sent Back to China, Man Washes Up Again." *New York Times* 4 June 1998: B1. Web. 26 Dec. 2004.

Düttmann, Alexander García. *Between Cultures: Tensions in the Struggle for Recognition*. London: Verso, 2001. Print.

Dworkin, Ronald. *Taking Rights Seriously*. London: Duckworth, 1978. Print.

Eberly, Rosa A. *Citizen Critics: Literary Public Spheres*. Chicago: U of Illinois P, 2000. Print.

Ebert, Teresa. *Ludic Feminism and After: Postmodernism, Desire, and Labor in Late Capitalism*. Ann Arbor: U of Michigan P, 1996. Print.

Edwards, Louise. "Chinese Women's Campaigns for Suffrage: Nationalism, Confucianism, and Political Agency." *Women's Suffrage in Asia: Gender, Nationalism, and Democracy*. Ed. Louise P. Edwards and Mina Roces. New York: RoutledgeCurzon, 2004. 59–78. Print.

———. "Women's Suffrage in China: Challenging Scholarly Conventions." *Pacific Historical Review* 69.4 (2000): 617–38. Web. 28 Dec. 2010.

Edwards, Louise, and Mina Roces. "Introduction: Orienting the Global Women's Suffrage Movement." *Women's Suffrage in Asia: Gender, Nationalism, and Democracy*. Ed. Louise Edwards and Mina Roces. New York: RoutledgeCurzon, 2004. 1–23. Print.

Engbers, Susanna Kelly. "With Great Sympathy: Elizabeth Cady Stanton's Innovative Appeals to Emotion." *Rhetoric Society Quarterly* 37.3 (2007): 307–32. Web. 6 May 2010.

Fanon, Frantz. *Black Skin, White Masks*. Trans. Charles Lam Markmann. New York: Grove, 1997. Print.

———. *Wretched of the Earth*. Trans. Richard Philcox. New York: Grove, 2005. Print.

Farrell, Amy, and Patrice McDermott. "Claiming Afghan Women: The Challenge of Human Rights Discourse for Transnational Feminism." *Just Advocacy? Women's Human Rights, Transnational Feminisms, and the Politics of Representation*. Ed. Wendy S. Hesford and Wendy Kozol. New Brunswick: Rutgers UP, 2005. 33–55. Print.

Ferguson, Ann. "Resisting the Veil of Privilege: Building Bridge Identities as an Ethico-politics of Global Feminisms." *Decentering the Center: Philosophy for a Multicultural, Postcolonial, and Feminist World*. Ed. Uma Narayan and Sandra Harding. Bloomington: Indiana UP, 2000. 189–207. Print.

Ferman, Claudia. "Textual Truth, Historical Truth, and Media Truth: Everybody Speaks About the Menchús." *The Rigoberta Menchú Controversy*. Ed. Arturo Arias. Minneapolis: U of Minnesota P, 2001. 156–76. Print.

Fiore, Robin N., and Hilde Lindemann Nelson, eds. *Recognition, Responsibility, and Rights: Feminist Ethics and Social Theory*. Lanham: Rowman and Littlefield, 2002. Print.

Fishkin, James S. *Democracy and Deliberation: New Directions for Democratic Reform*. New Haven: Yale UP, 1991. Print.

Fiss, Owen M. *The Irony of Free Speech*. Cambridge: Harvard UP, 1996. Print.

Fletcher, Ian Christopher, Laura E. Nym Mayhall, and Philippa Levine, eds. *Women's Suffrage in the British Empire: Citizenship, Nation, and Race*. London: Routledge, 2000. Print.

Flexner, Eleanor, and Ellen Fitzpatrick. *Century of Struggle: The Woman's Rights Movement in the United States*. Cambridge: Belknap P of Harvard UP, 1996. Print.

Fontana, Benedetto, Cary J. Nederman, and Gary Remer. "Introduction: Deliberative Democracy and the Rhetorical Turn." *Talking Democracy: Historical Perspectives on Rhetoric and Democracy*. Ed. Benedetto Fontana, Cary J. Nederman, and Gary Remer. University Park: Penn State UP, 2004. 1–25. Print.

Foster, Susan Leigh. "Choreographing History." *Choreographing History*. Ed. Susan Leigh Foster. Bloomington: Indiana UP, 1995. 3–21. Print.

Foucault, Michel. *Power/Knowledge: Selected Interviews and Other Writings, 1972–1977*. Ed. Colin Gordon. New York: Pantheon, 1980. Print.

Fox, Gregory H. "The Right to Political Participation in International Law." *Yale Journal of International Law* 17 (1992): 539–608. Web. 7 Aug. 2010.

Franck, Thomas M. "The Emerging Right to Democratic Governance." *American Journal of International Law* 86.1 (1992): 46–91. Print.

Franken, Al. *Lies and the Lying Liars Who Tell Them: A Fair and Balanced Look at the Right*. New York: Dutton, 2003. Print.

Fraser, Nancy. *Justice Interruptus: Critical Reflections on the "Postsocialist" Condition*. New York: Routledge, 1997. Print.

———. "Rethinking the Public Sphere: A Contribution to the Critique of Actually Existing Democracy." *The Phantom Public Sphere*. Ed. Bruce Robbins. Minneapolis: U of Minnesota P, 1993. 1–32. Print.

———. *Scales of Justice: Reimagining Political Space in a Globalizing World*. New York: Columbia UP, 2009. Print.

Fultner, Barbara, ed. "Communicative Action and Formal Pragmatics." Ed. Barbara Fultner. *Jürgen Habermas: Key Concepts*. Durham, U.K.: Acumen, 2011. 54–73. Print.

———. *Jürgen Habermas: Key Concepts*. Durham, U.K.: Acumen, 2011. Print.

Fusco, Coco. "The Other History of Intercultural Performance." *TDR* 38.1 (1994): 143–67. Web. 7 Jan. 2009.

Garber, Marjorie. "Compassion." *Compassion: The Culture and Politics of an Emotion*. Ed. Lauren Berlant. New York: Routledge, 2004. 15–28. Print.

Gardner, James A. "Shut Up and Vote: A Critique of Deliberative Democracy and the Life of Talk." *Tennessee Law Review* 63 (1996): 421–51. Print.

Garsten, Bryan. *Saving Persuasion: A Defense of Rhetoric and Judgment*. Cambridge: Harvard UP, 2006. Print.

Garver, Eugene. *Aristotle's Rhetoric: An Art of Character*. Chicago: U of Chicago P, 1994. Print.

Gaus, Gerald F. "Reason, Justification, and Consensus: Why Democracy Can't Have It All." *Deliberative Democracy: Essays on Reason and Politics*. Ed. James Bohman and William Rehg. Cambridge: MIT P, 1997. 205–42. Print.

Gilmore, Leigh. *Autobiographies: A Feminist Theory of Women's Self-Representation*. Ithaca: Cornell UP, 1994. Print.

────. "Jurisdictions: *I, Rigoberta Menchú, The Kiss,* and Scandalous Self-Representation in the Age of Memoir and Trauma." *Signs: Journal of Women in Culture and Society* 28.2 (2003): 695–718. Web. 8 Jan. 2010.

────. *The Limits of Autobiography: Trauma and Testimony.* Ithaca: Cornell UP, 2000. Print.

Glendon, Mary Ann. *A World Made New: Eleanor Roosevelt and the Universal Declaration of Human Rights.* New York: Random House, 2002. Print.

Goldberg, Elizabeth Swanson. *Beyond Terror: Gender, Narrative, Human Rights.* New Brunswick: Rutgers UP, 2007. Print.

Goldin, Paul R. *After Confucius: Studies in Early Chinese Philosophy.* Honolulu: U of Hawai'i P, 2005. Print.

Goldsmith, Barbara. *Other Powers: The Age of Suffrage, Spiritualism, and the Scandalous Victoria Woodhull.* New York: Harper Perennial, 1999. Print.

Grewal, Inderpal. "On the New Global Feminism and the Family of Nations: Dilemmas of Transnational Feminist Practice." *Talking Visions: Multicultural Feminism in a Transnational Age.* Ed. Ella Shohat. New York: MIT P, 1998. 501–30. Print.

Grewal, Inderpal, and Caren Kaplan. "Introduction: Transnational Feminist Practices and Questions of Postmodernity." *Scattered Hegemonies: Postmodernity and Transnational Feminist Practices.* Ed. Inderpal Grewal and Caren Kaplan. Minneapolis: U of Minnesota P, 1994. 1–33. Print.

Guilmoto, Christophe Z. "The Sex Ratio Transition in Asia." Working Papers du CEPED 5. Paris: Centre Population et Développement, 2009. 5 March 2011.

Guinier, Lani. *Tyranny of the Majority: Fundamental Fairness in Representative Democracy.* New York: Free, 1995. Print.

Gunn, Giles. *The Culture of Criticism and the Criticism of Culture.* New York: Oxford UP, 1987. Print.

Gurko, Miriam. *The Ladies of Seneca Falls: The Birth of the Woman's Rights Movement.* New York: Schocken, 1976. Print.

Gutmann, Amy, and Dennis Thompson. *Democracy and Disagreement: Why Moral Conflict Cannot Be Avoided in Politics, and What Should be Done About It.* Cambridge: Belknap P of Harvard UP, 1996. Print.

────. *Why Deliberative Democracy?* Princeton: Princeton UP, 2004. Print.

Habermas, Jürgen. "Actions, Speech Acts, Linguistically Mediated Interactions, and the Lifeworld." *Philosophical Problems Today.* Ed. G. Fløistad. Vol. 1. Dordrecht: Kluwer Academic, 2010. 45–74. Print.

────. *Between Facts and Norms: Contributions to a Discourse Theory of Law and Democracy.* Trans. William Rehg. Cambridge: MIT P, 1998. Print.

────. *Between Naturalism and Religion: Philosophical Essays.* Cambridge: Polity, 2008. Print.

────. *Inclusion of the Other: Studies in Political Theory.* Ed. Ciaran Cronin and Pablo De Greiff. Cambridge: MIT P, 2000. Print.

────. *Moral Consciousness and Communicative Action.* Trans. Christian Lenhardt and Shierry Weber Nicholsen. Cambridge: MIT P, 2001. Print.

────. *Postmetaphysical Thinking: Philosophical Essays.* Trans. William Mark Hohengarten. Cambridge: MIT P, 1994. Print.

────. *The Theory of Communicative Action.* Vol. 1, *Reason and the Rationalization of Society.* Trans. Thomas McCarthy. Boston: Beacon, 1981. Print.

────. "Three Normative Models of Democracy." *Democracy and Difference: Contesting the Boundaries of the Political.* Ed. Seyla Benhabib. Princeton: Princeton UP, 1996. 21–45. Print.

Hacking, Ian. *Rewriting the Soul: Multiple Personality and the Sciences of Memory.* Princeton: Princeton UP, 1995. Print.

Hall, David L., and Roger T. Ames. *The Democracy of the Dead: Dewey, Confucius, and the Hope for Democracy in China*. Chicago: Open Court, 1999. Print.

———. *Thinking Through Confucius*. Albany: SUNY P, 1987. Print.

Hamlin, Alan, and Philip Pettit, eds. *The Good Polity: Normative Analysis of the State*. New York: Blackwell, 1989. 1–13. Print.

Hancher, Michael. "Three Kinds of Intention." *Modern Language Notes* 87.7 (1972): 827–51. Print.

Haraway, Donna. *Simians, Cyborgs, and Women*. New York: Routledge, 1991. Print.

Harding, John Wesley. "An Israelite Indeed" [Sermon 90]. *Global Ministries—The United Methodist Church*. Web. 1 Dec. 2011.

Hariman, Robert. "Status, Marginality, and Rhetorical Theory." *Quarterly Journal of Speech* 72 (1986): 38–54. Web. 23 July 2009.

Hasian, Marouf, Jr. *Rhetorical Vectors of Memory in National and International Holocaust Trials*. East Lansing: Michigan State UP, 2006. Print.

Hauser, Gerald A. "The Moral Vernacular of Human Rights Discourse." *Philosophy and Rhetoric* 41.4 (2008): 440–66. Web. 6 Dec. 2010.

Hawhee, Debra. *Moving Bodies: Kenneth Burke at the Edges of Language*. Columbia: U of South Carolina P, 2009. Print.

Haworth, Abigail. "The Baby We Can't Ignore." *Marie Claire*. June 2001: 72–75. Print.

Heller, Agnes. "The Discourse Ethics of Habermas: Critique and Appraisal." *Thesis Eleven* 10–11 (1984–85): 5–17. Web. 7 Jan. 2008.

Henderson, Greig. "Dramatism and Deconstruction: Burke, de Man, and the Rhetorical Motive." *Kenneth Burke and the 21st Century*. Ed. Bernard L. Brock. Albany: SUNY P, 1999. 151–65. Print.

Hesford, Wendy S. *Spectacular Rhetorics: Human Rights Visions, Recognitions, Feminisms*. Durham: Duke UP, 2011. Print.

Hesford, Wendy S., and Wendy Kozol, eds. *Just Advocacy? Women's Human Rights, Transnational Feminisms, and the Politics of Representation*. New Brunswick,: Rutgers UP, 2005. Print.

Holmes, Stephen. "Precommitment and the Paradox of Democracy." *Constitutionalism and Democracy*. Ed Jon Elster and Rune Slagstad. New York: Cambridge UP, 1988. 185–240. Print.

Honig, Bonnie. "Democracy and Foreignness: Democratic Cosmopolitanism and the Myth of an Immigrant America." *Multiculturalism and Political Theory*. Ed. Anthony Simon Laden and David Owen. New York: Cambridge UP, 2007. 373–407. Print.

———. *Emergency Politics: Paradox, Law, Democracy*. Princeton: Princeton UP, 2009. Print.

Honneth, Axel. *The Struggle for Recognition: The Moral Grammar of Social Conflicts*. Cambridge: Polity, 1995. Print.

hooks, bell. *Yearning: Race, Gender, and Cultural Politics*. Boston: South End, 1990. 145–53. Print.

Howard-Hassmann, Rhoda E. *Can Globalization Promote Human Rights?* University Park: Penn State UP, 2010. Print.

Hua, Julietta. *Trafficking Women's Human Rights*. Minneapolis: U of Minnesota P, 2011. Print.

Hunt, Lynn. *Inventing Human Rights: A History*. New York: Norton, 2007. Print.

Ignatieff, Michael. *Human Rights as Politics and Idolatry*. Ed. Amy Gutmann. Princeton: Princeton UP, 2001. Print.

Ingram, David. *Habermas: Introduction and Analysis*. Ithaca: Cornell UP, 2010. Print.

Isin, Engin F., and Greg M. Nielsen, eds. *Acts of Citizenship*. New York: Zed, 2008. Print.

Jarratt, Susan C. "Feminism and Composition: The Case for Conflict." *Contending with Words: Composition and Rhetoric in a Postmodern Age*. Ed. Patricia Harkin and John Schilb. New York: MLA, 1991. 104–24. Print.

———. *Rereading the Sophists: Classical Rhetoric Refigured*. Carbondale: Southern Illinois UP, 1991. Print.

Jay, Martin. "The Ambivalent Virtues of Mendacity: How Europeans Taught (Some of) Us to Learn to Love the Lies of Politics." *The Humanities and the Dynamics of Inclusion Since World War II*. Ed. David A. Hollinger. Baltimore: John Hopkins UP, 2006. 107–25. Print.

Jullien, François. *The Propensity of Things: Toward a History of Efficacy in China*. New York: Zone, 1995. Print.

Kamp, Marianne. *The New Woman in Uzbekistan: Islam, Modernity, and Unveiling Under Communism*. Seattle: U of Washington P, 2006. Print.

Kapur, Ratna. "The Tragedy of Victimization Rhetoric: Resurrecting the 'Native' Subject in International/Post-Colonial Feminist Legal Politics." *Harvard Human Rights Journal* 15 (2002): 1–38. Web. 14 June 2012.

Kastely, James L. *Rethinking the Rhetorical Tradition: From Plato to Postmodernism*. New Haven: Yale UP, 1997. Print.

Keenan, Thomas. "Mobilizing Shame." *The South Atlantic Quarterly* 103.2/3 (2004): 435–49. Web. 30 Dec. 2009.

Kennedy, David. *The Dark Sides of Virtue: Reassessing International Humanitarianism*. Princeton: Princeton UP, 2004. Print.

Kennedy, Duncan. "The Critique of Rights in Critical Legal Studies." *Left Legalism/Left Critique*. Ed. Wendy Brown and Janet E. Halley. Durham: Duke UP, 2002. 373–419. Print.

Kent, Ann. *Between Freedom and Subsistence: China and Human Rights*. New York: Oxford UP, 1993. Print.

Kimball, Bruce. *Orators and Philosophers: A History of the Idea of Liberal Education*. New York: Teachers College, 1986. Print.

Kiss, Elizabeth. "Alchemy or Fool's Gold." *Vital Speeches of the Day* 62.24 (1 Oct. 1996): 755–60. *Academic Search Complete*. Web. 3 Nov. 2012.

Klasen, Stephan, and Claudia Wink. "'Missing Women': Revisiting the Debate." *Feminist Economics* 9.2–3 (2003): 263–99. Web. 26 Dec. 2004.

———. "A Turning Point in Gender Bias in Mortality? An Update on the Number of Missing Women." *Population and Development Review* 28 (2002): 285–312. Web. 26 Dec. 2004.

Koh, Harold Hongju, and Ronald C. Slye, eds. *Deliberative Democracy and Human Rights*. New Haven: Yale UP, 1999. Print.

Korsgaard, Christine M. *The Sources of Normativity*. Ed. Onora O'Neill. New York: Cambridge UP, 1996. Print.

Koshy, Susan. "From Cold War to Trade War: Neocolonialism and Human Rights." *Social Text* 58 (Spring 1999): 1–32. Web. 26 Aug. 2008.

Kottman, Paul A. "Introduction." *Relating Narratives: Storytelling and Selfhood*. By Adriana Cavarero. Trans. Paul A. Kottman. New York: Routledge, 1997. vii–xxxii. Print.

Kristeva, Julia. *Strangers to Ourselves*. Trans. Leon S. Roudiez. New York: Columbia UP, 1991. Print.

Kristof, Nicholas D. "Bush vs. Women." *New York Times* 16 Aug. 2002: A17. Web. 26 Dec. 2004.

———. "China's Super Kids." *New York Times* 22 Nov. 2002: A27. Web. 26 Dec. 2004.

———. "Devastated Women." *New York Times* 26 Aug. 2002: A29. Web. 26 Dec. 2004.

Kymlicka, William. *Multicultural Citizenship: A Liberal Theory of Minority Rights*. New York: Oxford UP, 1995. Print.

Laden, Anthony Simon. "Negotiation, Deliberation, and the Claims of Politics." *Multiculturalism and Political Theory*. Ed. Anthony Simon Laden and David Owen. New York: Cambridge, 2007. 198–217. Print.

Landes, Joan B. *Women and the Public Sphere in the Age of the French Revolution*. Ithaca: Cornell UP, 1988. Print.

Lavely, William. "First Impressions from the 2000 Census of China." *Population and Development Review* 27.4 (2001): 755–69. Web. 26 Dec. 2004.

Lentricchia, Frank. *Criticism and Social Change*. Chicago: U of Chicago P, 1983. Print.

Li, Chenyang. "The Confucian Concept of Jen and the Feminist Ethics of Care: A Comparative Study." *Hypatia* 9.1 (1994): 70–89. *Project MUSE*. Web. 11 June 2005.

Li, David Leiwei. *Imagining the Nation: Asian American Literature and Cultural Consent*. Stanford: Stanford UP, 1998. Print.

Lobel, Jules. *Success Without Victory: Lost Legal Battles and the Long Road to Justice in America*. New York: New York UP, 2003. Print.

Lovell, W. George, and Christopher H. Lutz. "The Primacy of Larger Truths: Rigoberta Menchú and the Tradition of Native Testimony in Guatemala." *The Rigoberta Menchú Controversy*. Ed. Arturo Arias. Minneapolis: U of Minnesota P, 2001. 171–97. Print.

Lu, Xing. *Rhetoric in Ancient China, Fifth to Third Century B.C.E.: A Comparison with Classical Greek Rhetoric*. Columbia: U of South Carolina P, 1998. Print.

Lugones, Maria. "Playfulness, "World"-Travelling, and Loving Perception." *Pilgramages/Peregrinajes: Theorizing Coalition Against Multiple Oppressions*. Lanham: Rowman and Littlefield, 2003. Print.

Luo, Shirong. "Relation, Virtue, and Relational Virtue: Three Concepts of Caring." *Hypatia* 22.3 (2007): 92–110. *Project MUSE*. Web. 11 June 2005.

Lutz, Alma. *Susan B. Anthony: Rebel, Crusader, Humanitarian*. Boston: Beacon, 1959. Print.

Lynch, Dennis A., Diane George, and Marilyn M. Cooper. "Moments of Argument: Agonistic Inquiry and Confrontational Cooperation." *College Composition and Communication* 48.1 (1997): 61–85. Print.

Lyon, Arabella. "Confucian Silence and Remonstration: A Basis for Deliberation?" *Rhetoric Before and Beyond the Greeks*. Ed. Carol Lipson and Roberta A. Binkley. Albany: SUNY P, 2004. 131–45. Print.

———. *Intentions: Negotiated, Contested, and Ignored*. University Park: Penn State UP, 1998. Print.

———. "Rhetorical Authority in Athenian Democracy and the Chinese Legalism of Han Fei." *Philosophy and Rhetoric* 41.1 (2008): 51–71. Print.

———. "'Why Do the Rulers Listen to the Wild Theories of Speech-Makers?': Or *Wuwei, Shi*, and Methods of Comparative Rhetoric." *Ancient Non-Greek Rhetorics*. Ed. Carol Lipson and Roberta A. Binkley. West Lafayette, Ind.: Parlor Press, 2009. 176–96. Print.

———. "Writing an Empire: Cross-Talk on Authority, Act, and Relationships with the Other in the *Analects, Daodejing*, and *HanFeizi*." *Search for the Way: How Chinese Engaged the Other*. Ed. LuMing Mao. Special issue of *College English* 72.4 (2010): 350–66. Print.

Lyon, Arabella, and Lester C. Olson. "Human Rights Rhetoric: Traditions of Testifying and Witnessing." *Human Rights Rhetoric: Traditions of Testifying and Witnessing*. Ed. Arabella Lyon and Lester C. Olson. New York: Routledge, 2012. 1–10. Print.

Lyotard, Jean-François. *The Differend: Phrases in Dispute*. Trans. Georges Van Den Abbeele. Minneapolis: U of Minnesota P, 1988. Print.

———. "Memorandum on Legitimation." *The Political*. Ed. David Ingram. Malden: Blackwell, 2002. 229–39. Print.

————. *The Postmodern Condition: A Report on Knowledge.* Trans. Geoff Bennington and Brian Massumi. Minneapolis: U of Minnesota P, 1984. Print.

MacKinnon, Catharine. *Only Words.* Cambridge: Harvard UP, 1996. Print.

Madison, G. B. "Critical Theory and Hermeneutics: Some Outstanding Issues in the Debate." *Perspectives on Habermas.* Ed. Lewis Edwin Hahn. Chicago: Open Court, 2000. 463–85. Print.

Magnus, Kathleen Dow. "The Unaccountable Subject: Judith Butler and the Social Conditions of Intersubjective Agency." *Hypatia* 21.2 (2006): 81–103. *Project MUSE.* 17 Oct. 2011.

Mahbubani, Kishore. *Can Asians Think?* 4th ed. Singapore: Marshall Cavendish Editions, 2010. Print.

Mahmood, Saba. *The Politics of Piety: The Islamic Revival and the Feminist Subject.* Princeton: Princeton UP, 2004. Print.

Mailloux, Steven. *Disciplinary Identities: Rhetorical Paths of English, Speech, and Composition.* New York: MLA, 2006. Print.

Malinowski, Bronislaw. "The Problems of Meaning in Primitive Language." *The Meaning of Meaning: A Study of the Influence of Language upon Thought and of the Science of Symbolism.* Ed. C. K. Ogden and I. A. Richards. New York: Harcourt, Brace and World, 1923. 296–336. Print.

Mann, James. "Framing China." *Covering China.* Ed. Robert Giles, Robert W. Snyder, and Lisa DeLisle. New Brunswick, N.J.: Transaction, 2001. 101–6. Print.

Mansbridge, Jane. "Everyday Talk in the Deliberative System." *Deliberative Politics: Essays on Democracy and Disagreement.* Ed. Stephen Macedo. New York: Oxford UP, 1999. 211–39. Print.

Markell, Patchen. "Contesting Consensus: Rereading Habermas on the Public Sphere." *Constellations* 3.3 (1997): 377–400. *Project Muse.* 17 October 2011.

McCarthy, Thomas. *Ideals and Illusions: On Reconstruction and Deconstruction in Contemporary Critical Theory.* Boston: MIT P, 1993. Print.

————. "On Reconciling Cosmopolitan Unity and National Diversity." *Alternative Modernities.* Ed. Dilip Parameshwar Gaonkar. Durham: Duke UP, 2001. 197–235. Print.

McMillen, Sally G. *Seneca Falls and the Origins of the Women's Rights Movement.* New York: Oxford UP, 2008. Print.

Meiklejohn, Alexander. "The First Amendment Is an Absolute." *Supreme Court Review* (1961): 245–66. Web. 4 April 2007.

————. *Political Freedom: The Constitutional Powers of the People.* New York: Oxford UP, 1948. Print.

Menchú, Rigoberta. *I, Rigoberta Menchú: An Indian Woman in Guatemala.* Ed. Elisabeth Burgos-Debray. Trans. Ann Wright. London: Verso, 1984. Print.

————. "Those Who Attack Me Humiliate the Victims: Interview With Juan Jesús Aznárez." *The Rigoberta Menchú Controversy.* Ed. Arturo Arias. Minneapolis: U of Minnesota P, 2001. 109–17. Print.

Merry, Sally Engle. *Human Rights and Gender Violence: Translating International Law into Local Justice.* Chicago: U of Chicago P, 2006. Print.

Mill, John Stuart. *On Liberty; Representative Government; The Subjection of Women: Three Essays.* London: Oxford UP, 1966. Print.

Miller, J. Hillis. "Performativity as Performance/Performativity as Speech Act: Derrida's Special Theory of Performativity." *South Atlantic Quarterly* 106.2 (2007): 219–35. Web. 23 Dec. 2009.

Missouri v Holland. 252 U.S. 416. (1920). *Lexis Nexis Academic.* Web. 18 June 2012.

Modleski, Tania. *Loving with a Vengeance: Mass-Produced Fantasies for Women.* New York: Routledge, 2007. Print.

Moeller, Susan D. *Compassion Fatigue: How the Media Sell Disease, Famine, War, and Death*. New York: Routledge, 1999. Print.

Mohanty, Chandra Talpade. *Feminism Without Borders: Decolonizing Theory, Practicing Solidarity*. Durham: Duke UP, 2003. Print.

———. "Feminist Encounters: Locating the Politics of Experience." *Copyright* 1 (1987): 30–44. Print.

Molony, Barbara. "Citizenship and Suffrage in Interwar Japan." *Women's Suffrage in Asia: Gender, Nationalism, and Democracy*. Ed. Louise Edwards and Mina Roces. New York: RoutledgeCurzon, 2004. 127–51. Print.

Montejo, Victor D. "Truth, Human Rights, and Representation." *The Rigoberta Menchú Controversy*. Ed. Arturo Arias. Minneapolis: U of Minnesota P, 2001. 372–91. Print.

Moon, J. Donald. "Practical Discourse and Communicative Ethics." *The Cambridge Companion to Habermas*. Ed. Stephen K. White. New York: Cambridge UP, 143–64. Print.

Moore, Michael. *Act and Crime: The Philosophy of Action and Its Implications for Criminal Law*. Oxford: Clarendon, 1993. Print.

Morales, Mario Roberto. "Menchú After Stoll and the Truth Commission." *The Rigoberta Menchú Controversy*. Ed. Arturo Arias. Minneapolis: U of Minnesota P, 2001. 351–71. Print.

Morley, Barry. *Beyond Consensus: Salvaging Sense of the Meeting*. Wallingford, Pa.: Pendle Hill, 1993. Print.

Moruzzi, Norma Claire. *Speaking Through the Mask: Hannah Arendt and the Politics of Social Identity*. Ithaca: Cornell UP, 2001. Print.

Mouffe, Chantal. "Deconstruction, Pragmatism, and the Politics of Democracy." *Deconstruction and Pragmatism*. Ed. Chantal Mouffe. London: Routledge, 1996. 1–12. Print.

———. *The Democratic Paradox*. New York: Verso, 2009. Print.

———. *The Return of the Political*. New York: Verso, 2005. Print.

Moyn, Samuel. *The Last Utopia: Human Rights in History*. Cambridge: Harvard UP, 2010. Print.

Mutua, Makau. "Savages, Victims, and Saviors: The Metaphor of Human Rights." *Harvard International Law Journal* 42.1 (2001): 201–45. *HeinOnline*. Web. 7 July 2009.

Narayan, Uma. "Essence of Culture and a Sense of History: A Feminist Critique of Cultural Essentialism." *Hypatia* 13.2 (2001): 86–106. *Project MUSE*. Web. 11 June 2005.

Nelson, Hilde Lindemann. *Damaged Identities: Narrative Repair*. Ithaca: Cornell UP, 2001. Print.

Nino, Carlos Santiago. *The Ethics of Human Rights*. New Haven: Yale UP, 1996. Print.

Noland, Carrie. *Agency and Embodiment: Performing Gestures/Producing Culture*. Cambridge: Harvard UP, 2009. Print.

Norgren, Jill. *Belva Lockwood: The Woman Who Would Be President*. New York: New York UP, 2007. Print.

Nussbaum, Martha C. *The Fragility of Goodness: Luck and Ethics in Greek Tragedy and Philosophy*. New York: Cambridge UP, 2001. Print.

———. *Upheavals of Thought: The Intelligence of Emotions*. New York: Cambridge UP, 2001. Print.

———. *Women and Human Development: The Capabilities Approach*. New York: Cambridge UP, 2000. Print.

Ober, Josiah. *Political Dissent in Democratic Athens: Intellectual Critics of Popular Rule*. Princeton: Princeton UP, 1998. Print.

Ong, Aihwa. *Flexible Citizenship: The Cultural Logics of Transnationality*. Durham: Duke UP, 1999. Print.

Oliver, Kelly. *Witnessing: Beyond Recognition*. Minneapolis: U of Minnesota P, 2001. Print.

Patton, Cindy. "Rights Language and HIV Treatment: Universal Care or Population Control?" *Human Rights Rhetoric: Traditions of Testifying and Witnessing*. Ed. Arabella Lyon and Lester C. Olson. Philadelphia: Routledge, 2012. 48–64. Print.

Payne, Leigh A. *Unsettling Accounts: Neither Truth nor Reconciliation in Confessions of State Violence*. Durham: Duke UP, 2008. Print.

Pendas, Devin O. "'Law, Not Vengeance': Human Rights, the Rule of Law, and the Claims of Memory in German Holocaust Trials." *Truth Claims: Representation and Human Rights*. Ed. Mark Philip Bradley and Patrice Petro. New Brunswick: Rutgers UP, 2002. 23–41. Print.

Phelan, James. *Living to Tell About It: A Rhetoric and Ethics of Character Narration*. Ithaca: Cornell UP, 2004. Print.

Pinker, Steven. *The Better Angels of Our Nature: Why Violence Has Declined*. New York: Viking, 2011. Print.

Pippin, Robert. "What Is the Question for Which Hegel's Theory of Recognition Is the Answer?" *European Journal of Philosophy* 8.2 (2000): 155–72. Web. 9 Jan. 2010.

Portnoy, Alisse. *Their Right to Speak: Women's Activism in the Indian and Slave Debates*. Cambridge: Harvard UP, 2005. Print.

Przeworski, Adam. *Democracy and the Market: Political and Economic Reforms in Eastern Europe and Latin America*. New York: Cambridge UP, 1991. Print.

Ratcliffe, Krista. "Rhetorical Listening: A Trope for Interpretive Invention and a 'Code of Cross-Cultural Conduct.'" *College Composition and Communication* 51.2 (1999): 195–224. Web. 10 Dec. 2009.

Rawls, John. *The Law of Peoples*. Cambridge: Harvard UP, 1999. Print.

———. *Political Liberalism*. New York: Columbia UP, 1993. Print.

Rehg, William, and James Bohman. "Discourse and Democracy: The Formal and Informal Bases of Legitimacy in *Between Facts and Norms*." *Discourse and Democracy: Essays on Habermas's* Between Facts and Norms. Ed. René von Schomberg and Kenneth Baynes. Albany: SUNY P, 2002. 31–60. Print.

Rich, Adrienne. "The Burning of Paper Instead of Children." *Collected Early Poems, 1950–1970*. New York: Norton, 1993. Print.

Ricoeur, Paul. *The Course of Recognition*. Cambridge: Harvard UP, 2005. Print.

Roberts-Miller, Patricia. *Deliberate Conflict: Argument, Political Theory, and Composition Classes*. Carbondale: U of Southern Illinois P, 2004. Print.

Robin, Ron. *Scandals and Scoundrels: Seven Cases that Shook the Academy*. Berkeley: U of California P, 2004. Print.

Robinson, Eric W. *The First Democracies: Early Popular Government Outside Athens*. Stuttgart: Franz Steiner Verlag, 1997. Print.

Rorty, Amélie Oksenberg, ed. *Essays on Aristotle's* Rhetoric. Berkeley: U of California P, 1996. Print.

Rorty, Richard. *Contingency, Irony, and Solidarity*. New York: Cambridge UP, 1989. Print.

———. "Response." *Rorty and His Critics*. Ed Robert D. Brandom. Malden, Mass.: Blackwell, 2000. 56–65. Print.

Rosenthal, Elisabeth. "Rural Flouting of One-Child Policy Undercuts China's Census." *New York Times* 14 April 2000: A6. Web. 26 Dec. 2004.

Roth, Abraham Sesshu. "Shared Agency." *The Stanford Encyclopedia of Philosophy* (Spring 2011 ed.). Ed. Edward N. Zalta. Web. 10 Nov. 2011.

Rousseau, Jean-Jacques. *The Social Contract, or Principles of Political Right*. Constitution Society. Web. 11 Oct. 2011.

Royster, Jacqueline Jones, and Molly Cochran. "Human Rights and Civil Rights: The Advocacy and Activism of African-American Women Writers." *Human Rights Rhetoric: Traditions of Testifying and Witnessing.* Ed. Arabella Lyon and Lester C. Olson. Philadelphia: Routledge, 2012. 11–28.

Rupp, Leila J. *Worlds of Women: The Making of an International Women's Movement.* Princeton: Princeton UP, 1997. Print.

Ryle, Gilbert. *Dilemmas.* New York: Cambridge UP, 1954. Print.

Sangtin Writers and Richa Nagar. *Playing with Fire: Feminist Thought and Activism Through Seven Lives in India.* Minneapolis: U of Minnesota P, 2006. Print.

Saussy, Haun. *Great Walls of Discourse and Other Adventures in Cultural China.* Cambridge: Harvard UP, 2001. Print.

Saxonhouse, Arlene. *Fear of Diversity: The Birth of Political Science in Ancient Greek Thought.* Chicago: U of Chicago P, 1992. Print.

Scarry, Elaine. *The Body in Pain: The Making and Unmaking of the World.* New York: Oxford UP, 1987. Print.

Schaffer, Kay, and Sidonie Smith. *Human Rights and Narrated Lives: The Ethics of Recognition.* New York: Palgrave Macmillan, 2004. Print.

Schenck v United States. 249 U.S. 47. (1919). *Lexis Nexis Academic.* Web. 18 June 2012.

Scharping, Thomas. *Birth Control in China, 1949–2000: Population Policy and Demographic Development.* New York: RoutledgeCurzon, 2003. Print.

Scott, Joan Wallach. *Only Paradoxes to Offer: French Feminists and the Rights of Man.* Cambridge: Harvard UP, 1996. Print.

Sen, Amartya. *Development as Freedom.* New York: Oxford UP, 1999. Print.

———. *The Idea of Justice.* Cambridge: Belknap P of Harvard UP, 2009. Print.

———. "More than 100 Million Women Are Missing." *New York Review of Books* 20 Dec. 1990. Web. 30 May 2004.

Sheeran, Michael J. *Beyond Majority Rule: Voteless Decisions in the Religious Society of Friends.* Philadelphia: Philadelphia Yearly Meeting, 1983. Print.

Shiffman, Gary. "Deliberation Versus Decision: Platonism in Contemporary Democratic Theory." *Talking Democracy: Historical Perspectives on Rhetoric and Democracy.* Ed. Benedetto Fontana, Cary J. Nederman, and Gary Remer. University Park: Penn State UP, 2004. 87–113. Print.

Singer, Beth J. *Pragmatism, Rights, and Democracy.* New York: Fordham UP, 1999. Print.

Singer, Peter. *The Life You Save: How to Do Your Part to End World Poverty.* New York: Random House, 2010. Print.

Skinnell, Ryan. "Elizabeth Cady Stanton's 1854 'Address to the Legislature of New York' and the Paradox of Social Reform Rhetoric." *Rhetoric Review* 29.2 (2010): 129–44. Web. 6 May 2010.

Sklodowska, Elzbieta. "The Poetics of Remembering, the Politics of Forgetting: Rereading *I, Rigoberta Menchú.*" *The Rigoberta Menchú Controversy.* Ed. Arturo Arias. Minneapolis: U of Minnesota P, 2001. 251–69. Print.

Slaughter, Joseph R. *Human Rights, Inc.: The World Novel, Narrative Form, and International Law.* New York: Fordham UP, 2007. Print.

Smith, Carol A. "Why Write an Exposé of Rigoberta Menchú?" *The Rigoberta Menchú Controversy.* Ed. Arturo Arias. Minneapolis: U of Minnesota P, 2001. 141–55. Print.

Smith, Sidonie. "Performativity, Autobiographical Practice, Resistance." *Women, Autobiography, Theory: A Reader.* Ed. Sidonie Smith and Julia Watson. Madison: U of Wisconsin P, 1998. 108–15. Print.

Sommer, Doris. "Las Casas's Lies and Other Language Games." *The Roberta Menchú Controversy.* Ed. Arturo Arias. Minneapolis: U of Minnesota P, 2001. 237–50. Print.

————. "Sacred Secrets: A Strategy for Survival." *Women, Autobiography, Theory: A Reader.* Ed. Sidonie Smith and Julia Watson. Madison: U of Wisconsin P, 1998. 197–207. Print.

Sorensen, Roy. *A Brief History of the Paradox: Philosophy and the Labyrinths of the Mind.* New York: Oxford UP, 2003. Print.

Southwell, Samuel B. *Kenneth Burke and Martin Heidegger: With a Note Against Deconstruction.* Gainesville: UP of Florida, 1987. Print.

Spelman, Elizabeth V. *Fruits of Sorrow: Framing Our Attention to Suffering.* Boston: Beacon, 1997. Print.

Spivak, Gayatri Chakravorty. "Can the Subaltern Speak?" *Marxism and the Interpretation of Culture.* Ed. Cary Nelson and Lawrence Grossberg. Chicago: U of Illinois P, 1988. 271–313. Print.

————. "Righting Wrongs." *Human Rights, Human Wrongs: The Oxford Amnesty Lectures, 2001.* Ed. Nicholas Owen. New York: Oxford UP, 2003. 164–227. Print.

Stanton, Elizabeth Cady. *Eighty Years and More (1815–1897): Reminiscences of Elizabeth Cady Stanton.* New York: Source Book, 1970. Print.

Stanton, Elizabeth Cady, Susan B. Anthony, and Matilda Joslyn Gage, eds. *History of Woman Suffrage.* Vol. 1, 1848–61. New York: Arno, 1969. Print.

Stanton, Elizabeth Cady, Theodore Stanton, and Harriot Stanton Blatch. *Elizabeth Cady Stanton: As Revealed in Her Letters, Diary, and Reminiscences.* Whitefish, Mont.: Kessinger P, 2007. Print.

Star, Daniel. "Do Confucians Really Care? A Defense of the Distinctiveness of Care Ethics: A Reply to Chenyang Li." *Hypatia* 17.1 (2002): 77. *Project MUSE.* Web. 11 June 2005.

Stoll, David. *Rigoberta Menchú and the Story of All Poor Guatemalans.* Boulder: Westview, 1998. Print.

Sunzi. *Sun-Tzu: The Art of Warfare.* Trans. Roger Ames. New York: Ballantine Books, 1993. Print.

Tan, Amy. *The Joy Luck Club.* New York: Vintage, 1989. Print.

Taracena, Arturo. "Arturo Taracena Breaks His Silence." *The Rigoberta Menchú Controversy.* Ed. Arturo Arias. Minneapolis: U of Minnesota P, 2001. 82–94. Print.

Taylor, Charles. *Sources of the Self: The Making of the Modern Identity.* Cambridge: Cambridge UP, 1989. Print.

Taylor, Diana. "A Savage Performance: Guillermo Gómez-Peña and Coco Fusco's 'Couple in the Cage.'" *TDR* 42.2 (1998): 160–75. *JSTOR.* Web. 2 Aug. 2010.

Terpstra, Timothy. "The 1848 Seneca Falls Convention: Initial American Public Reaction." M.A. thesis, Mississippi State University, 1975. Web. 8 Aug. 2011.

Tien, Charles, and James A. Nathan. "The Polls—Trends: American Ambivalence Toward China." *Public Opinion Quarterly* 65 (2001): 124–38. Print.

Tu Weiming. "Human Rights as Confucian Moral Discourse." *Confucianism and Human Rights.* Ed. Wm. Theodore de Bary and Tu Weiming. New York: Columbia UP, 1998. 299–302. Print.

Vickers, Brian. *In Defence of Rhetoric.* New York: Oxford UP, 1988. Print.

Von Schomberg, René, and Kenneth Baynes, eds. *Discourse and Democracy: Essays on Habermas's Between Facts and Norms.* Albany: SUNY P, 2002. Print.

Waldron, Jeremy. "Arendt on the Foundations of Equality." *Politics in Dark Times: Encounters with Hannah Arendt.* Ed. Seyla Benhabib. New York: Cambridge UP, 2010. 17–38. Print.

Walker, Nancy A. *Women's Magazines, 1940–1960.* New York: Bedford, 1998. Print.

Walton, Douglas. "Criteria of Rationality for Evaluating Democratic Public Rhetoric." *Talking Democracy: Historical Perspectives on Rhetoric and Democracy.* Ed. Benedetto

Fontana, Cary J. Nederman, and Gary Remer. University Park: Penn State UP, 2004. 295–330. Print.

Walzer, Michael. *Spheres of Justice: A Defense of Pluralism and Equality.* New York: Basic, 1983. Print.

Wardy, Robert. "Mighty Is the Truth and It Shall Prevail?" *Essays on Aristotle's* Rhetoric. Ed. Amélie Oksenberg Rorty. Berkeley: U of California P, 1996. 56–87. Print.

Warnke, Georgia. "Communicative Rationality and Cultural Values." *The Cambridge Companion to Habermas.* Ed. Stephen K. White. New York: Cambridge UP, 1995. 120–42. Print.

Warren, Mark E. "The Self in Discursive Democracy." *The Cambridge Companion to Habermas.* Ed. Stephen K. White. New York: Cambridge UP, 1995. 167–200. Print.

Wasserstrom, Jeffrey N. "Big Bad China and the Good Chinese: An American Fairy Tale." *China Beyond the Headlines.* Ed. Timothy B. Weston and Lionel M. Jensen. Lanham: Rowman and Littlefield, 2000. 13–35. Print.

Webster, Daniel. "A Discourse in Commemoration of the Lives and Services of John Adams and Thomas Jefferson." *Webster's Great Speeches.* Boston: Little, Brown, 1879. 156–78. Print.

Weir, Allison. "Global Feminism and Transformative Identity Politics." *Hypatia* 23.4 (2008): 110–33. *Project MUSE.* Web. 3 Aug. 2008.

Wellman, Judith. *The Road to Seneca Falls: Elizabeth Cady Stanton and the First Woman's Rights Convention.* Chicago: U of Illinois P, 2004. Print.

Wellmer, Albrecht. "Ethics and Dialogue: Elements of Moral Judgment in Kant and Discourse Ethics." *The Persistence of Modernity: Essays on Aesthetics, Ethics, and Postmodernism.* Trans. David Midgley. Cambridge: Polity, 1991. 113–31. Print.

Wells, Susan. *Sweet Reason: Rhetoric and the Discourses of Modernity.* Chicago: U of Chicago P, 1996. Print.

Wess, Robert. *Kenneth Burke: Rhetoric, Subjectivity, Postmodernism.* New York: Cambridge UP, 1996. Print.

Whitlock, Gillian. *Soft Weapons: Autobiography in Transit.* Chicago: U of Chicago P, 2007. Print.

Wong, Sau-ling. "'Sugar Sisterhood': Situating the Amy Tan Phenomenon." *The Ethnic Canon: Histories, Institutions, and Interventions.* Ed. David Palumbo-Liu. Minneapolis: U of Minnesota P, 1995. 174–210. Print.

Yack, Bernard. "Rhetoric and Public Reasoning: An Aristotelian Understanding of Political Deliberation." *Political Theory* 34.4 (2006): 417–38. Web. 5 May 2012.

Young, Iris Marion. "Asymmetrical Reciprocity: On Moral Respect, Wonder, and Enlarged Thought." *Judgment, Imagination, and Politics: Themes from Kant and Arendt.* Ed. Ronald Beiner and Jennifer Nedelsky. New York: Rowman and Littlefield, 2001. 205–28. Print.

———. "Communication and the Other: Beyond Deliberative Democracy." *Democracy and Difference: Contesting the Boundaries of the Political.* Ed. Seyla Benhabib. Princeton: Princeton UP, 1996. 120–35. Print.

———. "Difference as a Resource for Democratic Communication." *Deliberative Democracy: Essays on Reason and Politics.* Ed. James Bohman and William Rehg. Cambridge: MIT P, 1997. 383–406. Print.

———. *Inclusion and Democracy.* New York: Oxford UP, 2002. Print.

———. *Justice and the Politics of Difference.* Princeton: Princeton UP, 1990. Print.

———. "Throwing Like a Girl: A Phenomenology of Feminine Body Comportment, Motility, and Spatiality." *Throwing Like A Girl and Other Essays in Feminist Philosophy and Social Theory.* Indianapolis: Indiana UP, 1990. 141–59. Print.

Yu, Anthony C. "Reading The *Daodejing*: Ethics and Politics of the Rhetoric." *Chinese Literature: Essays, Articles, Reviews* 25 (2003): 165–87. Web. 28 May 2008.

Yuan, Lijun. "Ethics of Care and Concept of *Jen:* A Reply to Chenyang Li." *Hypatia* 17.1 (2002): 107–29. *Project MUSE.* Web. 11 June 2005.

Yunis, Harvey. *Taming Democracy: Models of Political Rhetoric in Classical Athens.* Ithaca: Cornell UP, 1996. Print.

Zappen, James P. "Kenneth Burke on Dialectical-Rhetorical Transcendence." *Philosophy and Rhetoric* 41.3 (2009): 279–330. *Project Muse.* Web. 1 Aug. 2011.

Ziarek, Ewa Plonowska. *An Ethics of Dissensus: Postmodernity, Feminism, and the Politics of Radical Democracy.* Stanford: Stanford UP, 2001. Print.

Žižek, Slavoj. "The Obscenity of Human Rights: Violence as Symptom." *Lacan.com.* Web. <http://www.lacan.com/zizviol.htm>.

Zoelle, Diana G. *Globalizing Concern for Women's Human Rights: The Failure of the American Model.* New York: St. Martin's, 2000. Print.

www.ingramcontent.com/pod-product-compliance
Lightning Source LLC
Chambersburg PA
CBHW021901020426
42334CB00013B/432